THE BEST OF

BAKER BOOK HOUSE
Grand Rapids, Michigan

First published 1945 by Fleming H. Revell
Company under the title
The Treasury of C. H. Spurgeon

Mass market edition published 1977
by Baker Book House under the title
The Best of C. H. Spurgeon

Trade paperback edition first
published 1986 by Baker Book House

Sixth printing, April 1991

Printed in the United States of America

Contents

6

Foreword

Fortunately, much of Spurgeon's work has been preserved in print. So prolific a producer was he that the volumes of his sermons alone constitute a considerable library. To these need be added many works, such as *The Treasury of David,* which were not only carefully written but personally edited.

Our task in preparing this volume was to sift Spurgeon's works so as to present his message and emphasis and at the same time reflect the diversity of his mind and interests. The Table of Contents indicates this. Because Spurgeon was preeminently a preacher, we have given most space to his sermons.

The first part of the book is of a miscellaneous character and reflects the distant horizons of Spurgeon's interests and the practical application he made of his knowledge in his pulpit ministry. There are sermon outlines, illustrations for preachers and teachers, quotable quotes, daily devotional messages, examples of wisdom and wit, and those searching, scholarly expositions of Scripture for which he was famous. "Harvest Time" is Spurgeon's first printed sermon, while "John Ploughman's Pictures" reflects the quaint style of rustic England a century ago. "Vanity Fair" is based on *Pilgrim's Progress.* His son Thomas says that Spurgeon read this classic at least a hundred times and wove it into a series of prayer-meeting addresses designed for young converts.

The second part consists of sermons chosen not only because they demonstrate the preacher's artistry, but because they illustrate the subjects with which he was most concerned. They are typical both of his message and method.

THE PUBLISHERS

Introduction

The unique combination of six major factors pertaining to the publication, circulation and influence of the sermons of Charles H. Spurgeon makes this body of sermonic material the most significant phenomenon of such type of publication to proceed from any one man in the history of the Christian church. The six factors are: his early age when his sermons began to appear in print—continuing with uninterrupted regularity down to the time of his death, and for some years thereafter; the enormous audiences which heard these sermons when originally preached; the sheer bulk of Mr. Spurgeon's output of sermonic and religious literature; the astonishing circulation which these printed sermons attained, and still continue to enjoy; the world-wide influence which the sermons exercised; and, finally, the variety and richness of their contents. However superlative this statement might be, even a brief examination of the facts will reveal its undeniable truthfulness.

Born on June 19, 1834, Charles H. Spurgeon began preaching in 1850, at the age of sixteen in the little village of Tevesham, three miles from the University city of Cambridge. By the time he had reached eighteen years of age, he says that he had preached 412 times, and that by 1853, he had preached over 600 times, though not yet twenty years old. It is true that other men have begun preaching in their teens, but I am not acquainted with anyone else, who later became a world-famous figure, who began publishing his sermons when but twenty years of age, and continued this without interruption for thirty-four years. He later said, "Before I ever entered a pulpit, the thought had occurred to me that I should one day preach sermons which would be printed. While reading the Penny Sermons of Joseph Irons, which were great fav-

9

orites with me, I conceived in my heart the idea that some time or other, I should have a Penny Pulpit of my own." His first printed effort appeared while he was pastor of the Baptist Church in Waterbeach, also near Cambridge, and was designated no. I of the Waterbeach Tracts, published in 1853. It was, however, immediately after his call to London that the great river of printed sermons commenced, with the publication of an address given at New Park Street Chapel, on August 20, 1854, from the text of I Samuel 12:17. So famous did Mr. Spurgeon become at once, upon arriving in London, that as early as 1856, when he was but twenty-two years old, a volume of his sermons was issued in New York entitled *The Modern Whitefield, the Rev. C. H. Spurgeon of London, His Sermons, with An Introduction and Sketch of His Life.* (This volume is said to have reached fifty editions. By 1862, when Spurgeon was not yet thirty years of age, six volumes of his sermons had been published *in America*!) Such men as John Henry Jowett, Alexander Maclaren, and G. Campbell Morgan were hardly out of school at the age that Spurgeon began publishing his sermons.

While it may be true that D. L. Moody preached to more people in his lifetime than did Mr. Spurgeon, I think it can be safely said that no man in modern times who remained pastor of one church has preached to as many people face to face as did Charles H. Spurgeon. His own Metropolitan Tabernacle seated about 5,500, and was always full. He often spoke in Surrey Music Hall, with a seating capacity of 10,000, occasionally in the Agricultural Hall, seating 20,000, and in Crystal Palace, London, where 23,000 people gathered. Dr. Arthur T. Pierson once estimated that Mr. Spurgeon preached to not less than 10,000,000 people in his thirty-four years of ministry.

The significance of the great crowds that attended Spurgeon's ministry is enhanced when one recalls the conditions prevailing in London at the time he was called to the New Park Street pulpit in 1854. The city itself was being ravaged with cholera, and a contemporary clergyman wrote, "We could not walk the streets but we saw the doctors hither and thither, hearses, mourning coaches, and funeral processions at almost every turn . . . our faces have turned pale; our spirits have trembled." The condition of the New Park Street Church, which had known in former days the ministry of some of the most distinguished Baptist preachers of England, was pitiful. The membership had dropped to one hundred and fifty, and the attendance normally was under one hundred. The church itself was in a location very difficult to find. Moreover, there were some very able preachers in the various pulpits of London when this young lad of twenty went up to the metropolis: Thomas Binney, whom Dargan called "unquestionably the greatest Congregational preacher of the period," was at King's Weigh House Chapel, and at first opposed Spurgeon's work. The well-known Anglican, Edward Meyrick Goulbourn, was at St. John's, Paddington, later to become Dean of Norwich. The famous lecturer on prophecy, John Cumming, was at the National Scottish Church, Covent Garden. During much of the period of Mr. Spurgeon's ministry, Archibald G. Brown was at the East London Tabernacle, William Brock was at Bloomsbury Chapel, and Baptist W. Noel drew large crowds at John Street Baptist Chapel. In the latter part of his ministry, Spurgeon was to have even keener competition, if one might so refer to it, with Joseph Parker at City Temple, Canon Liddon at St. Paul's and F. B. Meyer at Regent's Park Chapel. Within a year after his arrival in the city, however, his church was so crowded week by week that it was necessary first to enlarge it, and then to erect an entirely new building; and those audiences never left him until illness compelled his retirement from the pulpit.

The quantity of sermonic, devotional, and literary material that flowed from the lips and pen of Charles H. Spurgeon is beyond anything of equal quality produced by any other preacher of modern times. Figures can best help us appreciate this particular factor. Mr. Spurgeon began publishing one sermon every week in 1854, a practice continued to the time of his death. The *New*

Park Street Pulpit and *The Metropolitan Tabernacle Pulpit* (its successor), even appeared some years after his death, with sermons that had not yet been printed, and contained a total of not less than 18,000,000 words; *The Treasury of David* (7 vols.) about 2,250,000 words; his *Lectures to Students,* 400,000 words; and *Sermon Notes,* 375,000 words. These, together with all the other books he issued, apart from sermons, make a total of more than 23,000,000 words. For twenty-two years he edited *Sword and Trowel,* by which there passed through his critical eye, and much of it through his pen, another 10,000,000 words. Thus, the sheer bulk of the literary productions of Charles Spurgeon are equal to twenty-seven volumes of the ninth edition of the *Encyclopedia Britannica.* We should remember that all this was done not by some recluse hidden away on a beautiful estate (though he did have a lovely estate), but by a man who sometimes spoke ten times a week, who read hundreds of books every year, who saw thousands of candidates for baptism, often spending days at interviewing them (in one ten-year period, Mr. Spurgeon interviewed and baptized 3,569 people), who organized, and saw to the support of several large orphanages, of the well-kown Colportage Association of the Pastor's College, and of many other institutions.

Bulk, of course, can be had, and often is, at the expense of quality—but not so with the publications of Mr. Spurgeon, which were not only enormous in quantity, but of the very highest quality, vivacious, practical, expository, the result of constant meditation upon the Word of God, crowded with telling illustrations such as no other man in the English world at his time could command.

The extent of the output was only surpassed, one might say, by the circulation figures for these sermons. It is utterly impossible to estimate accurately the number of sermons, and other works, by Mr. Spurgeon that have appeared in print. As early as 1880 in America, an edition of his sermons had sold something over 500,000 volumes. In addition to the hundreds of volumes of separately-published sermons sold each week, and the annual bound volumes of the *Metropolitan Tabernacle Pulpit,* these sermons were often reprinted in periodicals, such as the (London) *Christian Herald.* Before his death, and after, many of the sermons were brought together in various volumes of particular studies; e.g., on the Miracles of Christ, on the Parables of Christ and on the Names, Titles, and Attributes of our Lord (a marvelous work), in addition to the famous series of twelve sermons each on innumerable subjects such as Christmas, the Resurrection of Christ, the Second Advent, etc. Extracts from his sermons were brought together under interesting titles, *Gleanings Among the Sheaves, Barbed Arrows From the Quiver of C. H. Spurgeon,* etc., etc.

In compiling this data, one must reckon with the large number of translations of these sermons. A Welch translation, issued once each month, was the first to appear, followed by the Dutch edition, at which time the Queen of Holland herself requested copies, read them, and entertained Mr. Spurgeon when he was traveling on the Continent. More than a score of publishers in Germany issued translations. The Swedish editions resulted in the conversion of multitudes, among whom were some of noble birth. Mr. Spurgeon himself was never able to discover into how many languages his sermons had been translated, but his own collection of translations included the following languages: Arabic, Armenian, Bengali, Bulgarian, Castilian (for the Argentine Republic), Chinese, Congo, Czech, Danish, Dutch, Esthonian, French, Gaelic, German, Hindi, Hungarian, Italian, Japanese, Kaffir, Karen, Lettish, Maori, Norwegian, Polish, Russian, Servian, Spanish, Swedish, Syriac, Tamil, Telugu, Urdu, Welsh, as well as Moon's and and Braille type for the blind. How many collections of sermons, apart from the *Metropolitan Tabernacle Pulpit* series, have been made, I do not know. One of these in my own library is that published by Funk and Wagnall some years ago embracing nineteen volumes. A few years ago a London publishing house rearranged in textual order hundreds of the sermons included in the *Metropolitan Tabernacle Pulpit* and issued them in seven quarto volumes—

The Treasury of the Old Testament (4 vols.) and, *The Treasury of the New Testament* (3 vols.), 6300 double-column pages, a storehouse of the very best in preaching. I have not tried to draw up a complete bibliography here.

In addition to all this sermonic material, the eminent preacher wrote a number of other books, e.g., his familiar *Commenting and Commentaries, Eccentric Preachers,* the four-volume series, *Lectures to My Students,* the now rarely seen *Teachings of Nature in the Kingdom of Grace,* and a work with the peculiar, suggestive title, *The Salt Sellars, Proverbs of All Nations with Homely Themes Thereon.* His two works of meditations, *Morning by Morning,* and *Evening by Evening* had sold over 220,000 copies by the end of the nineteenth century. Innumerable smaller volumes also issued from his pen, so that Mrs. Spurgeon at one time said she thought that, apart from the *Metropolitan Tabernacle Pulpit,* one could list perhaps one hundred and fifty titles of Mr. Spurgeon's writings. In his excellent life of Spurgeon, Dr. W. Y. Fullerton more accurately analyzes this: "The whole Spurgeon Library, taking no count of tractates, consists of no less than 135 volumes, of which he was the author, and twenty-eight which he edited, 163 volumes in all, or including the reprints, 176! If we add the albums and the pamphlets, we get an output of 200 books!

The variety in subject matter continually displayed throughout Spurgeon's productions has already been referred to. He was thoroughly acquainted with agriculture and horticulture, and used thousands of illustrations from nature. He traveled extensively and read voluminously on the places visited, and constantly used this material in his preaching. Sailors were often amazed at his intimate knowledge of nautical subjects. Mr. Spurgeon lived vigorously every day, reading widely, interviewing men and women concerning matters of the soul, entertaining many of the distinguished Christian servants of that age, absorbing everything that was of interest, meeting life face to face, with all of its richness and infinite possibility, both for good and for evil—all this was poured out graphically in his writings. His sermons moved through the Word of God from Genesis to Revelation, and a classification of his texts will reveal the proclamation of the gospel of the grace of God from almost every page of the Holy Scriptures, especially the Book of Psalms, from which 389 sermons were drawn; Isaiah, 233; the Gospel of Luke, 213; the Gospel of John, 274; the Epistle to the Romans, 128; the Epistle to the Hebrews, 127; the Book of Revelation, 71; the Song of Solomon, 58; the brief First Epistle of John, 50; and from the one-chapter Book of Jude, 10 sermons.

I believe it cannot be questioned but that Mr. Spurgeon's printed sermons had a greater influence over the souls and minds of men than did those of any other preacher of Great Britain or America. Thousands of men and women all over the world, some of them deep in sin, came to know Christ as Saviour through the reading of these pages. Upon investigating this matter at the beginning of our century, Dr. Pierson gave as his conviction that not less than ten thousand men and women had been saved through the reading of these sermons. One friend, whose name has not been revealed, distributed over 250,000 copies of the sermons, had volumes of them bound in the most attractive style and presented them to every crowned head in Europe, and gave volumes containing twelve or more sermons to all students of the universities of England, and to all members of the two houses of Parliament.

The sermon having the greatest repercussion was perhaps the one preached against baptisimal regeneration, from Mark 16:5. Before the year of Spurgeon's death, 225,000 copies of this one address had been sold. The Catalog of the Library of the British Museum contains fourteen columns of Spurgeon's works alone— more, I think, than on any other clergyman in the history of Great Britain—and in this bibliography, nearly four columns are devoted to pamphlets and books, issued by others, *resulting from this one sermon* on baptismal regeneration. The monumental four-volume autobiography, begun by Mr. Spurgeon and finished by his wife, contains scores of accounts of conversions following the reading of his printed messages, but there is no time available for repeating even one of them here.

No other minister of modern times has received such superlative encomiums as did Charles Haddon Spurgeon. Dr. R. F. Horton of London, who did not accept all of Spurgeon's views by any means, said that he might be "finally linked with Chrysostom, Bossuet, and Liddon, in the very front of the masters of the Christian pulpit." On one occasion Joseph Parker went so far as to say that Spurgeon was "the only pulpit name of the nineteenth century that will be remembered." "It is my humble judgment," said Dr. John Watson (Ian Maclaren), "and I rejoice to express it, that Mr. Spurgeon was God's chief preacher to the English-speaking race of our day." Sir Robertson Nicoll, a severe critic, who knew everything important in literature, and never praised unless he meant it, paid this tribute before the Baptist Union: "Read, above all things your Bible; and whatever books you add to your Bible, add some volumes of your great apostle Charles Spurgeon—not to preach out of them, for you might almost as well talk of plagiarising from the Epistle to the Romans as of plagiarising from Spurgeon. Read him because he is the unrivaled interpreter of the mysteries of the New Covenant. I take him up constantly and find myself repeating Browning's words—

> A turn and we stand in the heart of things:
> The woods are round us heaped and dim."

There have been many attempts—some of them quite successful—to account for the tremendous success and influence of Spurgeon's sermons, and I do not here intend to offer a fresh analysis. Fundamentally, however, we should remember that Spurgeon was born to preach: he had to preach. He began preaching when a boy, even to the children in the neighborhood, and throughout his life the pulpit was his throne, and preaching his greatest joy. Nothing could divert him from that major task. As a young man, even though he may have had some premonition of coming greatness, he did not spurn minor opportunities. In March, 1861, in an address to the Young Men's Christian Association, he remarked, "Do not think of waiting until you can do some great thing for God; do little things, and then the Master will bid you go up higher. Eleven years ago, I was addressing Sunday school children and these alone. Ten—nine years ago, I was preaching in little insignificant rooms here and there, generally going out and coming back on foot, and occasionally getting a lift in a cart. It has often happened that, when I have been going out to certain villages, the brooks would be so swollen that they could not be crossed in the usual way, so I would pull off my shoes and stockings, wade through up to my knees, then try to make myself tidy again as I best could, and go on to the little chapel to preach, and return home in the same way. Now, I am perfectly sure that, if I had not been willing to preach to those small gatherings of people in obscure country places, I should never have had the privilege of preaching to thousands of men and women in large buildings all over the land. If one wishes to be a steward in God's house, he must first be prepared to serve as a scullion in the kitchen, and be content to wash out the pots and clean the boots. Remember our Lord's rule, 'Whosoever exalteth himself shall be abased; and he that humbleth himself shall be exalted.' "

Spurgeon prepared his sermons with the greatest care, constantly collecting material, ever keeping in mind the needs of his people, and waiting upon God for the right text for each service. "To me, still, I must admit, my text-selection is a very great embarrassment—*embarras de richesse,* as the French say—an embarrassment of riches, very different from the bewilderment of poverty— the anxiety of attending to the most pressing of so many truths, all clamouring for a hearing, so many duties all needing enforcing, and so many spiritual needs of the people all demanding supply. I confess that I frequently sit hour after hour, praying and waiting for a subject, and that this is the main part of my study; much hard labour have I spent in manipulating topics, ruminating upon points of doctrine, making skeletons out of verses, and then burying every bone of them in the catacombs of oblivion, drifting on and on over leagues of broken water, till I see the red lights, and make sail direct to the desired haven. I believe that, almost any Saturday in my life, I prepared enough outlines of Sermons, if I felt at liberty to preach them, to last me for a month, but I no more dare to use them than an honest mariner would run to shore a cargo of contraband goods."

Above all, this servant of God kept close to the Word of God. His tributes to the Scriptures alone would fill an entire volume. Preaching once from Jeremiah 13:15-17, he said, "The voice which we are bidden to hear is *a Divine voice,* it is the voice of Him that made the heavens and the earth, whose creatures we are. Jehovah hath spoken! If it were but the voice of prophets apart from their Master, it might be but a slight sin to refuse what they say; but since Jehovah hath spoken, shall men dare to be deaf to Him? Shall they turn away from Him that speaketh from heaven? He that spake us into being hath spoken to our being. He by whose word the heavens stand, and at whose word both heaven and earth shall pass away, hath spoken, and His voice is to the sons of men. It is God who says, 'I have written to him the great things of my law.' The sacred Scriptures are the record of what God hath spoken: receive them with the reverence which they deserve as coming from God only, and as being, therefore, pure truth, fixed certainty, and unerring right."

Spurgeon believed what he preached, lived what he preached, and every day saw abundant results from his messages, to the glory of God. I know of no one in the nineteenth century of whom the words of St. Mark concerning Jesus would be quite so true— "The common people heard him gladly." He spoke in language that all could easily understand, and each person in the audience felt that the messenger was talking to him personally, and understood his problems and needs. He had a profound understanding of the grace of God, and hundreds of passages of Scripture entered into his soul through experience, some of them bitter experiences. Then, of course, Spurgeon had great natural gifts—gifts for expression, for pointed illustrations, for smooth-flowing sentences, for awakening the interest of his audiences everywhere; and, because he was so filled with a sense of the glory of Christ, and of the wonders of His Word, he could soar off into oratorical flights (not flights of fancy) such as come, generally, not from toil and preparation, but from a certain mysterious bestowment of power by the Holy Spirit Himself. None of us has been called to be a Spurgeon—would to God some were—and it is foolish to attempt to imitate such a preacher as he, but we should never permit our own laziness, or love of sin, or anything else, to keep us from yielding all we have to this glorious task, and privilege of preaching, of being constant students of the Word of God, of allowing ourselves to be channels of divine grace, a voice for God through whom many may come to eternal life.

In preparing for this Introduction, I have tried to read again most of the significant autobiographical and biographical volumes of Charles H. Spurgeon, and in so doing, I have come to the strong conviction that the Christian church today has not yet seen a fully adequate, definitive life of this mighty preacher of the grace of God that should not be written. There are probably more sources of material available for such a work than for any other preacher of the nineteenth century, apart from Dwight L. Moody.

THE BEST OF

Spurgeon's Gems

HEAVEN

HAPPY ARE the spirits who have ended their fight of faith and now live in the raptures of a sight of Him; yea, thrice happy are the lowest of those seraphs who fly at his bidding, and do forever behold the face of our Father which is in heaven. The drought of these dry plains stirreth us to desire the river of the water of life; the barren fig trees of this weary land urge us to pursue a speedy path to the immortal trees upon the banks of the river of God; our clouds exhort us to fly above this lower sky up where unclouded ages roll; the very thorns and briers, the dust and heat of this world's pilgrimage and strife, are powerful orators to excite our highest thoughts to the things which are unseen and eternal.

THE GREAT ATONEMENT

Look! Look! look with solemn eye through the shades that part us from the world of spirits, and see that house of misery which men call hell! Ye cannot endure the spectacle. Remember that in that place there are spirits forever paying their debt to divine justice; but though some of them have been for these four thousand years sweltering in the flame, they are no nearer a discharge than when they began; and when ten thousand times ten thousand years shall have rolled away, they will no more have made satisfaction to God for their guilt than they have done up till now. And now can you grasp the thought of the greatness of your Saviour's meditation when He paid your debt and paid it all at once; so that there now remaineth not one farthing of debt owing from Christ's people to their God, except a debt of love? To justice the believer oweth nothing; though he owed originally so much that eternity would not have been long enough to suffice for the paying of it, yet in one moment Christ did pay it all, so that the man who believeth is entirely justified from all guilt, and set free from all punishment, through what Jesus hath done. Think ye, then, how great His atonement if He hath done all this.

GREEN PASTURES

Blessed be God, the green pastures and the still waters, the shepherd's crook and pleasant company, are objects which are quite as familiar to the believer's mind as the howling wilderness and the brandished rod.

LAMBS

The meanest lamb of the blood-bought flock shall be preserved securely by the "strength of Israel" unto the day of His appearing, and shall, through every season of tribulation and distress, continue to be beloved of the Lord.

CHURCH ATTENDANCE

Fire will not tarry in a single coal, but if many be laid together, it will be long before it is clean gone. A single tree may not afford much shelter for a traveler, but he will rest beneath the thick boughs of the grove: so will Jesus often sit longer where many of "the trees of the Lord" are planted. Go to the assemblies of the saints if you would keep the arm of the King of saints. Those who dwell most with the daughters of Jerusalem are most likely to have a goodly share of Emmanuel's company.

SINS

A little filth acquired every day, if it be left unwashed, will make us as black as if we had been plunged in the mire; and as sin upon the conscience turns Christ's joy out of the heart, it will be impossible for us to feel the delights of communion until all our everyday sins have been washed from the conscience by a fresh application of the atoning blood.

A Lost Christ

As plants thrive not when the light is kept from them, but become blanched and unhealthy, so souls deprived of the light of God's countenance are unable to maintain the verdure of their piety or the strength of their graces. What a loss is a lost Christ!

Sun of the Soul

When the Lord Jesus is present in the soul and is beheld by it, ambition, covetousness, and worldliness flee apace; for such is His apparent glory that earthly objects fade away like the stars in noonday; but when He is gone, they will show their false glitter, as the stars, however small, will shine at midnight.

Trust the Lord

Trust the Lord much while He is with you. Keep no secrets from Him. His secrets are with you; let your secrets be with Him. Jesus admires confidence and if it be not afforded Him, He will say, "Farewell," until we can trust Him better.

Keys to the Heart

If thou desirest Christ for a perpetual guest, give Him all the keys of thine heart; let not one cabinet be locked up from Him; give Him the range of every room and the key of every chamber; thus you will constrain Him to remain.

On Bridges

I had rather put my foot upon a bridge as narrow as Hungerford, which went all the way across, than on a bridge that was as wide as the world if it did not go all the way across the stream.

Offerings

Princes have melted pearls into the wine wherewith they entertained monarchs; let us do the same. Let us make rich offerings to Jesus; let our duties be more faithfully discharged, our labors more willingly performed, and let our zeal be more eminently fervent.

The Love of Jesus

Whatever our frame or feeling, the heart of Jesus is full of love—love which was not caused by our good behavior and is not diminished by our follies—love which is as sure in the night of darkness, as in the brightness of the day of joy.

With Christ

When Christ is with the Christian, the means of grace are like flowers in the sunshine, smelling fragrantly and smiling beauteously; but without Christ they are like flowers by night, their fountains of fragrance are sealed by the darkness.

A Divided Heart

Jesus will never tarry in a divided heart. He must be all or nothing. Search thy heart; dethrone its idols; eject all interlopers; chastise all trespassers; yea, slay the Diabolians who lurk in thy soul.

Troubles

There is a story told that in the olden times Artaxerxes and another great king were engaged in a furious fight. In the middle of the battle a sudden eclipse happened, and such was the horror of all the warriors that they made peace then and there. Oh, if an eclipse of trouble should induce you to ground arms and seek to be reconciled unto God! Sinner, you are fighting against God, lift-

ing the arm of your rebellion against Him. Happy shall you be if
that trouble which is now fallen upon you should lead you to
throw down the weapons of your rebellion, and fly to the arms of
God and say, "Lord have mercy upon me a sinner." It will be the
best thing that thou hast ever had. Thy trouble will be far better
to thee than joys could have been if thy sorrows shall induce thee
to fly to Jesus who can make peace through the blood of His cross.

SHADED PLANTS

A portion of the Lord's family live usually in the shade: they
are like those sweet flowers which bloom nowhere so well as in
the darkest and thickest glades of the forest.

BACKSLIDERS

The sun will shine on the dunghill, but Christ will not shine
on the backslider while he is indulging in his lusts.

THE PULPIT

If there be a place under high heaven more holy than another,
it is the pulpit whence the gospel is preached. This is the Ther-
mopylae of Cristendom; here must the great battle be fought between Christ's church and the invading hosts of a wicked world.
This is the last vestige of anything sacred that is left to us. We
have no altars now; Christ is our altar: but we have a pulpit still
left, a place which, when a man entereth, he might well put off
his shoes from his feet, for the place whereon he standeth is holy.
Consecrated by a Saviour's presence, established by the clearness
and the force of an apostle's eloquence, maintained and upheld
by the faithfulness and fervor of a succession of evangelists who,
like stars, have marked the era in which they lived and stamped
it with their names, the pulpit is handed down to those of us who
occupy it now with a prestige of everything that is great and holy.
Yet I have seen the wicked come and go from it. Alas! if there be

a sinner that is hardened, it is the man that sins and occupies his pulpit. We have heard of such a man living in the commission of the foulest sins and who at length has been discovered; and yet such is the filthiness of mankind that when he began to preach to the people again, they clustered round the beast for the mere sake of hearing what he would say to them. We have known cases, too, where men, when convicted to their own forehead, have unblushingly persevered in proclaiming a gospel which their lives denied. And perhaps these are the hardest of all sinners to deal with. But if the garment be once defiled, away with all thoughts of the pulpit then! He must be clean who ministers at the altar. Every saint must be holy, but he the holiest of all who seeks to serve his God. Yet, we must mourn to say it, the church of God every now and then has had a sun that was black instead of white, and a moon that was as a clot of blood instead of being full of fairness and beauty. Happy the church when God gives her holy ministers; but unhappy the church where wicked men preside. I know ministers to this day, however, who know more about fishing rods than they do about chapters in the Bible; more about fox-hounds than about hunting after men's souls; who understand a great deal more of the spring and the net than they do of the net for catching souls or of earnest exhortations to men to flee from the wrath to come. We know such even now: still uproarious at a farmer's dinner, still the very loudest to give the toast and clash the glass, still mightiest among the mighty, fond of the gay, the wild, and the dissolute. Pity on the church that still allows it! Happy the day when all such persons shall be purged from the pulpit; then shall it stand forth "clear as the sun, fair as the moon, and terrible as an army with banners."

Honey in the Rock

You need not dispute divine decrees, but sit down and draw honey out of this rock and wine of this flinty rock. Oh, it is a hard, hard doctrine to a man who has no interest in it, but when a man has once a title to it, then it is like the rock in the wilderness; it streams with refreshing water whereat myriads may drink and never thirst again. Well does the Church of England say of that doctrine, it "is full of sweet, pleasant, and unspeakable comfort to godly persons." And though it be like the Tarpeian rock, whence many a malefactor has been dashed to pieces in presumption, yet is it like Pisgah, from whose lofty summit the spires of heaven may be seen in the distance.

THE REFORMATION

One reformation will never serve the church; she needs continually to be wound up and set a-going afresh; for her works run down, and she does not act as she used to do. The bold, bald doctrines that Luther brought out began to be a little modified until layer after layer was deposited upon them, and at last the old rocky truth was covered up, and there grew upon the superficial subsoil an abundance of green and flowery errors that looked fair and beautiful, but were in no way whatever related to the truth, except as they were the products of its decay. Then there came bold men who brought the truth out again and said, "Clear away this rubbish; let the light blast upon these deceitful beauties; we want them not; bring out the old truth once more!" And it came out. But the tendency of the church is perpetually to be covering up its own naked simplicity, forgetting that the truth is never so beautiful as when it stands in its own unadorned, God-given glory. And now, at this time, we want to have the old truths restored to their places. The subtleties and the refinements of the preacher must be laid aside. We must give up the grand distinctions of the schoolmen and all the lettered technicalities of men who have studied theology as a system but have not felt the power of it in their hearts; and when the good old truth is once more preached by men whose lips are touched as with a live coal from off the altar, this shall be the instrument in the hand of the Spirit for bringing about a great and thorough revival of religion in the land.

The Place of the Holy

Little do we know when we look here from this pulpit, it looks like one great field of flowers, fair to look upon, how many a root of deadly henbane and noxious nightshade groweth here; and though you all look fair and goodly, yet "I have seen the wicked come and go from the place of the holy."

The Note of Victory

Soldier of the cross! the hour is coming when the note of victory shall be proclaimed throughout the world. The battlements of the enemy must soon succumb; the swords of the mighty must soon be given up to the Lord of lords. What! soldier of the cross! in the day of victory wouldst thou have it said that thou didst turn thy back in the day of battle? Dost thou not wish to have a share in the conflict that thou mayest have a share in the victory? If thou hast even the hottest part of the battle, wilt thou flinch and fly? Thou shalt have the brightest part of the victory if thou art in the fiercest of the conflict. Wilt thou turn and lose thy laurels? Wilt thou throw down thy sword? Shall it be with thee as when a standard-bearer fainteth? Nay, man, up to arms again! for the victory is certain. Though the conflict be severe, I beseech you, on to it again! On, on, ye lion-hearted men of God, to the battle once more! for ye shall yet be crowned with immortal glory.

Feathers for Arrows

Abasement

WHEN LATIMER resigned his bishopric, Foxe tells us that as he put off his rochet from his shoulders he gave a skip on the floor for joy, "feeling his shoulders so light at being discharged of such a burden." To be relieved of our wealth or high position is to be unloaded of weighty responsibilities and should not cause us to fret, but rather to rejoice like those who are lightened of a great load. If we cease from office in the church, or from public honors, or from power of any sort, we may be consoled by the thought that there is just so much the less for us to answer for at the great audit when we must give an account of our stewardship.

Absence from Week-night Services

"Prayer-meeting and lecture as usual on Wednesday evening in the lecture-room. Dear brethren, I urge you all to attend the weekly meetings. 'Forsake not the assembling of yourselves together.'" Some of the "dear brethren" deported themselves in this way. Brother A. *thought it looked like rain* and concluded that his family, including himself of course, had better remain at home. On Thursday evening it was raining very hard, and the same brother hired a carriage and took his whole family to the Academy of Music to hear M. Agassiz lecture on the "Intelligence of the Lobster." Brother B. *thought he was too tired to go,* so he stayed at home and *worked* at the sledge he had promised to make for Billy. Sister C. *thought the pavements were too slippery.* It would be very dangerous for her to venture out. I saw her next

31

morning going down street to get her old bonnet "done up." She had an old pair of stockings drawn over her shoes. Three-fourths of the members stayed at home. God was at the prayer-meeting. The pastor was there, and God blessed them. The persons who stayed at home were each represented by a vacant seat. God doesn't bless empty seats.

Age—No Cure for Sin

According to Æsop, an old woman found an empty jar which had lately been full of prime old wine and which still retained the fragrant smell of its former contents. She greedily placed it several times to her nose, and drawing it backwards and forwards said, "Oh, most delicious! How nice must the wine itself have been when it leaves behind in the very vessel which contained it so sweet a perfume!"

Men often hug their vices when their power to enjoy them is gone. The memories of reveling and wantonness appear to be sweet to the ungodly in their old age. They sniff the empty bottles of their follies and only wish they could again be drunken with them. Age cures not the evil heart, but exhibits in a ridiculous but deeply painful light the indelible perversity of human nature.

Young Should Be Trained

The question is often asked how shall we get our working-classes to attend public worship. The answer may be supplied by an incident of my boyhood. On the mantel-shelf of my grandmother's best parlor, among other marvels, was an apple in a phial. It quite filled up the body of the bottle, and my wondering inquiry was, "How could it have been got into its place?" By stealth I climbed a chair to see if the bottom would unscrew, or if there had been a join in the glass throughout the length of the phial. I was satisfied by careful observation that neither of these theories could be supported, and the apple remained to me an enigma and a mystery. But as it was said of that other wonder, the source of the Nile—"Nature well known no mystery remains,"—so was it here. Walking in the garden, I saw a phial placed on a tree bearing within it a tiny apple growing within the crystal; now I saw it all; the apple was put into the bottle while it was little, and it grew there. Just so must we catch the little men and women who swarm our streets—we call them boys and girls—and introduce them within the influence of the church, for alas! it is hard indeed to reach them when they have ripened in carelessness and sin.

THE BIBLE

The *historical* matters of Scripture, both narrative and prophecy, constitute as it were the *bones* of its system; whereas the *spiritual* matters are as its muscles, blood vessels and nerves. As the *bones* are necessary to the human system, so Scripture *must* have its *historical* matters. The expositor who nullifies the *historical* ground-work of Scripture for the sake of finding only spiritual truths everywhere, brings death on all correct interpretation.

INTEREST IN THE BIBLE

The lifeboat may have a tasteful bend and beautiful decoration, but these are not the qualities for which I prize it; it was my salvation from the howling sea! So the interest which a regenerate soul takes in the Bible is founded on a personal application to the heart of the saving truth which it contains. If there is no taste for this truth, there can be no relish for the Scriptures.

HOW TO DEAL WITH BIBLE DIFFICULTIES

An old man once said, "For a long period I puzzled myself about the difficulties of Scripture, until at last I came to the resolution that reading the Bible was like eating fish. When I find a difficulty, I lay it aside and call it a bone. Why should I choke on the bone when there is so much nutritious meat for me? Some day, perhaps, I may find that even the bone may afford me nourishment."

JUDGED BY ITS FRUITS

A Roman Catholic priest in Belgium rebuked a young woman and her brother for reading that "bad book," pointing to the Bible. "Mr. Priest," she replied, "a little while ago my brother was an idler, a gambler, a drunkard, and made such a noise in the house that no one could stay in it. Since he began to read the Bible, he works with industry, goes no longer to the tavern, no longer touches cards, brings home money to his poor old mother, and our life at home is quiet and delightful. How comes it, Mr. Priest, that a bad book produces such good fruits?"

THE MARROW OF THEOLOGY

The late venerable and godly Dr. Archibald Alexander, of Princeton, United States, had been a preacher of Christ for sixty years and a professor of divinity for forty. On his death-bed, he was heard to say to a friend, "All my theology is reduced to this narrow compass—Jesus Christ came into the world to save sinners."

A ROYAL PERSONAGE

A poor but pious woman called upon two elegant young ladies, who, regardless of her poverty, invited her to sit down with them in the drawing-room and thereupon entered into conversation with her upon religious subjects. While thus employed, their brother, a dashing youth, by chance entered and appeared astonished to see his sisters thus engaged. One of them instantly exclaimed, "Brother, don't be surprised; this is a king's daughter, though she has not yet put on her fine clothes."

COMING TO CHRIST—AS A SINNER

A great monarch was accustomed on certain set occasions to entertain all the beggars of the city. Around him were placed his courtiers, all clothed in rich apparel; the beggars sat at the same table in their rags of poverty. Now it came to pass that on a certain day one of the courtiers had spoiled his silken apparel so that he dared not put it on, and he felt, "I cannot go to the king's feast today for my robe is foul." He sat weeping till the thought struck him, "Tomorrow when the king holds his feast, some will come as courtiers happily decked in their beautiful array, but others will come who will be dressed in rags, and be made quite as welcome. "Well, well," said he, "so long as I may see the king's face and sit at the royal table, I will enter among the beggars." So without mourning because he had not his silken habit, he put on the rags of a beggar and he saw the king's face as well as if he had worn his scarlet and fine linen. My soul has done this full many a time when her evidences of salvation have been dim; and I bid you do the same when you are in like case: if you cannot come to Jesus as a saint, come as a sinner; only do come with simple faith to Him and you shall receive joy and peace.

COMMUNION OF SAINTS

Communion is strength, solitude is weakness. Alone, the fine old beech yields to the blast and lies prone upon the sward: in the forest, supporting each other, the trees laugh at the hurricane. The sheep of Jesus flock together; the social element is the genius of Christianity.

WORKS AND OUR SALVATION

William Wickham being appointed by King Edward to build a stately church, wrote in the windows, *"This work made William Wickham."* When charged by the king for assuming the honor of that work to himself as the author, whereas he was only the overseer, he answered that he meant not that he made the work, but that the work made him, having before been very poor and then in great credit. Lord, when we read in Thy Word that we must work out our own salvation, Thy meaning is not that our salvation should be the effect of our work, but our work the evidence of our salvation.

DECEPTION OF THE WORLD

Æsop's fable says: "A pigeon oppressed by excessive thirst, saw a goblet of water painted on a sign-board. Not supposing it to be only a picture, she flew towards it with a loud whirr, and unwittingly dashed against the signboard, and jarred herself terribly. Having broken her wings by the blow, she fell to the ground and was killed by one of the bystanders."

The mockeries of the world are many, and those who are deluded by them not only miss the joys they looked for, but in their eager pursuit of vanity bring ruin upon their souls. We call the dove silly to be deceived by a picture, however cleverly painted, but what epithet shall we apply to those who are duped by the transparently false allurements of the world!

CAUSING UNITY

There was a blacksmith once who had two pieces of iron which he wished to weld into one, and he took them just as they were, all cold and hard, and putting them on the anvil, began to hammer with all his might, but they were two pieces still and would not unite. At last he remembered what he ought never to have forgotten; he thrust both of them into the fire, took them out red-hot, laid the one upon the other, and by one or two blows of the hammer they very soon became one.

Barbed Arrows

Abide after cleansing where you were before cleansing.

A bushelful of resolutions is of small value; a single grain of practice is worth the whole.

A cake made of memories will do for a bite now and then, but it makes poor daily bread.

A change of life alone can prove a change of heart.

A Christian's life should be the Decalogue written large.

Additions and subtractions are weeds which it is hard to keep out of the garden of conversation.

Adversity has less power to harm than prosperity.

A faith look at Jesus breaks the heart both for sin and from sin.

A faith that never wept is a faith that never lived.

A frequent hearer is likely to become a fervent believer.

A gash in the conscience may disfigure a soul forever.

A gospel that does not suit everybody does not suit anybody.

A groundless hope is a mere delusion.

A living argument is invincible.

All true hearts are not fit for fight.

Balance your duties, and let not one press out another.

Baptize your heart in devotion ere you wade into the stream of daily care.

Better in the abyss of truth than on the summit of falsehood.

Better the smitings of truth than the kisses of deceit.

Better to be God's dog than the devil's darling.

Beware of aptness in making an excuse.

Beware of contentment with shallow grace.
Beware of ill company in the evening.

Children of shame may be made heirs of glory.
Christ is a great frequenter of cottages.
Christ is ready for every emergency.
Communion with God is a great maker of music.
Constancy is the proof of sincerity.
Continued delay of duty is a continuous sin.
Conversion days are our high holidays.
Conversions are not run into moulds.
Cries are not for musicians but for mourners.

Despair of spirit has fled when you have leaned hard on the Cross-Bearer.

"*Deus Vult*"—God wills it—is a grand cry to produce a crusade.

Do not please the devil by distrusting your faithful God.

Empty buckets are fittest for the well of grace.

Every ungodly man may have his life-lease run out tomorrow.

Every day wear the red cross on your arm by avowing your faith in the atoning blood.

Everything it will honestly bear, you may pile upon the back of a divine promise.

Every believer in the cross must bear the cross.

Faith gathers the handfuls of sacred corn from which contemplation threshes out the ears and prepares soul-sustaining bread.

Faith is a salamander that lives in the fire, a star which moves in a lofty sphere, a diamond which bores its way through the rock.

Faith is the acorn from which the oak of holiness will grow.

Faith is the fountain, the foundation, and the fosterer of obedience.

Faith is the mother of holiness and the nurse of virtue.

Faith knows that whenever she gets a black envelope from the heavenly post office, there is a treasure in it.

Faith laughs at that which fear weeps over.

Get right within, and you will be right without.

God blesses us many times every time He blesses us.

God can use inferior persons for grand purposes.

God gives small creatures great delight.

God has no thunderbolts for those who hate their sins.

Godliness is not a rack nor a thumbscrew.

Godly people are thoughtful people. Indeed, it is often a sign of the beginning of grace in a man when he begins to consider.

Good delayed is evil indulged.

Grace baptizes us into blessedness.

Grace does not exempt us from activity.

Grace makes the servant of God to be in the highest sense a true gentleman.

Grace personally received must be personally acknowledged.

Grief has small regard for the laws of the grammarian.

Half-way house godliness is wretched stuff.

Hannibal, it is said, dissolved the rocks of the Alps with vinegar; but Christ dissolves our hearts with love.

Have the blood-mark very visibly on all your mercies.

Heaven hides itself away within the gospel.

He that can stand on the hilltop can stand in the valley.

Holiness is the royal road to Scriptural knowledge.

How can a soul make progress if it is evermore changing its course? Do not sow in Beersheba and then rush off to reap in Dan.

Idle words are in the speech of man, not in the writings of Jehovah.

If the devil never roars, the church will never sing.

If we do not praise Him, we deserve to be banished to the Siberia of despair.

If your life pleases God, let it please *you.*

I have heard of Latter-day Saints; I far more admire Everyday Saints.

In a dewdrop the sun may be reflected.

It needs more grace to lead than to follow.

I would rather obey God, than rule an empire.

Jesus will never be a part-Saviour.

Let your wishes blaze up into prayers.

Like a young bird in its nest, glory dwells in grace.

Longing follows on the heels of loving.

Look you well to your integrity, and the Lord will look to your prosperity.

Make inscrutable mysteries into footstools for faith to kneel upon.

Man's security is the devil's opportunity.

Maturity comes by affliction.

Mechanical worship is easy, but worthless.

Men may fast from bread that they may gorge themselves on pride.

Men of faith are not idle men.

Men's pennies and God's promises don't very well go together to buy heaven.

Mount like the lark to your God, and sing as you mount.

Never be afraid of your Bibles.

Never get an inch beyond the cross.

No man need stick in the mud because he becomes a Christian.

Nothing holds a man like the silken cord of gratitude.

Nothing shakes prison-walls and breaks jailers hearts like the praises of the Lord.

Obedience is for the present tense.

One of the best positions in which our heart can be found is at Jesus' feet.

Our littleness does not alter God's promise.

Our motto is, "With God anywhere: without God, nowhere."

Our vessels are never full till they run over. The little over proves our zeal, tries our faith, casts us upon God, and wins His help.

Periodical godliness is perpetual hypocrisy.

Personal experience is more convincing than observation.

Pleasures which block the road to heaven ought to be given up.

Praise makes the happy man the strong man.

Pray down the sermon, and then pray up the sermon.

Prayer can never be in excess.

Prayer is the promise utilized.

Prayer is the thermometer of grace.

Preach the cross, and plead the blood.

Providence is God's business.

Prudence prays with Moses, while it fights for Joshua.

Question mars all melody.

Real faith will find a way out of perplexity or will make one.

Religion without a heart is a wretched affair.

Remove grace from the gospel, and the gospel is gone.

Repentance, apart from Christ, will need be repented of.

Repentance puts us in a lowly seat.

Revivals are our jubilees.

Safe walking can only come of careful walking.

Saintly souls should not be lodged in filthy bodies.

Sanctified adversity quickens our spiritual sensitiveness.

Saving faith is a life-long act.

Show religion is a vain show.

Simple trust and grateful service make a link more precious than gold.

Sin in satin is as great a rebel as sin in rags.

Sin may drive you *from* Sinai; it ought to draw you *to* Calvary.

Some saints can be lead with a hair-thread.

Sorrow unsettles the judgment.

Soul music is the soul of music.

Style the fiend an angel of light, and he is none the less a devil.

Sympathy in sin is conspiracy in crime.

Take Christ to be the sole Saviour of your soul.

Take no rest from prayer, and give Him no rest.

Temporal things are as the mirage in the desert.

The accent of conviction is indispensable if you would convince.

The approbation of God is more than the admiration of nations.

The arrows of calamity are aimed at your sins.

The believer has abiding arguments for abiding consolation.

The Bible in the memory is better than the Bible in the bookcase.

The Bible is the treasury of heavenly knowledge, the cyclopedia of divine science.

The Bible is, to many a man, God's unopened letter.

The blank of nothingness stood not in God's way when He came to create.

The cross is the last argument of God.

The cure for vain glory is true glory.

The devil's bread is all bran.

The divine blesses the human, or the human could not bless the divine.

The door of repentance opens into the halls of joy.

The doorstep of the palace of wisdom is a humble sense of ignorance.

Weak faith is a great fabricator of terrors.

We could do with less paint if we had more power.

We need faith in every step of a holy life.

We need less varnish and more verity.

We need workshop faith, as well as prayer-meeting faith.

We play the man today, and the mouse tomorrow.

We shall not be muzzled like dogs either to please the world or its masters.

When the devil is not troubled by us, he does not trouble us.

When the Lord's black horses call at our door, they bring us double loads of blessing.

When you are out for a holiday, be holy.

Who wants to paddle about in a duck pond all his life? Launch out into the deep.

Wilful ignorance will bring terrible damnation.

You cannot get a gross of conversions like you can a gross of steel pens.

You have the milk of faith, but God wills that you should have the cream of assurance.

You lose the leverage of power if you fail in holiness.

You may wash sin in eau-de-Cologne, but it smells none the sweeter.

Your Father's kisses will make you forget your brother's frowns.

Gleanings Among the Sheaves

THE PRECIOUSNESS OF THE PROMISES

THE PROMISES of God are to the believer an inexhaustible mine of wealth. Happy is it for him if he knows how to search out their secret veins and enrich himself with their hid treasures. They are an armory containing all manner of offensive and defensive weapons. Blessed is he who has learned to enter into the sacred arsenal, to put on the breastplate and the helmet, and to lay his hand to the spear and to the sword. They are a surgery in which the believer will find all manner of restoratives and blessed elixirs; nor lacks there an ointment for every wound, a cordial for every faintness, a remedy for every disease. Blessed is he who is well skilled in heavenly pharmacy and knoweth how to lay hold on the healing virtues of the promises of God. The promises are to the Christian a storehouse of food. They are as the granaries which Joseph built in Egypt, or as the golden pot wherein the manna was preserved. Blessed is he who can take the five barley loaves and fishes of promise and break them till his five thousand necessities shall all be supplied, and he is able to gather up baskets full of fragments. The promises are the Christian's Magna Charta of liberty; they are the title deeds of his heavenly estate. Happy is he who knoweth how to read them well and call them all his own. Yea, they are the jewel room in which the Christian's crown treasures are preserved. The regalia are his, secretly to admire today, which he shall openly wear in Paradise hereafter. He

44

is already privileged as a king with the silver key that unlocks the strong room; he may even now grasp the scepter, wear the crown, and put upon his shoulders the imperial mantle. O, how unutterably rich are the promises of our faithful, covenant-keeping God! If we had the tongue of the mightiest of orators, and if that tongue could be touched with a live coal from off the altar, yet still it could not utter a tenth of the praises of the exceeding great and precious promises of God. Nay, they who have entered into rest, whose tongues are attuned to the lofty and rapturous eloquence of cherubim and seraphim, even they can never tell the height and depth, the length and breadth of the unsearchable riches of Christ, which are stored up in the treasure house of God —the promises of the covenant of His grace.

The Privileges of Trial

It is said that when the stars cannot be seen during the day from the ordinary level of the earth, if one should go down into a dark well, they would be visible at once. And certainly it is a fact that the best of God's promises are usually seen by His church when she is in her darkest trials. As sure as ever God puts His children in the furnace, He will be in the furnace with them. I do not read that Jacob saw the angel until he came into a position where he had to wrestle, and then the wrestling Jacob saw the wrestling angel. I do not know that Joshua ever saw the angel of God till he was by Jericho; and then Joshua saw the angelic warrior. I do not know that Abraham ever saw the Lord till he had become a stranger and a wanderer in the plains of Mamre, and then the Lord appeared unto him as a wayfaring man. It is in our most desperate sorrows that we have our happiest experiences. You must go to Patmos to see the revelation. It is only on the barren, storm-girt rock, shut out from all the world's light, that we can find a fitting darkness in which we can view the light of heaven undistracted by the shadows of earth.

The Joy of Victory

The Christian's battlefield is here, but the triumphal procession is above. This is the land of the sword and the spear: that is the land of the wreath and the crown. This is the land of the garment rolled in blood and of the dust of the fight: that is the land of the trumpet's joyful sound, the place of the white robe and of the shout of conquest. O, what a thrill of joy shall be felt by all the blessed when their conquests shall be complete in heaven; when death itself, the last of foes, shall be slain; when Satan shall be dragged captive at the chariot wheels of Christ; when the great shout of universal victory shall rise from the hearts of all the redeemed! What a moment of pleasure shall that be!

Something of the joy of victory we know even here. Have you ever struggled against an evil heart and at last overcome it? Have you ever wrestled hard with a strong temptation and known what it was to sing with thankfulness, "When I said my feet slipped, Thy mercy, O Lord, held me up."? Have you, like Bunyan's Christian, fought with Apollyon, and after a fierce contest, put him to flight? Then you have had a foretaste of the heavenly triumph—just an imagining of what the ultimate victory will be. God gives you these partial triumphs that they may be earnests of the future. Go on and conquer, and let each conquest, though a harder one and more strenuously contested, be to you as a pledge of the victory of heaven.

A Quiet Heart

Unless the heart be kept peaceable, the life will not be happy. If calm doth not reign over that inner lake within the soul which feeds the rivers of our life, the rivers themselves will always be in storm. Our outward acts will always tell that they were born in tempests by being tempestuous themselves. We all desire to lead a joyous life; the bright eye and the elastic foot are things which we each of us desire; to carry about a contented mind is that to which most men are continually aspiring. Let us remember that the only way to keep our life peaceful and happy is to keep the heart at rest; for come poverty, come wealth, come honor, come shame, come plenty, or come scarcity, if the heart be quiet, there will be happiness anywhere. But whatever the sunshine and the brightness, if the heart be troubled, the whole life must be troubled too.

A Rich Life

When one of our kings came back from captivity, as old chroniclers tell, there were fountains in Cheapside which flowed with wine. So bounteous was the king and so glad the people, that instead of water, they made wine flow free to everybody. There is a way of making our life so rich, so full, so blessed to our fellowmen, that the metaphor may be applicable to us, and men may say that our life flows with wine when other men's lives flow with water. You have known some such men. John Howard's life was not like our poor, common lives: he was so benevolent, his sympathy with the race so self-denying that the streams of his life were like generous wine. You have known personally, it may be, some eminent saint, one who lived very near to Jesus: when he talked, there was an unction and a savor about his words, a solidity and a strength about his utterances which you could appreciate, though you could not attain unto it. You have sometimes said, "I wish my words were as full, as sweet, as mellow, and as unctuous as the words of such a one. I wish my actions were just as rich, had as deep a color, and as pure a taste, as the acts of some other to whom you point. All I can do seems but little and empty when compared with his high attainments. O, that I could do more! O, that I could send streams of pure gold into every house, instead of my poor dross!" Well, Christian, this should stimulate thee to keep thine heart full of rich things.

Never, never neglect the Word of God; that will make thy heart rich with precept, thy head rich with understanding, and thy bowels rich with compassion; then, thy conversation, when it flows through thy mouth, will be from thy soul, and, like all that is within thee, rich, unctuous, and savory. Only let thy heart be full of sweet, generous love, and the stream that flows from thy lips will be sweet and generous. Above all, get Jesus to live in thine heart, and then out of thee shall flow rivers of living water, more exhilarating, purer, and more satiating than the water of the well of Sychar of which Jacob drank. Go forth, with Christian, to the great mine of unsearchable riches and cry unto the Holy Spirit to make thy heart rich unto salvation. So shall thy life and conversation be a boon to thy fellows; and when they see thee, thy visage shall shine, and thy face shall be as the angel of God.

The Lord's Jewels

Goldsmiths make exquisite forms from precious material: they fashion the bracelet and the ring from gold. God maketh His precious things out of base material and from the black pebbles of the defiling brooks, He hath taken up stones which He hath set in the golden ring of His immutable love to make them gems to sparkle on His finger forever.

Self

Faith will never be weak if *self* be weak, but when self is strong, faith cannot be strong; for "self" is very much like what the gardener calls the "sucker," at the bottom of the tree, which never bears fruit but only draws away the nourishment from the tree itself. Now, self is that sucker which diverts the nourishment from faith, and you must cut it up or else your faith will always be "little faith," and you will have difficulty in maintaining any comfort in your soul.

STRENGTH THROUGH JOY

It is when the mind is happy that it can be laborious. "The joy of the Lord is your strength."

THE REFINER'S FIRE

There is not an ingot of silver in heaven's treasury which has not been in the furnace on earth and been purified seven times; there is not a gem which the Divine Jeweler has not exposed to every sort of test; there is not an atom of gold in the Redeemer's crown which has not been molten among the hottest coals so as to rid it of its alloy. It is universal to every child of God. If you are a servant of the Lord, you must be tried "as gold is tried."

HEART-LEARNING

We can learn nothing of the gospel except by feeling its truths. There are some sciences that may be learned by the head, but the science of Christ crucified can only be learned by the heart.

THE HOPE OF HEAVEN

Believers are not only to be with Christ and to behold His glory, but they are to be like Christ and to be glorified with Him. Is He glorious? So shall they be. Is He enthroned? So shall they be. Does He wear a crown? So shall they. Is He a priest? So shall they be kings to share His dominion and priests to offer acceptable sacrifices forever. Mark, that in all Christ has, believers participate. They are to reign with Christ and have a portion of His joy; to be honored with Him, to be accepted in Him. This is heaven indeed! If you have this hope, I beseech you hold it fast, live on it, rejoice in it.

A hope so much divine,
  May trials well endure;
May purge your soul from sense and sin,
  As Christ the Lord is pure.

Live near your Master now, so shall your evidences be bright; and when you come to cross the flood, you shall see Him face to face, and what *that is* only they can tell who enjoy it every hour. But if you have *not* this bright hope, how is it that you can live content? You are going through a dark world to a darker eternity. I beeseech you stop and pause. Consider for a moment whether it is worth while to lose heaven for this poor earth. What! pawn eternal glories for the pitiful pence of a few moments of the world's enjoyments? No, stop, I beseech you; weigh the bargain ere you accept it. What shall it profit you to gain the whole world and lose your soul? What wailing and gnashing of teeth shall there be over the carelessness or misadventure by which men lose *such a heaven as this!*

Using the Promises for This Life

Godliness is profitable unto all things, having promise of the life that now is, and of that which is to come.—I Tim. 4:8.

A SORT of affection prevents some Christians from treating religion as if its sphere lay among the common places of daily life. It is to them transcendental and dreamy; rather a creation of pious fiction than a matter of fact. They believe in God, after a fashion, for things spiritual and for the life which is to be; but they totally forget that true godliness hath the promise of the life which now is, as well as of that which is to come. To them it would seem almost a profanation to pray about the small matters of which daily life is made up. Perhaps they will be startled if I venture to suggest that this should make them question the reality of their faith. If it cannot bring them help in little troubles of life, will it support them in the greater trials of death? If it cannot profit them as to food and raiment, what can it do for them as to the immortal spirit?

In the life of Abraham we perceive that his faith had to do with all the events of his earthly pilgrimage; it was connected with his removals from one country to another, with the separation of a nephew from his camp, with fighting against invaders, and specially with the birth of the long-promised son. No part of the patriarch's life was outside the circle of his faith in God. Towards the close of his life it is said, "and the Lord had blessed Abraham in all things," which includes temporals as well as spirituals.

In Jacob's case the Lord promised him bread to eat, and raiment to put on, and the bringing of him to his father's house in peace; and all these things are of a temporal and earthly character. Assuredly these first believers did not spirit away the present blessings of the covenant, or regard it as an airy, mystical matter to believe in God. One is struck with the want of any line of demarcation between secular and sacred in their lives; they journeyed as pilgrims, fought like Crusaders, ate and drank like saints, lived as priests, and spake as prophets. Their life was their religion and their religion was their life. They trusted God, not merely about certain things of higher import, but about everything, and hence, even a servant from one of their houses when he was sent on an errand, prayed, "O Lord God of my master, prosper the way which I go!" This was genuine faith, and it is ours to imitate it, and no longer to allow the substance of the promise, and the life of faith, to evaporate in mere sentimental and visionary fancies. If trust in God is good for everything, it is good for everything within the line of the promise, and it is certain that the life which now is lies within that region.

Let my reader observe and use practically such words of God as these, "Ye shall serve the Lord your God, and he shall bless thy bread, and thy water; and I will take sickness away from the midst of thee" (Ex. 23:25). "Trust in the Lord, and do good; so shalt thou dwell in the land, and verily thou shalt be fed" (Ps. 37: 3). "Surely he shall deliver thee from the snare of the fowler, and from the noisome pestilence. He shall cover thee with his feathers, and under his wings shalt thou trust: his truth shall be thy shield and buckler, Thou shalt not be afraid for the terror by night; nor for the arrow that flieth by day; nor for the pestilence that walketh in darkness; nor for the destruction that wasteth at noonday. A thousand shall fall at thy side, and ten thousand at thy right hand; but it shall not come nigh thee" (Ps. 91:3–7). "He shall deliver thee in six troubles: yea, in seven there shall no evil touch thee" (Job 5:19). "He that walketh righteously, and speaketh uprightly; he that despiseth the gain of oppressions, that shaketh his hands from holding of bribes, that stoppeth his ears from hearing of blood, and shutteth his eyes from seeing evil; he shall dwell on high: his place of defence shall be the munitions of rocks: bread shall be given him; his waters shall be sure" (Is. 33:15, 16). "For the Lord God is a sun and shield: the Lord will give grace and glory: no good thing will he withhold from them that walk uprightly" (Ps. 84:11). "No weapon that is formed against thee shall prosper; and every tongue that shall rise against thee in judgment thou shalt condemn. This is the heritage of the servants of the Lord, and their righteousness is of me, saith the Lord" (Is. 54:17).

Our Saviour intended faith to be our *quietus* concerning daily cares, or he would not have said, "Therefore I say unto you, take no thought for your life, what ye shall eat, or what ye shall drink; nor yet for your body, what ye shall put on. Is not the life more than meat, and the body than raiment? Behold the fowls of the air: for they sow not, neither do they reap, nor gather into barns; yet your heavenly Father feedeth them. Are ye not much better than they?" (Mat. 6:25, 26.) What else but the exercise of faith concerning temporal things could he have meant when he used the following language? "And seek not ye what ye shall eat, or what ye shall drink, neither be ye of doubtful mind. For all these things do the nations of the world seek after: and your Father knoweth that ye have need of these things" (Luke 12:29, 30).

Paul meant the same when he wrote, "Be careful for nothing; but in every thing by prayer and supplication with thanksgiving let your requests be made known unto God. And the peace of God, which passeth all understanding, shall keep your hearts and minds through Christ Jesus" (Phil. 4:6, 7).

He who is gone to prepare heaven for us will not leave us without provision for the journey thither. God does not give us heaven as the Pope gave England to the Spanish King—*if he could get it:* but he makes the road sure, as well as the end. Now, our earthly necessities are as real as our spiritual ones, and we may rest sure that the Lord will supply them. He will send us those supplies in the way of promise, prayer, and faith, and so make them a means of education for us. He will fit us for Canaan by the experience of the wilderness.

To suppose that temporal things are too little for our condescending God is to forget that he observes the flight of sparrows and counts the hairs of his people's heads. Besides, everything is so little to him, that, if he does not care for the little, he cares for nothing. Who is to divide affairs by size or weight? The turning-point of history may be a minute circumstance. Blessed is the man to whom nothing is too small for God; for certainly nothing is too small to cause us sorrow or to involve us in peril. A man of God once lost a key: he prayed about it and found it. It was reported of him as a strange circumstance. Indeed, it was nothing unusual: some of us pray about everything and tremble lest the infinitesimal things should not be sanctified by the Word of God and prayer. It is not the including of trifles which is any trouble to our consciences, but the omission of them. We are assured that when our Lord gave his angels charge to guard our feet from stones in the way, he placed all the details of our life under heavenly care, and we are glad to commit all things to his keeping.

It is one of the abiding miracles of the present dispensation that in Christ we have continual peace under all trials, and through him we have power in prayer to obtain from the Lord all things necessary for this life and godliness. It has been the writer's lot to test the Lord hundreds of times about temporal needs, being driven thereto by the care of orphans and students. Prayer has many, many times brought opportune supplies and cleared away serious difficulties. I know that faith can fill a purse, provide a meal, change a hard heart, procure a site for a building, heal sickness, quiet insubordination, and stay an epidemic. Like money in the worldling's hand, faith in the hand of the man of God "answereth all things." All things in heaven, and earth, and under the earth answer to the command of prayer. Faith is not to be imitated by a quack, nor simulated by a hypocrite; but where it is real and can grasp a divine promise with firm grip, it is a great wonder-worker. How I wish that my reader would so believe in God as to lean upon him in all the concerns of his life! This would lead him into a new world, and bring to him such confirmatory evidence as to the truth of our holy faith that he would laugh sceptics to scorn. Child-like faith in God provides sincere hearts with a practical prudence, which I am inclined to call-sanctified common-sense. The simple-minded believer, though laughed at as an idiot, has a wisdom about him which cometh from above and effectually baffles the cunning of the wicked. Nothing puzzles a malicious enemy like the straightforward unguardedness of an out-and-out believer.

He that believes his God is not afraid of evil tidings, for his heart has found a calm fixity in trusting in the Lord. In a thousand ways this faith sweetens, enlarges, and enriches life. Try it, dear reader, and see if it does not yield you an immeasurable wealth of blessedness! It will not save you from trouble, for the promise is, "These things I have spoken unto you, that in me ye might have peace. In the world ye shall have tribulation: but be of good cheer; I have overcome the world" (John 16:33): but it will cause you to glory in tribulations also, "knowing that tribulation worketh patience, and patience, experience; and experience, hope: and hope maketh not ashamed; because the love of God is shed abroad in our hearts by the Holy Ghost which is given unto us" (Rom. 5:3-5).

> My faith not only flies to heaven,
>   But walks with God below;
> To me are all things daily given,
>   While passing to and fro.
>
> The promise speaks of worlds above,
>   But not of these alone;

It feeds and clothes me *now* with love,
And makes this world my own.

I trust the Lord, and he replies,
In things both great and small.
He honours faith with prompt supplies;
Faith honours *him* in all.

An Exposition of Psalm 19

SUBJECT.—It would be idle to inquire into the particular period when this delightful poem was composed, for there is nothing in its title or subject to assist us in the inquiry. The heading, "To the chief Musician, a Psalm of David," informs us that David wrote it, and that it was committed to the Master of the service of song in the sanctuary for the use of the assembled worshipers. Is his earliest days the psalmist, while keeping his father's flock, had devoted himself to the study of God's two great books—nature and Scripture; and he had so thoroughly entered into the spirit of these only two volumes in his library that he was able with a devout criticism to compare and contrast them, magnifying the excellency of the Author as seen in both. How foolish and wicked are those who instead of accepting the two sacred tomes and delighting to behold the same divine hand in each, spend all their wits in endeavoring to find discrepancies and contradictions. We may rest assured that the true "Vestiges of Creation" will never contradict Genesis, nor will a correct "Cosmos" be found at variance with the narrative of Moses. He is wisest who reads both the world-book and the Word-book as two volumes of the same work, and feels concerning them, "My Father wrote them both."

DIVISION.—This song very distinctly divides itself into three parts, well described by the translators in the ordinary heading of our version. The creatures shew God's glory, 1–6. The word sheweth his grace, 7–11. David prayeth for grace, 12–14. Thus praise and prayer are mingled, and he who here sings the work of God in the world without, pleads for a work of grace in himself within.

EXPOSITION

1. The heavens declare the glory of God; and the firmament sheweth his handywork.

2. Day unto day uttereth speech, and night unto night sheweth knowledge.

3. *There is* no speech nor language, *where* their voice is not heard.

4. Their line is gone out through all the earth, and their words to the end of the world. In them hath he set a tabernacle for the sun.

5. Which is as a bridegroom coming out of his chamber, and rejoiceth as a strong man to run a race.

6. His going forth *is* from the end of the heaven, and his circuit unto the ends of it: and there is nothing hid from the heat thereof.

COMMENT

1. *"The heavens declare the glory of God."* The book of nature has three leaves, heaven, earth, and sea, of which heaven is the first and the most glorious, and by its aid we are able to see the beauties of the other two. Any book without its first page would be sadly imperfect, and especially the great Natural Bible since its first pages, the sun, moon, and stars, supply light to the rest of the volume, and are thus the keys, without which the writing which follows would be dark and undiscerned. Man walking erect was evidently made to scan the skies, and he who begins to read creation by studying the stars begins the book at the right place.

The *heavens* are plural for their variety, comprising the watery heavens with their clouds of countless forms, the aerial heavens with their calms and tempests, the solar heavens with all the glories of the day, and the starry heavens with all the marvels of the night; what the Heaven of heavens must be hath not entered into the heart of man, but there in chief all things are telling the glory of God. Any part of creation has more instruction in it than human mind will ever exhaust, but the celestial realm is peculiarly rich in spiritual lore. The heavens *declare,* or are declaring, for the continuance of their testimony is intended by the participles employed; every moment God's existence, power, wisdom, and goodness, are being sounded abroad by the heavenly heralds which shine upon us from above. He who would guess at divine sublimity should gaze upward into the starry vault; he who would imagine infinity must peer into the bound-less expanse; he who desires to see divine wisdom should consider the balancing of the orbs; he who would know divine fidelity must mark the regularity of the planetary motions; and he who would attain some conceptions of divine power, greatness, and majesty, must estimate the forces of attraction, the magnitude of the fixed stars, and the brightness of the whole celestial train. It is not merely glory that the heavens declare, but the *"glory of God,"* for they deliver to us such unanswerable arguments for a conscious, intelligent, planning, controlling, and presiding Cre-ator, that no unprejudiced person can remain unconvinced by them. The testimony given by the heavens is no mere hint, but a plain, unmistakable declaration; and it is a declaration of the most constant and abiding kind. Yet for all this, to what avail is the loudest declaration to a deaf man, or the clearest showing to one spiritually blind? God the Holy Ghost must illuminate us, or all the suns in the milky way never will.

"The firmament sheweth his handywork;" not *handy,* in the vulgar use of that term, but hand-work. The expanse is full of the works of the Lord's skilful, creating hands; hands being attributed to the great creating Spirit to set forth His care and workmanlike action, and to meet the poor comprehension of mortals. It is humbling to find that even when the most devout and elevated minds are desirous to express their loftiest thoughts of God, they must use words and metaphors drawn from the earth. We are children, and must each confess, "I think as a child, I speak as a child." In the expanse above us God flies, as it were, His starry flag to show that the King is at home, and hangs out His es-

cutcheon that atheists may see how He despises their denuncia-
tions of Him. He who looks up to the firmament and then writes
himself down an atheist, brands himself at the same moment as
an idiot or a liar. Strange is it that some who love God are yet
afraid to study the God-declaring book of nature; the mock-spir-
ituality of some believers who are too heavenly to consider the
heavens has given color to the vaunts of infidels that nature
contradicts revelation. The wisest of men are those who with
pious eagerness trace the goings forth of Jehovah as well in cre-
atio₁ as in grace; only the foolish have any fears lest the honest
study of the one should injure our faith in the other. Dr. M'Cosh
has well said, "We have often mourned over the attempts made to
set the works of God against the Word of God, and thereby excite, propagate, and perpetuate jealousies fitted to separate parties
that ought to live in closest union. In particular, we have always
regretted that endeavors should have been made to depreciate
nature with a view of exalting revelation; it has always appeared
to us to be nothing else than the degrading of one part of God's
works in the hope thereby of exalting and recommending another.
Let not science and religion be reckoned as opposing citadels,
frowning defiance upon each other and their troops brandishing
their armor in hostile attitude. They have too many common
foes, if they would but think of it, in ignorance and prejudice, in
passion and vice, under all their forms, to admit of their lawfully
wasting their strength in a useless warfare with each other. Science has a foundation, and so has religion; let them unite their
foundations, and the basis will be broader, and they will be two
compartments of one great fabric reared to the glory of God. Let
the one be the outer and the other the inner court. In the one, let
all look, and admire and adore; and in the other, let those who
have faith kneel, and pray, and praise. Let the one be the sanctuary where human learning may present its richest incense as an
offering to God, and the other the holiest of all, separated from
it by a veil now rent in twain, and in which, on a blood-sprinkled

mercy seat, we pour out the love of a reconciled heart, and hear the oracles of the living God."

2. *"Day unto day uttereth speech, and night unto night sheweth knowledge."* As if one day took up the story where the other left it, and each night passed over the wondrous tale to the next. The original has in it the thought of pouring out, or welling over, with speech; as though days and nights were but as a fountain flowing evermore with Jehovah's praise. Oh to drink often at the celestial well and learn to utter the glory of God! The witnesses above cannot be slain or silenced; from their elevated seats they constantly preach the knowledge of God, unawed and unbiased by the judgments of men. Even the changes of alternating night and day are mutely eloquent, and light and shade equally reveal the Invisible One; let the vicissitudes of our circumstances do the same, and while we bless the God of our days of joy, let us also extol Him who giveth "songs in the night."

The lesson of day and night is one which it were well if all men learned. It should be among our day thoughts and night thoughts to remember the flight of time, the changeful character of earthly things, the brevity both of joy and sorrow, the preciousness of life, our utter powerlessness to recall the hours once flown, and the irresistible approach of eternity. Day bids us labor, night reminds us to prepare for our last home; day bids us work for God, and night invites us to rest in him; day bids us look for endless day, and night warns us to escape from everlasting night.

3. *"There is no speech nor language, where their voice is not heard."* Every man may hear the voices of the stars. Many are the languages of terrestrials, to celestials there is but one, and that one may be understood by every willing mind. The lowest heathen are without excuse if they do not discover the invisible things of God in the works which he has made. Sun, moon, and stars are God's traveling preachers; they are apostles upon their

journey confirming those who regard the Lord, and judges on circuit condemning those who worship idols.

The margin gives us another rendering, which is more literal and involves less repetition; "*no speech, no words, their voice is not heard*"; that is to say, their teaching is not addressed to the ear, and is not uttered in articulate sounds; it is pictorial, and directed to the eye and heart; it touches not the sense by which faith comes, for faith cometh by hearing. Jesus Christ is called the Word, for He is a far more distinct display of Godhead than all the heavens can afford; they are, after all, but dumb instructors; neither star nor sun can arrive at a word, but Jesus is the express image of Jehovah's person, and His name is the Word of God.

4. "*Their line is gone out through all the earth, and their words to the end of the world.*" Although the heavenly bodies move in solemn silence, yet in reason's ear they utter precious teachings. They give forth no literal *words,* but yet their instruction is clear enough to be so described. Horne says that the phrase employed indicates a language of signs, and thus we are told that the heavens speak by their significant actions and operations. Nature's words are like those of the deaf and dumb, but grace tells us plainly of the Father. By their line is probably meant the *measure* of their domain which, together with their testimony, has gone out to the utmost end of the habitable earth. No man living beneath the cope of heaven dwells beyond the bounds of the diocese of God's Court-preachers; it is easy to escape from the light of ministers, who are as stars in the right hand of the Son of Man; but even then men, with a conscience yet unseared, will find a Nathan to accuse them, a Jonah to warn them, and an Elijah to threaten them in the silent stars of night. To gracious souls the voices of the heavens are more influential far, they feel the sweet influences of the Pleiades and are drawn towards their Father God by the bright bands of Orion.

"*In them hath he set a tabernacle for the sun.*" In the midst of the heavens the sun encamps and marches like a mighty monarch on his glorious way. He has no fixed abode, but as a traveler pitches and removes his tent, a tent which will soon be taken down and rolled together as a scroll. As the royal pavilion stood in the center of the host, so the sun in his place appears like a king in the midst of attendant stars.

5. *"Which is as a bridegroom coming out of his chamber."* A bridegroom comes forth sumptuously appareled, his face beaming with a joy which he imparts to all around; such, but with a mighty emphasis, is the rising sun. *"And rejoiceth as a strong man to run a race."* As a champion girt for running cheerfully addresses himself to the race, so does the sun speed onward with matchless regularity and unwearying swiftness in his appointed orbit. It is but mere play to him; there are no signs of effort, flagging, or exhaustion. No other creature yields such joy to the earth as her bridegroom the sun; and none, whether they be horse or eagle, can for an instant compare in swiftness with that heavenly champion. But all his glory is but the glory of God; even the sun shines in light borrowed from the Great Father of Lights.

> Thou sun, of this great world both eye and soul,
> Acknowledge Him thy greater; sound His praise
> Both when thou climb'st, and when high noon hast gained,
> And when thou fall'st.

6. *"His going forth is from the end of the heaven, and his circuit unto the ends of it."* He bears his light to the boundaries of the solar heavens, traversing the zodiac with steady motion, denying his light to none who dwell within his range. *"And there is nothing hid from the heat thereof."* Above, beneath, around, the heat of the sun exercises an influence. The bowels of the earth are stored with the ancient produce of the solar rays, and even yet earth's inmost caverns feel their power. Where light

is shut out, yet heat and other more subtle influences find their way.

There is no doubt a parallel intended to be drawn between the heaven of grace and the heaven of nature. God's way of grace is sublime and broad, and full of His glory; in all its displays it is to be admired and studied with diligence; both its lights and its shades are instructive; it has been proclaimed, in a measure, to every people, and in due time shall be yet more completely published to the ends of the earth. Jesus, like a sun, dwells in the midst of revelation, tabernacling among men in all His brightness; rejoicing, as the Bridegroom of His church, to reveal Himself to men; and, like a champion, to win unto Himself renown. *He* makes a circuit of mercy, blessing the remotest corners of the earth; and there are no seeking souls, however degraded and depraved, who shall be denied the comfortable warmth and benediction of His love—even death shall feel the power of His presence, and resign the bodies of the saints, and this fallen earth shall be restored to its pristine glory.

7. The law of the Lord *is* perfect, converting the soul: the testimony of the Lord *is* sure, making wise the simple.

8. The statutes of the LORD *are* right, rejoicing the heart: the commandment of the LORD *is* pure, enlightening the eyes.

9. The fear of the LORD *is* clean, enduring for ever; the judgments of the LORD *are* true *and* righteous altogether.

10. More to be desired *are they* than gold, yea, than much fine gold: sweeter also than honey and the honeycomb.

11. Moreover by them is thy servant warned: *and* in keeping of them *there is* great reward.

In the three following verses we have a brief but instructive hexapla containing six descriptive titles of the Word, six characteristic qualities mentioned and six divine effects declared. Names, nature, and effect are well set forth.

7. *"The law of the Lord is perfect"*; by which he means not

merely the law of Moses but the doctrine of God, the whole run and rule of sacred Writ. The doctrine revealed by God he declares to be perfect, and yet David had but a very small part of the Scriptures, and if a fragment, and that the darkest and most historical portion, be perfect, what must the entire volume be? How more than perfect is the book which contains the clearest possible display of divine love, and gives us an open vision of redeeming grace. The gospel is a complete scheme or law of gracious salvation, presenting to the needy sinner everything that his terrible necessities can possibly demand. There are no redundancies and no omissions in the Word of God and in the plan of grace; why then do men try to paint this lily and gild this refined gold? The gospel is perfect in all its parts, and perfect as a whole: it is a crime to add to it, treason to alter it, and felony to take from it.

"*Converting the soul.*" Making the man to be returned or restored to the place from which sin had cast him. The practical effect of the Word of God is to turn the man to himself, to his God, and to holiness; and the turn or conversion is not outward alone, "*the soul*" is moved and renewed. The great means of the conversion of sinners is the Word of God, and the more closely we keep to it in our ministry the more likely are we to be successful. It is God's Word rather than man's comment on God's Word which is made mighty with souls. When the law drives and the gospel draws, the action is different but the end is one, for by God's spirit the soul is made to yield and cries, "Turn me, and I shall be turned." Try men's depraved nature with philosophy and reasoning, and it laughs your efforts to scorn, but the Word of God soon works a transformation.

"*The testimony of the Lord is sure.*" God bears His testimony against sin and on behalf of righteousness; He testifies of our fall and of our restoration; this testimony is plain, decided, and infallible, and is to be accepted as sure. God's witness in His Word is so sure that we may draw solid comfort from it both for time and eternity, and so sure that no attacks made upon it however fierce or subtle can ever weaken its force. What a blessing that in a world of uncertainties we have something sure to rest upon! We hasten from the quicksands of human speculations to the *terra firma* of Divine Revelation.

"*Making wise the simple.*" Humble, candid, teachable minds receive the word and are made wise unto salvation. Things hidden from the wise and prudent are revealed unto babes. The persuadable grow wise, but the cavilers continue fools. As a law or plan, the Word of God converts and, then, as a testimony it instructs; it is not enough for us to be converts, we must continue to be disciples; and if we have felt the power of truth, we must go on to prove its certainty by experience. The perfection of the gospel converts, but its sureness edifies; if we would be edified, it becomes us not to stagger at the promise through unbelief, for a doubted gospel cannot make us wise, but truth of which we are assured will be our establishment.

8. "*The statutes of the Lord are right.*" His precepts and decrees are founded in righteousness and are such as are right or fitted to the right reason of man. As a physician gives the right medicine, and a counselor the right advice, so does the Book of God. "*Rejoicing the heart.*" Mark the progress; he who was converted was next made wise and is now made happy; that truth which makes the heart right then gives joy to the right heart. Free grace brings heart-joy. Earthborn mirth dwells on the lip and flushes the bodily powers; but heavenly delights satisfy the inner nature and fill the mental faculties to the brim. There is no cordial of comfort like that which is poured from the bottle of Scripture. "Retire and read thy Bible to be gay."

"*The commandment of the Lord is pure.*" No mixture of error defiles it, no stain of sin pollutes it; it is the unadulterated milk, the undiluted wine. "*Enlightening the eyes,*" purging away by its own purity the earthly grossness which mars the intellectual discernment: whether the eye be dim with sorrow or with sin, the Scripture is a skilful oculist and makes the eye clear and bright. Look at the sun and it puts out your eyes, look at the more than sunlight of Revelation and it enlightens them; the purity of snow causes snow-blindness to the Alpine traveler, but the purity of God's truth has the contrary effect and cures the natural blindness of the soul. It is well again to observe the gradation; the convert became a disciple and next a rejoicing soul, he now obtains a discerning eye and as a spiritual man discerneth all things, though he himself is discerned of no man.

9. "*The fear of the Lord is clean.*" The doctrine of truth is here described by its spiritual effect, viz., inward piety, or the fear of the Lord; this is clean in itself, and cleanses out the love of sin, sanctifying the heart in which it reigns. Mr. Godly-fear is never satisfied till every street, lane, and alley, yea, and every house and every corner of the town of Mansoul is clean rid of the Diabolonians who lurk therein. "*Enduring for ever.*" Filth brings decay, but cleanness is the great foe of corruption. The grace of God in the heart being a pure principle is also an abiding and incorruptible principle, which may be crushed for a time, but cannot be utterly destroyed. Both in the Word and in the heart, when the Lord writes, He says with Pilate, "What I have written, I have written"; He will make no erasures Himself, much less suffer others to do so. The revealed will of God is never changed; even Jesus came not to destroy but to fulfil, and even the ceremonial law was only changed as to its shadow, the substance intended by it is eternal. When the governments of nations are shaken with revolution and ancient constitutions are being repealed, it is comforting to know that the throne of God is unshaken, and His law unaltered.

"*The judgments of the Lord are true and righteous altogether*"; jointly and severally the words of the Lord are true; that which is good in detail is excellent in the mass; no exception may be taken to a single clause separately, or to the book as a whole. God's judgments, all of them together, or each of them apart, are manifestly just, and need no laborious excuses to justify them. The judicial decisions of Jehovah, as revealed in the law or illustrated in the history of His providence, are truth itself and commend themselves to every truthful mind; not only is their power invincible, but their justice is unimpeachable.

10. *"More to be desired are they than gold, yea, than much fine gold."* Bible truth is enriching to the soul in the highest degree; the metaphor is one which gathers force as it is brought out; gold—fine gold—much fine gold; it is good, better, best, and therefore it is not only to be desired with a miser's avidity, but with more than that. As spiritual treasure is more noble than mere material wealth, so should it be desired and sought after with greater eagerness. Men speak of solid gold, but what is so solid as solid truth? For love of gold pleasure is forsworn, ease renounced, and life endangered; shall we not be ready to do as much for love of truth? *"Sweeter also than honey and the honeycomb."* Trapp says, "Old people are all for profit, the young for pleasure; here's gold for the one, yea, the finest gold in great quantity; here's honey for the other, yea, live honey dropping from the comb." The pleasures arising from a right understanding of the divine testimonies are of the most delightful order; earthly enjoyments are utterly contemptible if compared with them. The sweetest joys, yea, the sweetest of the sweetest falls to his portion who has God's truth to be his heritage.

11. *"Moreover by them is thy servant warned."* We are warned by the Word both of our duty, our danger, and our remedy. On the sea of life there would be many more wrecks, if it were not for the divine storm signals which give to the watchful a timely warning. The Bible should be our Mentor, our Monitor, our Memento Mori, our Remembrancer, and the Keeper of our Conscience. Alas, that so few men will take the warning so graciously given; none but servants of God will do so, for they alone regard their Master's will. Servants of God not only find his service delightful in itself, but they receive good recompense;

"In keeping of them there is great reward." There is a wage, and a great one; though we earn no wages of debt, we win great wages of grace. Saints may be losers for a time, but they shall be glorious gainers in the long run, and even now a quiet conscience is in itself no slender reward for obedience. He who wears the herb called heart's-ease in his bosom is truly blessed. However, the main reward is yet to come, and the word here used hints as much, for it signifies *the heel,* as if the reward would come to us at the end of life when the work was done; not while the labor was in the hand, but when it was gone, and we could see the heel of it. Oh the glory yet to be revealed! It is enough to make a man faint for joy at the prospect of it. Our light affliction, which is but for a moment, is not worthy to be compared with the glory which shall be revealed in us. Then shall we know the value of the Scriptures when we swim in that sea of unutterable delight to which their streams will bear us, if we commit ourselves to them.

12. Who can understand *his* errors? cleanse thou me from secret *faults.*

13. Keep back thy servant also from presumptuous *sins;* let them not have dominion over me: then shall I be upright, and I shall be innocent from the great transgression.

14. Let the words of my mouth, and the meditation of my heart, be acceptable in thy sight, O LORD, my strength, and my redeemer.

12. *"Who can understand his errors?"* A question which is its own answer. It requires, rather, a note of exclamation than of interrogation. By the law is the knowledge of sin, and in the presence of divine truth, the psalmist marvels at the number and heinousness of his sins. He best knows himself who best knows the Word, but even such an one will be in a maze of wonder as to what he does not know, rather than on the mount of congratulation as to what he does know. We have heard of a comedy of errors, but to a good man this is more like a tragedy. Many books

have a few lines of errata at the end, but our errata might well be as large as the volume if we could but have sense enough to see them. Augustine wrote in his older days a series of retractations; ours might make a library if we had enough grace to be convinced of our mistakes and to confess them. "*Cleanse thou me from secret faults.*" Thou canst mark in me faults entirely hidden from myself. It were hopeless to expect to see all my spots; therefore, O Lord, wash away in the atoning blood even those sins which my conscience has been able to detect. Secret sins, like private conspirators, must be hunted out, or they may do deadly mischief; it is well to be much in prayer concerning them. In the Lateran Council of the Church of Rome, a decree was passed that every true believer must confess his sins, all of them, once in a year to the priest, and they affixed to it this declaration, that there is no hope of pardon but in complying with that decree. What can equal the absurdity of such a decree as that? Do they suppose that they can tell their sins as easily as they can count their fingers? Why, if we could receive pardon for all our sins by telling every sin we have committed in one hour, there is not one of us who would be able to enter heaven, since, besides the sins that are known to us and that we may be able to confess, there is a vast mass of sins which are as truly sins as those which we lament but which are secret and come not beneath our eye. If we had eyes like those of God, we should think very differently of ourselves. The transgressions which we see and confess are but like the farmer's small samples which he brings to market when he has left his granary full at home. We have but a very few sins which we can observe and detect compared with those which are hidden from ourselves and unseen by our fellow creatures.

13. "*Keep back thy servant also from presumptuous sins; let them not have dominion over me.*" This earnest and humble prayer teaches us that saints may fall into the worst of sins unless restrained by grace, and that therefore they must watch and pray lest they enter into temptation. There is a natural proneness to

sin in the best of men, and they must be held back as a horse is held back by the bit or they will run into it. Presumptuous sins are peculiarly dangerous. All sins are great sins, but yet some sins are greater than others. Every sin has in it the very venom of rebellion and is full of the essential marrow of traitorous rejection of God; but there be some sins which have in them a greater development of the essential mischief of rebellion and which wear upon their faces more of the brazen pride which defies the Most High. It is wrong to suppose that because all sins will condemn us, that therefore one sin is not greater than another. The fact is, that while all transgression is a greatly grievous and sinful thing, yet there are some transgressions which have a deeper shade of blackness, and a more double scarlet-dyed hue of criminality than others. The presumptuous sins of our text are the chief and worst of all sins; they rank head and foremost in the list of iniquities. It is remarkable that though an atonement was provided under the Jewish law for every kind of sin, there was this one exception; "But the soul that sinneth presumptuously shall have no atonement; it shall be cut off from the midst of my people." And now under the Christian dispensation, although in the sacrifice of our blessed Lord there is a great and precious atonement for presumptuous sins, whereby sinners who have erred in this manner are made clean, yet without doubt, presumptuous sinners, dying without pardon, must expect to receive a double portion of the wrath of God, and a more terrible portion of eternal punishment in the pit that is digged for the wicked. For this reason is David so anxious that he may never come under the reigning power of these giant evils. *"Then shall I be upright, and I shall be innocent from the great transgression."* He shudders at the thought of the unpardonable sin. Secret sin is a steppingstone to presumptuous sin, and that is the vestibule of "the sin which is unto death." He who is not wilful in his sin will be in a fair way to be innocent so far as poor sinful man can be; but he who tempts the devil to tempt him is in a path which will lead him from bad to worse and from the worse to the worst.

14. "*Let the words of my mouth, and the meditation of my heart, be acceptable in thy sight, O Lord, my strength, and my Redeemer.*" A sweet prayer, and so spiritual that it is almost as commonly used in Christian worship as the apostolic benediction. *Words of the mouth* are mockery if the heart does not *meditate;* the shell is nothing without the kernel; but both together are useless unless *accepted;* and even if accepted by man, it is all vanity if not acceptable in *the sight of God.* We must in prayer view Jehovah as our *strength* enabling and our *Redeemer* saving, or we shall not pray aright, and it is well to feel our personal interest so as to use the word *my,* or our prayers will be hindered. Our near Kinsman's name, our Goel or Redeemer, makes a blessed ending to the Psalm; it began with the heavens, but it ends with Him whose glory fills heaven and earth. Blessed Kinsman, give us now to meditate acceptably upon Thy most sweet love and tenderness.

Vanity Fair

Then I saw in my dream, that when they were got out of the wilderness, they presently saw a town before them, and the name of that town is Vanity; and at the town there is a fair kept, called Vanity Fair. It is kept all the year long. It beareth the name of Vanity Fair, because the town where it is kept is lighter than vanity (Psa. 62:9), and also because all that is there sold, or that cometh thither, is vanity; as it is the saying of the wise, "All that cometh is vanity" (Eccl. 11:8).

THE HAPPIEST state of a Christian is the holiest state. As there is most heat nearest to the sun, so there is most happiness nearest to Christ. No Christian enjoys comfort when his eyes are fixed on vanity. I do not blame ungodly men for rushing to their pleasures. Let them have their fill. That is all they have to enjoy, but Christians must seek their delights in a higher sphere than the insipid frivolities of the world. Vain pursuits are dangerous to renewed souls.

Now, as I said, the way to the Celestial City lies just through this town where this lusty fair is kept; and he that would go to the city, and yet not go through this town, "must needs go out of the world" (I Cor. 5:10).

When weary of the strife and sin that meets you on every hand, consider that all the saints have endured the same trial. They were not carried on beds of down to heaven, and you must not expect to travel more easily than they. They had to hazard their lives unto the death in the high places of the field, and you will not be crowned till you also have endured hardness as a good soldier of Jesus Christ. Therefore, "stand fast in the faith, quit you like men, be strong."

Now these pilgrims, as I said, must needs go through this fair. Well, so they did; but, behold, even as they entered into the fair, all the people in the fair were moved, and the town itself, as it were, in a hubbub about them, and that for several reasons: For,

First, The pilgrims were clothed with such kind of raiment as was diverse from the raiment of any that traded in that fair. The people, therefore, of the fair made a great gazing upon them! some said they were fools; some, they were bedlams; and some they were outlandish men (I Cor. 4:9).

Secondly, And as they wondered at their apparel, so they did likewise at their speech; for few could understand what they said. They naturally spoke the language of Canaan; but they that kept the fair were the men of this world. So that from one end of the fair to the other, they seemed barbarians each to the other (I Cor. 2:7, 8).

If you follow Christ fully, you will be sure to be called by some ill name or other. They will say how singular you are. If you become a true Christian, you will soon be a marked man. They will say, "How odd he is!" "How singular she is!" They will think that we try to make ourselves remarkable, when in fact, we are only conscientious and are endeavoring to obey the will of God.

They will say, "Why you are old-fashioned! You believe the same old things that they used to believe in Oliver Cromwell's day—those old Puritanical doctrines." They laugh at our faith and assert that we have lost our liberty.

This fair is no new erected business, but a thing of ancient standing. I will show you the original of it.

Almost five thousand years ago there were pilgrims walking to the Celestial City, as these two honest persons are; and Beelzebub, Apollyon, and Legion, with their companions, perceiving by the path that the pilgrims made, that their way to the city lay through this town of Vanity, they contrived here to set up a fair; a fair wherein should be sold all sorts of vanity, and that it should last all the year long. Therefore at this fair are all such merchandise sold as houses, lands, trades, places, honours, preferments, titles, countries, kingdoms, lusts, pleasures; and delights of all sorts, as harlots, wives, husbands, children, masters, servants' lives, blood, bodies, souls, silver, gold, pearls, precious stones, and what not.

There are divers kinds of vanity. The cap and bells of the fool, the mirth of the world, the dance, the lyre, and the cup of the dissolute; all these men know to be vanities. They wear upon their forefront their proper name and title. Far more treacherous are those equally vain things, the cares of this world, and the deceitfulness of riches. A man may follow vanity as truly in the counting-house, as in the theatre. If he be spending his life in amassing wealth, he passes his days in a vain show. Unless we follow Christ and make our God the great object of life, we only differ in appearance from the most frivolous.

It is the sweetness of sin that makes it the more dangerous. Satan never sells his poisons naked; he always gilds them before he vends them. Beware of pleasures. Many of them are innocent and healthful, but many are destructive. It is said that where the most beautiful cacti grow, there the most venomous serpents lurk. It is so with sin. Your fairest pleasures will harbor your grossest sins. Take care! Cleopatra's asp was introduced in a basket of flowers. Satan offers to the dunkard the sweetness of the intoxicating cup. He gives to each of us the offer of our peculiar joy; he tickleth us with pleasures, that he may lay hold of us.

And moreover, at this fair, there are at all times to be seen jugglings, cheats, games, plays, fools, apes, knaves, and rogues, and that of every kind.

Here are to be seen, too, and that for nothing, thefts, murders, adulteries, false swearers, and that of a blood-red colour.

Banish forever all thought of indulging the flesh if you would live in the power of your risen Lord. It were ill that a man who is alive in Christ should dwell in the corruption of sin. "Why seek ye the living among the dead?" said the angel to Magdalene. Should the living dwell in the sepulcher? Should divine life be immured in the charnel house of fleshly lust? How can we partake of the cup of the Lord and yet drink the cup of Belial? Surely, believer, from open lusts and sins you are delivered; have you also escaped from the more secret and delusive lime-twigs of the Satanic fowler? Have you come forth from the lust of pride? Have you escaped from slothfulness? Have you clean escaped from carnal security? Are you seeking day by day to live above worldliness, the pride of life, and the ensnaring vice of avarice? Follow after holiness; it is the Christian's crown and glory.

Thirdly, But that which did not a little amuse the merchandisers was, that these pilgrims set very light by all their wares. They cared not so much as to look upon them: and if they called upon them to buy, they would put their fingers in their ears, and cry, "Turn away mine eyes from beholding vanity," and look upwards signifying that their trade and traffic was in heaven (Phil. 3:20, 21).

One chanced, mockingly, beholding the carriage of the men to say unto them, "What will ye buy?" But they, looking gravely upon him said, "We buy the truth."

The common religion of the day is a mingle-mangle of Christ and Belial.

"If God be God serve Him; if Baal be God, serve him." There can be no alliance between the two. Jehovah and Baal can never be friends. "Ye cannot serve God and Mammon." "No man can serve two masters." All attempts at compromise in matters of truth and purity are founded on falsehood. May God save us from such hateful double-mindedness. You must have no fellowship with the unfruitful words of darkness, but rather reprove them. Walk worthy of your high calling and dignity. Remember, O Christian, that thou art a son of the King of kings. Therefore, keep thyself unspotted from the world. Soil not the fingers which are soon to sweep celestial strings; let not those eyes become the windows of lust which are soon to see the King in His beauty; let not those feet, which are soon to walk the golden streets be defiled in miry places; let not those hearts be filled with pride and bitterness which are ere long to be filled with heaven and to overflow with ecstatic joy:

> Rise where eternal beauties bloom,
> And pleasures all divine;
> Where wealth that never can consume,
> And endless glories shine!

At that there was an occasion taken to despise the men the more; some mocking, some taunting, some speaking reproachfully, and some calling upon others to smite them. At last things came to a hubbub and great stir in the fair, insomuch that all order was confounded. Now was word presently brought to the great one of the fair, who quickly came down, and deputed some of his most trusty friends to take those men into examination about whom the fair was almost overturned. So the men were brought to examination; and they that sat upon them asked whence they came, whither they went, and what they did there in such an unusual garb. The men told them that they were pilgrims and strangers in the world, and that they were going to their own country, which was the heavenly Jerusalem, and that they had given no occasion to the men of the town, nor yet to the merchandisers, thus to abuse them, and to let them in their journey, except it was for that, when one asked them what they would buy, they said they would buy the truth. But they that were appointed to examine them, did not believe them to be any other than bedlams and mad, else such as came to put all things into a confusion in the fair. Therefore they took them and beat them, and besmeared them with dirt, and then put them into a cage, that they might be made a spectacle to all the men of the fair. There, therefore, they lay for some time, and were made the objects of any man's sport, or malice, or revenge; the great one of the fair laughing still at all that befell them.

Pilgrims travel as suspected persons through Vanity Fair. Not only are we under surveillance, but there are more spies than we reck of. The espionage is everywhere, at home and abroad. If we fall into the enemies' hands, we may sooner expect generosity from a wolf, or mercy from a fiend, than anything like patience with our infirmities from men who spice their infidelity towards God with scandals against His people. Live a godly gracious life, and you will not escape persecution. You may be happily circumstanced so as to live among earnest Christians and so escape persecution; but take the average Christian man, and he will have a hard time of it if he is faithful. The ungodly will revile those who are true to the Lord Jesus. Christians are ridiculed in the workshop, they are pointed out in the street, and an opprobrious name is hooted at them. Now we shall know who are God's elect and who are not. Persecution acts as a winnowing fan, and those who are light as chaff are driven away by its blast; but those who are true corn remain and are purified. Careless of man's esteem, the truly God-fearing man holds on his way and fears the Lord forever.

"Let us hear the conclusion of the whole matter." My longing is that the churches may be more holy. I grieve to see so much of worldly conformity. How often wealth leads men astray; how many Christians follow the fashion of this wicked world. Alas! with all my preaching, many wander, and try to be members of the church, and citizens of the world too. We have among us avowed lovers of Christ who act too much like "lovers of pleasure."

It is a shameful thing for a professor of Christianity to be found in those music halls, saloons, and places of revelry where you cannot go without your morals being polluted, for you can neither open your eyes nor your ears without knowing at once that you are in the purlieus of Satan.

I charge you by the living God, if you cannot keep good

company and avoid the circle of dissipation, do not profess to be followers of Christ, for He bids you come out from among them and be separate. If you can find pleasure in lewd society and lascivious songs, what right have you to mingle with the fellowship of saints or to join in the singing of psalms?

Keep the best company. Be much with those who are much with God. Let them be thy choicest companions who have made Christ their choicest companion; let Christ's love be thy love. With whom shall believers be, but believers? Our English proverb says, "Birds of a feather flock together." To see a saint and a sinner associating is to see the living and the dead keeping house together. It is better to be with Lazarus in rags, than with Dives in robes. Dwell where God dwells. Make those your companions on earth who will be your companions in heaven.

An unholy church! it is useless to the world and of no esteem among men. It is an abomination, hell's laughter, heaven's abhorrence. The worst evils which have ever come upon the world have been brought upon her by an unholy church. O Christian, the vows of the Lord are upon you. You are God's priest: act as such. You are God's king: reign over your lusts. You are God's chosen: do not associate with Belial. Heaven is your portion: live like a heavenly spirit. So shall you prove that you have true faith in Jesus, for there cannot be faith in the heart unless there be holiness in the life:

> Lord, I desire to live as one
>   Who bears a blood-bought name;
> As one who fears but grieving Thee,
>   And knows no other shame.

John Ploughman's Pictures

If the Cap Fits, Wear It

FRIENDLY READERS: Last time I made a book I trod on some people's corns and bunions, and they wrote me angry letters asking, "Did you mean me!" This time, to save them the expense of a halfpenny card, I will begin my book by saying,

> Whether I please or whether I tease,
> I'll give you my honest mind;
> If the cap should fit, pray wear it a bit;
> If not you can leave it behind.

No offence is meant; but if anything in these pages should come home to a man, let him not send it next door but get a coop for his own chickens. What is the use of reading or hearing for other people? We do not eat and drink for them; why should we lend them our ears and not our mouths? Please then, good friend, if you find a hoe on these premises, weed your own garden with it.

I was speaking with Will Shepherd the other day about our master's old donkey, and I said, "He is so old and stubborn, he really is not worth his keep." "No," said Will, "and worse still, he is so vicious, that I feel sure he'll do somebody a mischief one of these days." You know they say that walls have ears; we were talking rather loud, but we did not know that there were ears in haystacks. We stared, I tell you, when we saw Joe Scroggs come from behind the stack, looking red as a turkey-cock and raving like mad. He burst out swearing at Will and me like a cat spitting at a dog. His monkey was up and no mistake. He'd let us know

80

that he was as good a man as either of us, or the two put together for the matter of that. Talk about *him* in that way; He'd do—I don't know what. I told old Joe we never thought of him nor said a word about him, and he might just as well save his breath to cool his porridge, for nobody meant him any harm. This only made him call me a liar and roar the louder. My friend, Will, was walking away holding his sides, but when he saw that Scroggs was still in a fume, he laughed outright and turned round on him and said, "Why, Joe, we were talking about master's old donkey and not about you; but I shall never see that donkey again without thinking of Joe Scroggs." Joe puffed and blowed, but perhaps he thought it a hard job for he backed out of it, and Will and I went off to our work in rather a merry cue, for Old Joe had blundered on the truth about himself for once in his life.

The aforesaid Will Shepherd has sometimes come down rather heavy upon me in his remarks, but it has done me good. It is partly through his home thrusts that I have come to write this new book, for he thought I was idle; perahps I am, and perhaps I am not. Will forgets that I have other fish to fry and tails to butter; and he does not recollect that a ploughman's mind wants to lie fallow a little and can't give a crop every year. It is hard to make rope when your hemp is all used up, or pancakes without batter, or rook pie without the birds; and so I found it hard to write more when I had said just about all I knew.

Burn a Candle at Both Ends and It Will Soon Be Gone

He came in to old Alderman Greedy's money for he was his nephew; but, as the old saying is, the fork followed the rake, the spender was heir to the hoarder. God has been very merciful to some of us in never letting money come rolling in upon us, for most men are carried off their legs if they meet with a great wave of fortune. Many of us would have been bigger sinners if we had been trusted with larger purses. Poor Jack had plenty of pence but little sense. Money is easier made than made use of. What is hard to gather is easy to scatter. The old gentleman had lined his nest well, but Jack made the feathers fly like flakes of snow in winter time. He got rid of his money by shovelfuls and then by cartloads. After spending the interest he began swallowing the capital and so killed the goose that laid the golden eggs. He squandered his silver and gold in ways which must never be told. It would not go fast enough, and so he bought race horses to run away with it. He got into the hands of backlegs and fell into company of which we shall say but little; only when such madams smile, men's purses weep; these are a well without a bottom, and the more a fool throws in, the more he may. The greatest beauty often causes the greatest ruin. Play, women, and wine are enough to make a prince a pauper.

Always taking out and never putting back soon empties the biggest sack, and so Jack found it; but he took no notice till his last shilling bade him good-by, and then he said he had been robbed; like silly Tom who put his finger in the fire and said it was his bad luck.

It Is Hard for an Empty Sack to Stand Upright

Sam may try a fine while before he will make one of his empty sacks stand upright. If he were not half daft, he would have left off that job before he began it and not have been an Irishman either. He will come to his wit's end before he sets the sack on its end. The old proverb printed at the top was made by a man who had burned his fingers with debtors, and it just means that when folks have no money and are over head and ears in debt, as often as not they leave off being upright and tumble over one way or another. He that has but four and spends five will soon need no purse, but he will most likely begin to use his wits to keep himself afloat and take to all sorts of dodges to manage it.

Nine times out of ten they begin by making promises to pay on a certain day when it is certain they have nothing to pay with. They are as bold at fixing the time as if they had my lord's income. The day comes round as sure as Christmas, and then they haven't a penny in the world, and so they make all sorts of excuses and begin to promise again. Those who are quick to promise are generally slow to perform. They promise mountains and perform molehills. He who gives you fair words and nothing more feeds you with an empty spoon, and hungry creditors soon grow tired of that game. Promises don't fill the belly. Promising men are not great favorites if they are not performing men. When such a fellow is called a liar, he thinks he is hardly done by; and yet he is so, as sure as eggs are eggs, and there's no denying it, as the boy said when the gardener caught him up the cherry tree.

A Handsaw Is a Good Thing, But Not To Shave With

Our friend will cut more than he will eat and shave off something more than hair, and then he will blame the saw. His brains don't lie in his beard, nor yet in the skull above it, or he would see that his saw will only make sores. There's sense in choosing your tools, for a pig's tail will never make a good arrow, nor will his ear make a silk purse. You can't catch rabbits with drums, nor pigeons with plums. A good thing is not good out of its place. It is much the same with lads and girls; you can't put all boys to one trade nor send all girls to the same service. One chap will make a London clerk, and another will do better to plough and sow and reap and mow and be a farmer's boy. It's no use forcing them; a snail will never run a race nor a mouse drive a wagon.

> Send a boy to the well against his will,
> The pitcher will break and the water spill.

With unwilling hounds it is hard to hunt hares. To go against nature and inclination is to row against wind and tide. They say you may praise a fool till you make him useful; I don't know so much about that, but I do know that if I get a bad knife I generally cut my finger, and a blunt axe is more trouble than profit. No, let me shave with a razor if I shave at all and do my work with the best tools I can get.

Never set a man to work he is not fit for; he will never do it well. They say that if pigs fly they always go with their tails forward, and awkward workmen are much the same. Nobody expects cows to catch crows or hens to wear hats. There's reason in roasting eggs, and there should be reason in choosing servants.

Hunchback Sees Not His Own Hump, But He Sees His Neighbor's

He points at the man in front of him, but he is a good deal more of a guy himself. He should not laugh at the crooked until he is straight himself and not then. I hate to hear a raven croak at a crow for being black. A blind man should not blame his brother for squinting, and he who has lost his legs should not sneer at the lame. Yet so it is, the rottenest bough cracks first, and he who should be the last to speak is the first to rail. Bespattered hogs bespatter others, and he who is full of fault finds fault. They are most apt to speak ill of others who do most ill themselves.

> We're very keen our neighbor's hump to see,
> We're blind to that upon our back alone;
> E'en though the lump far greater be,
> It still remains to us unknown.

It does us much hurt to judge our neighbors, because it flatters our conceit, and our pride grows quite fast enough without feeding. We accuse others to excuse ourselves. We are such fools as to dream that we are better because others are worse, and we talk as if we could get up by pulling others down. What is the good of spying holes in people's coats when we can't mend them? Talk of my debts if you mean to pay them; if not, keep your red rag behind your ivory ridge. A friend's faults should not be advertised, and even a stranger's should not be published. He who brays at an ass is an ass himself, and he who makes a fool of another is a fool himself. Don't get into the habit of laughing at people, for the old saying is, "Hanging's stretching and mocking's catching."

> Some must have their joke whoever they poke;
> For the sake of fun mischief is done,
> And to air their wit full many they hit.

He Has a Hole Under His Nose,
and His Money Runs Into It

This is the man who is always dry, because he takes so much heavy wet. He is a loose fellow who is fond of getting tight. He is no sooner up than his nose is in the cup, and his money begins to run down the hole which is just under his nose. He is not a blacksmith, but he has a spark in his throat, and all the publican's barrels can't put it out. If a pot of beer is a yard of land, he must have swallowed more acres than a ploughman could get over for many a day, and still he goes on swallowing until he takes to wallowing. All goes down Gutter Lane. Like the snipe, he lives by suction. If you ask him how he is, he says he would be quite right if he could moisten his mouth. His purse is a bottle, his bank is the publican's till and his casket is a cask; pewter is his precious metal, and his pearl (purl) is a mixture of gin and beer. The dew of his youth comes from Ben Nevis, and the comfort of his soul is cordial gin. He is a walking barrel, a living drainpipe, a moving swill tub. They say "loath to drink and loath to leave off," but he never needs persuading to begin, and as to ending—that is out of the question while he can borrow twopence. This is the gentleman who sings:

> He that buys land buys many stones,
> He that buys meat buys many bones,

> He that buys eggs buys many shells,
> He that buys good ale buys nothing else.

He will never be hanged for leaving his drink behind him. He drinks in season and out of season: in summer because he is hot, and in winter because he is cold.

Scant Feeding of Man or Horse
Is Small Profit and Sure Loss

What is saved out of food of cattle is a dead loss, for a horse can't work if he is not fed. If an animal won't pay for keeping, he won't pay for starving. Even the land yields little if not nourished, and it is just the same with the poor beast. You might as well try to run a steam engine without coals, or drive a water mill without water, as a horse without putting corn into him. Thomas Tusser, who wrote a book upon "Husbandry" in the olden time, said,

> Who starveth his cattle, and wearieth them out
> By carting and ploughing, his gain I much doubt;
> But he that in labor doth use them aright
> Has gain to his comfort and cattle in plight.

Poor dumb animals cannot speak for themselves, and therefore everyone who has his speech should plead for them. To keep them short of victuals is a crying shame. I hate cruelty, and above all things the cruelty which starves the laboring beast.

> A right good man is good to all,
> And stints not stable, rack or stall;
> Not only cares for horse and hog,
> But kindly thinks of cat and dog.

Is not a man better than a beast? Then, depend upon it, what is good for the ploughing horse is good for the ploughing boy. A bellyfull of plain food is a wonderful help to a laboring man. A starving workman is a dear servant. If you don't pay your men, they pay themselves or else they shirk their work. He who labors well should be fed well, especially a ploughman.

> Let such have enow
> That follow the plough.

A Looking-Glass Is of No Use
to a Blind Man

He who will not see is much the same as if he had no eyes; indeed, in some things, the man without eyes has the advantage, for he is in the dark *and knows it*. A lantern is of no use to a bat, and good teaching is lost on the man who will not learn. Reason is folly with the unreasonable. One man can lead a horse to the water, but a hundred cannot make him drink: it is easy work to tell a man the truth, but if he will not be convinced, your labor is lost. We pity the poor blind, we cannot do so much as that for those who shut their eyes against the light.

A man who is blind to his own faults is blind to his own interests. He who thinks that he never was a fool is a fool now. He who never owns that he is wrong will never get right. He'll mend, as the saying is, when he grows better, like sour beer in summer. How can a man take the smuts off his face if he will not look in the glass nor believe that they are there when he is told of them?

Prejudice shuts up many eyes in total darkness. The man knows already: he is positive and can swear to it, and it's no use your arguing. He has made up his mind, and it did not take him long, for there's very little of it, but when he has said a thing he sticks to it like cobbler's wax. He is wiser than seven men that can render a reason. He is as positive as if he had been on the other side of the curtain and looked into the back yard of the universe. He talks as if he carried all knowledge in his waistcoat pocket like a peppermint lozenge. Those who like may try to teach him, but I don't care to hold up a mirror to a mole.

Spurgeon's Prayers

O THOU who art King of kings and Lord of lords, we worship Thee.

> Before Jehovah's awful throne
> We bow with sacred joy.

We can truly say that we delight in God. There was a time when we feared Thee, O God, with the fear of bondage. Now we reverence, but we love as much as we reverence. The thought of Thine Omnipresence was once horrible to us. We said: "Whither shall we flee from His presence?" and it seemed to make hell itself more dreadful because we heard a voice, "If I make my bed in hell, behold, Thou art there." But now, O Lord, we desire to find Thee. Our longing is to feel Thy presence, and it is the heaven of heavens that Thou art there. The sick bed is soft when Thou art there. The furnace of affliction grows cool when Thou art there, and the house of prayer when Thou art present is none other than the house of God, and it is the very gate of heaven.

Come near, our Father, come very near to Thy children. Some of us are very weak in body and faint in heart. Soon, O God, lay Thy right hand upon us and say unto us, "Fear not." Peradventure, some of us are alike, and the world is attracting us. Come near to kill the influence of the world with Thy superior power.

Even to worship may not seem easy to some. The dragon seems to pursue them, and floods out of his mouth wash away their devotion. Give to them great wings as of an eagle, that each one may fly away into the place prepared for him and rest in the presence of God today.

Our Father, come and rest Thy children now. Take the helmet from our brow, remove from us the weight of our heavy armor for awhile, and may we just have peace, perfect peace, and be at rest. Oh! help us, we pray Thee, now. As Thou hast already washed Thy people in the fountain filled with blood and they are clean, now this morning wash us from defilement in the water. With the basin and with the ewer, O Master, wash our feet again. It will greatly refresh; it will prepare us for innermost fellowship with Thyself. So did the priests wash ere they went into the holy place.

Lord Jesus, take from us now everything that would hinder the closest communion with God. Any wish or desire that might hamper us in prayer remove, we pray Thee. Any memory of either sorrow or care that might hinder the fixing of our affection wholly on our God, take it away now. What have we to do with idols any more? Thou hast seen and observed us. Thou knowest where the difficulty lies. Help us against it, and may we now come boldly, not into the Holy place alone, but into the Holiest of all, where we should not dare to come if our great Lord had not rent the veil, sprinkled the mercy seat with His own blood, and bidden us enter.

Now, we have come close up to Thyself, to the light that shineth between the wings of the Cherubim, and we speak with Thee now as a man speaketh with his friends. Our God, we are Thine. Thou art ours. We are now concerned in one business, we are leagued together for one battle. Thy battle is our battle, and our fight is Thine. Help us, we pray Thee. Thou who didst strengthen Michael and his angels to cast out the dragon and his angels, help poor flesh and blood that to us also the word may be fulfilled: "The Lord shall bruise Satan under your feet, shortly."

Our Father, we are very weak. Worst of all we are very wicked if left to ourselves, and we soon fall a prey to the enemy.

Therefore help us. We confess that sometimes in prayer when we are nearest to Thee at that very time some evil thought comes in, some wicked desire. Oh! what poor simpletons we are. Lord help us. We feel as if we would now come closer to Thee still and hide under the shadow of Thy wings. We wish to be lost in God. We pray that Thou mayest live in us, and not we live, but Christ live in us and show Himself in us and through us.

Lord sanctify us. Oh! that Thy spirit might come and saturate every faculty, subdue every passion, and use every power of our nature for obedience to God.

Come, Holy Spirit, we do know Thee; Thou hast often overshadowed us. Come, more fully take possession of us. Standing now as we feel we are right up at the mercy seat our very highest prayer is for perfect holiness, complete consecration, entire cleansing from every evil. Take our heart, our head, our hands, our feet, and use us all for Thee. Lord take our substance, let us not hoard it for ourselves, nor spend it for ourselves. Take our talent, let us not try to educate ourselves that we may have the repute of being wise, but let every gain of mental attainment be still that we may serve Thee better.

May every breath be for Thee; may every minute be spent for Thee. Help us to live while we live and while we are busy in the world as we must be, for we are called to it, may we sanctify the world for Thy service. May we be lumps of salt in the midst of society. May our spirit and temper as well as our conversation be heavenly; may there be an influence about us that shall make the world the better before we leave it. Lord hear us in this thing.

And now that we have Thine ear we would pray for this poor world in which we live. We are often horrified by it. O, Lord, we could wish that we did not know anything about it for our own comfort. We have said, "Oh, for a lodge in some vast wilderness!" We hear of oppression and robbery and murder, and men seem let loose against each other. Lord, have mercy upon this great and wicked city. What is to be done with these millions? What can we do? At least help every child of Thine to do his utmost. May none of us contribute to the evil directly or indirectly, but may we contribute to the Good that is in it.

We feel we may speak with Thee now about this, for when Thy servant Abraham stood before Thee and spake with such wonderful familiarity to Thee, he pleaded for Sodom; and we plead for London. We would follow the example of the Father of the Faithful and pray for all great cities, and indeed for all the nations. Lord let Thy kingdom come. Send forth Thy light and Thy truth. Chase the old dragon from his throne with all his hellish crew. Oh! that the day might come when even upon earth the Son of the woman, the Man-child, should rule the nations, not with a broken staff of wood, but with an enduring scepter of iron, full of mercy, but full of power, full of grace, but yet irresistible. Oh! that that might soon come, the personal advent of our Lord! We long for the millennial triumph of His Word.

Until then, O Lord, gird us for the fight, and make us to be among those who overcome through the blood of the Lamb and through the word of our testimony, because we "love not our lives unto the death."

We lift our voice to Thee in prayer; also, for all our dear ones. Lord bless the sick and make them well as soon as it is right they should be. Sanctify to them all they have to bear. There are also dear friends who are very weak; some that are very trembling. God bless them. While the tent is being taken down, may the inhabitant within look on with calm joy, for we shall by and by "be clothed upon with our house that is from heaven." Lord help us to sit very loose by all these things here below. May we live here like strangers and make the world not a house but an inn in which we sup and lodge, expecting to be on our journey tomorrow.

Lord save the unconverted, and bring out, we pray Thee, from among them those who are converted, but who have not confessed Christ. May the church be built up by many who, having believed, are baptized unto the sacred name. We pray Thee go on and multiply the faithful in the land. Oh! that Thou wouldst turn the hearts of men to the gospel once more. Thy servant is often very heavy in heart because of the departures from the faith. Oh! bring them back; let not Satan take away any more of the stars with his tail, but may the lamps of God shine bright. Oh! Thou that walkest amongst the seven golden candlesticks trim the flame, pour forth the oil, and let the light shine brightly and steadily. Now, Lord, we cannot pray any longer, though we have a thousand things to ask for. Thy servant cannot, so he begs to leave a broken prayer at the mercy seat with this at the foot of it: We ask in the name of Jesus Christ Thy Son. Amen.

The Wonders of Calvary

Great God, there was a time when we dreaded the thought of coming near to Thee, for we were guilty and Thou wast angry with us, but now we will praise Thee because Thine anger is turned away and Thou comfortest us. Ay, and the very throne which once was a place of dread has now become the place of shelter. I flee unto Thee to hide me.

We long now to get away from the world, even from the remembrance of it and have fellowship with the world to come by speaking with Him that was, and is, and is to come, the Almighty. Lord we have been worried and wearied oftentimes with care, but with Thee care comes to an end, all things are with Thee, and when we live in Thee, we live in wealth, in sure repose, in constant joy.

We have to battle with the sons of men against a thousand errors and unrighteousnesses, but when we flee to Thee, there all is truth and purity and holiness, and our heart finds peace. Above all, we have to battle with ourselves, and we are very much ashamed of ourselves. After many years of great mercy, after tasting of the powers of the world to come, we still are so weak, so foolish; but oh! when we get away from self to God, there all is truth and purity and holiness, and our heart finds peace, wisdom, completeness, delight, joy, victory.

Oh! bring us, then, we pray Thee, now near to Thyself. Let us bathe ourselves in communion with our God. Blessed be the love which chose us before the world began. We can never sufficiently adore Thee for Thy sovereignty, the sovereignty of love which saw us in the ruins of the Fall, yet loved us notwithstanding all.

We praise the God of the Eternal Council Chamber and of the Everlasting Covenant, but where shall we find sufficiently fit words with which to praise Him who gave us grace in Christ His Son, before He spread the starry sky.

We also bless Thee, O God, as the God of our redemption, for Thou hast so loved us as to give even Thy dear Son for us. He gave Himself, His very life for us that He might redeem us from all iniquity and separate us unto Himself to be His peculiar people, zealous for good works.

Never can we sufficiently adore free grace and undying love. The wonders of Calvary never cease to be wonders, they are growingly marvelous in our esteem as we think of Him who washed us from our sins in His own blood. Nor can we cease to praise the God of our regeneration who found us dead and made us live, found us at enmity and reconciled us, found us loving the things of this world and lifted us out of the slough and mire of selfishness and worldliness into the love of divine everlasting things.

O Spirit of God, we love Thee this day, especially for dwelling in us. How canst Thou abide in so rude a habitation. How canst Thou make these bodies to be Thy temples, and yet Thou dost so, for which let Thy name be had in reverence so long as we live.

O Lord, we would delight ourselves in Thee this day. Give us faith and love and hope that with these three graces we may draw very near to the Triune God. Thou wilt keep us, Thou wilt preserve us, Thou wilt feed us, Thou wilt lead us, and Thou wilt bring us to the mind of God, and there wilt Thou show us Thy love, and in the glory everlasting and boundless, there wilt Thou make us know and taste and feel the joys that cannot be expressed.

But a little longer waiting and we shall come to the golden shore; but a little longer fighting and we shall receive the crown of life that fadeth not away.

Lord, get us up above the world. Come, Holy Spirit, heavenly Dove, and mount and bear us on Thy wings, far from these inferior sorrows and inferior joys, up where eternal ages roll. May we ascend in joyful contemplation, and may our spirit come back again, strong for all its service, armed for all its battles, armored for all its dangers, and made ready to live heaven on earth until by and by we shall live heaven in heaven. Great Father, be with Thy waiting people, any in great trouble do Thou greatly help; any that are despondent do Thou sweetly comfort and cheer; any that have erred and are smarting under their own sin, do Thou bring them back and heal their wounds; any that this day are panting after holiness do Thou give them the desire of their hearts; any that are longing for usefulness do Thou lead them into ways of usefulness.

Lord, we want to live while we live. We do pray that we may not merely groan out an existence here below, nor live as earthworms crawling back into our holes and dragging now and then a sere leaf with us; but oh! give us to live as we ought to live, with a new life that Thou hast put into us, with the divine quickening which has lifted us as much above common men as men are lifted above the beasts that perish.

Do not let us always be hampered like poor half-hatched birds within the egg; may we chip the shell today and get out into the glorious liberty of the children of God. Grant us this, we pray Thee.

Lord, visit our church. We have heard Thy message to the churches at Ephesus; it is a message to us also. Oh! do not let any of us lose our first love. Let not our church grow cold and dead. We are not, we fear, what once we were. Lord revive us!

All our help must come from Thee. Give back to the church its love, its confidence, its holy daring, its consecration, its liberality, its holiness. Give back all it ever had and give it much more. Take every member and wash his feet, sweet Lord, most tenderly, and set us with clean feet in a clean road, with a clean heart to guide them, and do Thou bless us as Thou art wont to do after a divine fashion.

Bless us, our Father, and let all the churches of Jesus Christ partake of like care and tenderness. Walking among the golden candlesticks trim every lamp and make every light, even though it burneth but feebly now, to shine out gloriously through Thy care.

Now bless the sinners. Lord convert them. O God, save men, save this great city, this wicked city, this slumbering dead city. Lord, arouse it, arouse it by any means, that it may turn unto its God. Lord save sinners all the world over, and let Thy precious Word be fulfilled. "Behold He cometh with clouds." Why dost Thou tarry? Make no tarrying, O, our Lord. And now unto Father, Son, and Holy Ghost be glory forever and ever. Amen.

The Wings of Prayer

Our Father, Thy children who know Thee delight themselves in Thy presence. We are never happier than when we are near Thee. We have found a little heaven in prayer. It has eased our load to tell Thee of its weight; it has relieved our wound to tell Thee of its smart; it has restored our spirit to confess to Thee its wanderings. No place like the mercy seat for us.

We thank Thee, Lord, that we have not only found benefit in prayer, but in the answers to it we have been greatly enriched. Thou hast opened Thy hid treasures to the voice of prayer; Thou hast supplied our necessities as soon as ever we have cried unto Thee; yea, we have found it true: "Before they call I will answer, and while they are yet speaking I will hear."

We do bless Thee, Lord, for instituting the blessed ordinance of prayer. What could we do without it, and we take great shame to ourselves that we should use it so little. We pray that we may be men of prayer, taken up with it, that it may take us up and bear us as on its wings towards heaven.

And now at this hour wilt Thou hear the voice of our supplication. First, we ask at Thy hands, great Father, complete forgiveness for all our trespasses and shortcomings. We hope we can say with truthfulness that we do from our heart forgive all those who have in any way trespassed against us. There lies not in our heart, we hope, a thought of enmity towards any man. However we have been slandered or wronged, we would, with our inmost heart, forgive and forget it all.

We come to Thee and pray that, for Jesus's sake, and through the virtue of the blood once shed for many for the remission of sins, Thou wouldest give us perfect pardon of every transgression of the past. Blot out, O God, all our sins like a cloud, and let them never be seen again. Grant us also the peace-speaking word of promise supplied by the Holy Spirit, that being justified by faith we may have peace with God through Jesus Christ our Lord. Let us be forgiven and know it, and may there remain no lingering question in our heart about our reconciliation with God, but by a firm, full asurance based upon faith in the finished work of Christ may we stand as forgiven men and women against whom transgression shall be mentioned never again forever.

And then, Lord, we have another mercy to ask which shall be the burden of our prayer. It is that Thou wouldest help us to live such lives as pardoned men should live. We have but a little time to tarry here, for our life is but a vapor; soon it vanishes away; but we are most anxious that we may spend the time of our sojourning here in holy fear, that grace may be upon us from the commencement of our Christian life even to the earthly close of it.

Lord, Thou knowest there are some that have not yet begun to live for Thee, and the prayer is now offered that they may today be born again. Others have been long in Thy ways and are not weary of them. We sometimes wonder that Thou are not weary of us, but assuredly we delight ourselves in the ways of holiness more than ever we did. Oh! that our ways were directed to keep Thy statutes without slip or flaw. We wish we were perfectly obedient in thought, and word, and deed, entirely sanctified. We shall never be satisfied till we wake up in Christ's likeness, the likeness of perfection itself. Oh! wake us to this selfsame thing, we beseech Thee. May experience teach us more and more how to avoid occasions of sin. May we grow more watchful; may we have a greater supremacy over our own spirit; may we be able to control ourselves under all circumstances, and so act that if the Master were to come at any moment we should not be ashamed to give our account into His hands.

Lord, we are not what we want to be. This is our sorrow. Oh! that Thou wouldest, by Thy Spirit, help us in the walks of life to adorn the doctrine of God our Saviour in all things. As men of business, as work-people, as parents, as children, as servants, as masters, whatever we may be, may we be such that Christ may look upon us with pleasure. May His joy be in us, for then only can our joy be full.

Dear Saviour, we are Thy disciples, and Thou art teaching us the art of living; but we are very dull and very slow, and beside, there is such a bias in our corrupt nature, and there are such examples in the world, and the influence of an ungodly generation tells even upon those that know Thee. O, dear Saviour, be not impatient with us, but still school us at Thy feet, till at last we shall have learned some of the sublime lessons of self-sacrifice, of meekness, humility, fervor, boldness, and love which Thy life is fit to teach us. O Lord, we beseech Thee mold us into Thine own image. Let us live in Thee and live like Thee. Let us gaze upon Thy glory till we are transformed by the sight and become Christlike among the sons of men.

Lord, hear the confessions of any that have back-slidden, who are rather marring Thine image than perfecting it. Hear the prayers of any that are conscious of great defects during the past.

Give them peace of mind by pardon, but give them strength of mind also to keep clear of such mischief in the future. O Lord, we are sighing and crying more and more after Thyself. The more we have of Thee the more we want Thee; the more we grow like Thee; the more we perceive our defects, and the more we pine after a higher standard to reach even unto perfection's self.

Oh! help us. Spirit of the living God, continue still to travail in us. Let the groanings that cannot be uttered be still within our Spirit, for these are growing pains, and we shall grow while we can sigh and cry, while we can confess and mourn; yet this is not without a blessed hopefulness that He that hath begun a good work in us will perfect it in the day of Christ.

Bless, we pray Thee, at this time, the entire church of God in every part of the earth. Prosper the work and service of Christian people, however they endeavor to spread the kingdom of Christ. Convert the heathen; enlighten those that are in any form of error. Bring the entire church back to the original form of Christianity. Make her first pure and then she shall be united. O Saviour, let Thy kingdom come. Oh! that Thou wouldest reign and Thy will be done on earth as it is in heaven.

We pray Thee use every one of us according as we have ability to be used. Take us, and let no talent lie to canker in the treasure house, but may every pound of Thine be put out in trading for Thee in the blessed market of soul-winning. Oh! give us success. Increase the gifts and graces of those that are saved. Bind us in closer unity to one another than ever. Let peace reign; let holiness adorn us.

Hear us as we pray for all lands, and then for all sorts of men, from the Sovereign on the throne to the peasant in the cottage. Let the benediction of heaven descend on men, through Jesus Christ our Lord. Amen.

Checkbook of the Bank of Faith

Is It Nothing to You?

Let not thine heart envy sinners: but be thou in the fear of the Lord all the day long. For surely there is an end; and thine expectation shall not be cut off.—Prov. 23:17, 18.

WHEN WE see the wicked prosper we are apt to envy them. When we hear the noise of their mirth and our own spirit is heavy, we half think that they have the best of it. This is foolish and sinful. If we knew them better, and especially if we remembered their end, we should pity them.

The cure for envy lies in living under a constant sense of the divine presence, worshiping God and communing with Him all the day long, however long the day may seem. True religion lifts the soul into a higher region where the judgment becomes more clear and the desires are more elevated. The more of heaven there is in our lives, the less of earth we shall covet. The fear of God casts out envy of men.

The death-blow of envy is a calm consideration of the future. The wealth and glory of the ungodly are a vain show. This pompous appearance flashes out for an hour, and then is extinguished. How is the prosperous sinner the better for his prosperity when judgment overtakes him? As for the godly man, his end is peace and blessedness, and none can rob him of his joy; wherefore, let him forego envy and be filled with sweet content.

And there shall cleave nought of the cursed thing to thine hand: that the Lord may turn from the fierceness of his anger, and show thee mercy, and have compassion upon thee, and multiply thee, as he hath sworn unto thy fathers.—Deut. 13:17.

Israel must conquer idolatrous cities and destroy all the spoil, regarding all that had been polluted by idolatry as an accursed thing to be burned with fire. Now, sin of all sorts must be treated by Christians in the same manner. We must not allow a single evil habit to remain. It is now war to the knife with sins of all sorts and sizes, whether of the body, the mind, or the spirit. We do not look upon this giving up of evil as deserving mercy, but we regard it as a fruit of the grace of God which we would on no account miss.

When God causes us to have no mercy on our sins, then he has great mercy on us. When we are angry with evil, God is no more angry with us. When we multiply our efforts against iniquity, the Lord multiplies our blessings. The way of peace, of growth, of safety, of joy in Christ Jesus, will be found by following out these words: "There shall nought of the cursed thing cleave to thine hand." Lord, purify me this day. Compassion, prosperity, increase, and joy, will surely be given to those who put away sin with solemn resolution.

The Tenses

But there the glorious Lord will be unto us a place of broad rivers and streams; wherein shall go no galley with oars, neither shall gallant ship pass thereby. —Isa. 33:21.

The Lord will be to us the greatest good without any of the drawbacks which seem necessarily to attend the best earthly things. If a city is favored with broad rivers, it is liable to be attacked by galleys with oars and other ships of war. But when the Lord represents the abundance of His bounty under this figure, He takes care expressly to shut out the fear which the metaphor might suggest. Blessed be His perfect love!

Lord, if Thou send me wealth like broad rivers, do not let

the galley with oars come up in the shape of worldliness or pride. If Thou grant me abundant health and happy spirits, do not let "the gallant ship" of carnal ease come sailing up the flowing flood. If I have success in holy service, broad as the German Rhine, yet let me never find the galley of self-conceit and self-confidence floating on the waves of my usefulness. Should I be so supremely happy as to enjoy the light of Thy countenance year after year, yet let me never despise Thy feeble saints, nor allow the vain notion of my own perfection to sail up the broad rivers of my full assurance. Lord, give me that blessing which maketh rich and neither addeth sorrow nor aideth sin.

For, lo, I will command, and I will sift the house of Israel among all nations, like as corn is sifted in a sieve, yet shall not the least grain fall upon the earth.—Amos 9:9.

The sifting process is going on still. Wherever we go, we are still being winnowed and shifted. In all countries God's people are being tried "like as corn is sifted in a sieve." Sometimes the devil holds the sieve and tosses us up and down at a great rate, with the earnest desire to get rid of us forever. Unbelief is not slow to agitate our heart and mind with its restless fears. The world lends a willing hand at the same process and shakes us to the right and to the left with great vigor. Worst of all, the church, so largely apostate as it is, comes in to give a more furious force to the sifting process.

Well, well! let it go on. Thus is the chaff severed from the wheat. Thus is the wheat delivered from dust and chaff. And how great is the mercy which comes to us in the text, "yet shall not the least grain fall upon the earth!" All shall be preserved that is good, true, gracious. Not one of the least of believers shall be lost, neither shall any believer lose anything worth calling a loss. We shall be so kept in the sifting that it shall be a real gain to us through Christ Jesus.

And it shall come to pass, that every thing that liveth, which moveth, whithersoever the rivers shall come, shall live.—Ezek. 47:9.

The living waters in the prophet's vision flowed into the Dead Sea, and carried life with them, even into that stagnant lake. Where grace goes, spiritual life is the immediate and the everlasting consequence. Grace proceeds sovereignly according to the will of God, even as a river in all its windings follows its own sweet will; and wherever it comes it does not wait for life to come to it, but it creates life by its own quickening flow. Oh that it would pour along our streets and flood our slums! Oh that it would now come into my house, and rise till every chamber were made to swim with it! Lord, let the living water flow to my family and my friends, and let it not pass *me* by. I hope I have drunk of it already; but I desire to bathe in it, yea, to swim in it. O my Saviour, I need life more abundantly. Come to me, I pray thee, till every part of my nature is vividly energetic and intensely alive. Living God, I pray thee, fill me with thine own life.

I am a poor, dry stick; come and make me so to live that, like Aaron's rod, I may bud and blossom and bring forth fruit unto thy glory. Quicken me, for the sake of my Lord Jesus. Amen.

JUDE'S DOXOLOGY

Look unto me, and be ye saved, all the ends of the earth: for I am God, and there is none else.—Isa. 45:22.

This is a promise of promises. It lies at the foundation of our spiritual life. Salvation comes through a look at Him who is "a just God and a Saviour." How simple is the direction! "Look unto me. How reasonable is the requirement! Surely the creature should look to the Creator. We have looked elsewhere long enough, it is time that we look alone to Him who invites our expectation and promises to give us His salvation.

Only a look! Will we not look at once? We are to bring nothing in ourselves, but to look outward and upward to our Lord on His throne, wither He has gone up from the cross. A look requires no preparation, no violent effort: it needs neither wit nor wisdom, wealth nor strength. All that we need is in the Lord our God, and if we look to Him for everything, that everything shall be ours, and we shall be saved.

Come, far-off ones, look hither! Ye ends of the earth, turn your eyes this way! As from the furthest regions men may see the sun and enjoy His light, so you who lie in death's borders at the very gates of hell may by a look receive the light of God, the life of heaven, the salvation of the Lord Jesus Christ who is God and therefore able to save.

In those days, and in that time, saith the Lord, the iniquity of Israel shall be sought for, and there shall be none; and the sins of Judah, and they shall not be found: for I will pardon them whom I reserve.—Jer. 1:20.

A glorious word indeed! What a perfect pardon is here promised to the sinful nations of Israel and Judah! Sin is to be so removed that it shall not be found, so blotted out that there shall be none. Glory be unto the God of pardons!

Satan seeks out sins wherewith to accuse us, our enemies seek them that they may lay them to our charge, and our own conscience seeks them even with a morbid eagerness. But when the Lord applies the precious blood of Jesus, we fear no form of search, for "there shall be none," "they shall not be found." The Lord hath caused the sins of His people to cease to be: He hath finished transgression and made an end of sin. The sacrifice of Jesus has cast our sins into the depths of the sea. This makes us dance for joy.

The reason for the obliteration of sin lies in the fact that Jehovah Himself pardons His chosen ones. His words of grace is not only royal, but divine. He speaks absolution, and we are absolved. He applies the atonement, and from that hour His people are beyond all fear of condemnation. Blessed be the name of the sin-annihilating God!

What Is It to Win a Soul?

Soul-winning is the chief business of the Christian minister; indeed, it should be the main pursuit of every true believer. We should each say with Simon Peter, "I go a fishing," and with Paul our aim should be, "That I might by all means save some."

What is it to win a soul? This may be instructively answered by describing what it is not. We do not regard it to be soul-winning to steal members out of churches already established and train them to utter our peculiar Shibboleth: we aim rather at bringing souls to Christ than at making converts to our synagogue. There are sheep-stealers abroad, concerning whom I will say nothing except that they are not "brethren," or, at least, they do not act in a brotherly fashion. To their own Master they must stand or fall. We count it utter meannesss to build up our own house with the ruins of our neighbors' mansions; we infinitely prefer to quarry for ourselves. I hope we all sympathize in the large-hearted spirit of Dr. Chalmers, who, when it was said that such and such an effort would not be beneficial to the special interests of the Free Church of Scotland although it might promote the general religion of the land, said, "What is the Free Church compared with the Christian good of the people of Scotland?" What, indeed, is any church or what are all the churches put together, as mere organizations, if they stand in conflict with the moral and spiritual advantage of the nation, or if they impede the kingdom of Christ? It is because God blesses men through the churches that we desire to see them prosper, and not merely for the sake of the churches themselves. There is such a thing as selfishness in our eagerness for the aggrandizement of our own party; and from this evil spirit may grace deliver us!

In the next place, we do not consider soul-winning to be accomplished by hurriedly inscribing more names upon our church roll in order to show a good increase at the end of the year. This is easily done, and there are brethren who use great pains, not to say arts, to effect it; but if it be regarded as the Alpha and Omega of a minister's efforts, the result will be deplorable. By all means let us bring true converts into the church, for it is a part of our work to teach them to observe all things whatsoever Christ has commanded them; but still, this is to be done to disciples and not to mere professors; and if care be not used, we may do more harm than good at this point. To introduce unconverted persons to the church is to weaken and degrade it; and therefore an apparent gain may be a real loss. I am not among those who decry statistics, nor do I consider that they are productive of all manner of evil; for they do much good if they are accurate and if men use them lawfully. It is a good thing for people to see the nakedness of the land through statistics of decrease, that they may be driven on their knees before the Lord to seek prosperity; and, on the other hand, it is by no means an evil thing for workers to be encouraged by having some account of results set before them. I should be very sorry if the practice of adding up, and deducting, and giving in the net result were to be abandoned, for it must be right to know our numerical condition. It has been noticed that those who object to the process are often brethren whose unsatisfactory reports should somewhat humiliate them: this is not always so, but it is suspiciously frequent. I heard of the report of a church the other day in which the minister, who was well known to have reduced his congregation to nothing, cleverly wrote, "Our church is looking up." When he was questioned with regard to this statement, he replied, "Everybody knows that the church is on its back, and it cannot do anything else but look up."

Do not consider that soul-winning is or can be secured by the multiplication of baptisms and the swelling of the size of your church. What mean these despatches from the battlefield? "Last night fourteen souls were under conviction, fifteen were justified, and eight received full sanctification." I am weary of this public bragging, this counting of unhatched chickens, this exhibition of doubtful spoils. Lay aside such numberings of the people, such idle pretence of certifying in half a minute that which will need the testing of a lifetime. Hope for the best, but in your highest excitements be reasonable. Inquiry rooms are all very well; but if they lead to idle boastings, they will grieve the Holy Spirit and work abounding evil.

Nor is it soul-winning merely to create excitement. Excitement will accompany every great movement. We might justly question whether the movement was earnest and powerful if it was quite as serene as a drawing-room Bible-reading. You cannot very well blast great rocks without the sound of explosions, nor fight a battle and keep everybody as quiet as a mouse. On a dry day, a carriage is not moving much along the roads unless there is some noise and dust; friction and stir are the natural result of force in motion. So, when the Spirit of God is abroad and men's minds are stirred, there must and will be certain visible signs of movement, although these must never be confounded with the movement itself.

Do not aim at sensation and "effect." Flowing tears and streaming eyes, sobs and outcries, crowded after-meetings and all kinds of confusion may occur and may be borne with as concomitants of genuine feeling; but pray do not plan their production.

It very often happens that the converts that are born in excitement die when the excitement is over. They are like certain insects which are the product of an exceedingly warm day, and die when the sun goes down. Certain converts live like salamanders, in the fire; but they expire at a reasonable temperature.

I delight not in the religion which needs or creates a hot head. Give me the Godliness which flourishes upon Calvary rather than upon Vesuvius. The utmost zeal for Christ is consistent with common-sense and reason: raving, ranting, and fanaticism are products of another zeal which is not according to knowledge. We would prepare men for the chamber of communion and not for the padded room at Bedlam.

What is the real winning of a soul for God? So far as this is done by instrumentality, what are the processes by which a soul is led to God and to salvation? I take it that one of its main operations consists *in instructing a man that he may know the truth of God.* Instruction by the gospel is the commencement of all real work upon men's minds. "Go ye, therefore, and teach all nations, baptizing them in the name of the Father, and of the Son, and of the Holy Ghost: teaching them to observe all things whatsoever I have commanded you: and, lo, I am with you always, even unto the end of the world." Teaching begins the work and crowns it, too.

The gospel, according to Isaiah, is, "Incline your ear, and come unto me: hear, and your soul shall live." It is ours, then, to give men something worth their hearing; in fact, to instruct them. We are sent to evangelize or to preach the gospel to every creature; and that is not done unless we teach them the great truths of revelation. The gospel is good news. To listen to some preachers you would imagine that the gospel was a pinch of sacred snuff to make them wake up, or a bottle of ardent spirits to excite their brains. It is nothing of the kind; it is news, there is information in it, there is instruction in it concerning matters which men need to know and statements in it calculated to bless those who hear it. It is not a magical incantation or a charm whose force consists in a collection of sounds; it is a revelation of facts and truths which require knowledge and belief. The gospel is a reasonable system, and it appeals to men's understanding; it is a matter for thought and consideration, and it appeals to the conscience and the reflecting powers. Hence, if we do not teach men something, we may shout, "Believe! Believe! Believe!" but what are they to believe? Each exhortation requires a corresponding instruction, or it will mean nothing. "Escape!" From what? This requires for its answer the doctrine of the punishment of sin. "Fly!" But whither? Then must you preach Christ and His wounds; yea, and the clear doctrine of atonement by sacrifice. "Repent!" Of what? Here you must answer such questions as, What is sin? What is the evil of sin? What are the consequences of sin? "Be converted!" But what is it to be converted? By what power can we be converted? What from? What to? The field of instruction is wide if men are to be made to know the truth which saves. "That the soul be without knowledge, it is not good," and it is ours as the Lord's instruments to make men so to know the truth that they may believe it and feel its power. We are not to try and save men in the dark, but in the power of the Holy Ghost we are to seek to turn them from darkness to light.

And, do not believe, dear friends, that when you go into revival meetings or special evangelistic services, you are to leave out the doctrines of the gospel, for you ought then to proclaim the doctrines of grace rather more than less. Teach gospel doctrines clearly, affectionately, simply, and plainly, and especially those truths which have a present and practical bearing upon man's condition and God's grace.

Second, to win a soul it is necessary not only to instruct our hearer and make him know the truth, but *to impress him so that he may feel it*. A purely didactic ministry which should always appeal to the understanding and should leave the emotions untouched would certainly be a limping ministry. "The legs of the lame are not equal," says Solomon; and the unequal legs of some ministries cripple them. We have seen such an one limping about with a long doctrinal leg but a very short emotional leg. It is a horrible thing for a man to be so doctrinal that he can speak cooly of the doom of the wicked, so that, if he does not actually praise God for it, it costs him no anguish of heart to think of the ruin of millions of our race. This is horrible! I hate to hear the terrors of the Lord proclaimed by men whose hard visages, harsh tones, and unfeeling spirit betray a sort of doctrinal desiccation: all the milk of human kindness is dried out of them. Having no feeling himself, such a preacher creates none, and the people sit and listen while he keeps to dry, lifeless statements, until they come to value him for being "sound," and they themselves come to be sound, too: and I need not add, sound asleep also, or what life they have is spent in sniffing out heresy and making earnest men offenders for a word. Into this spirit may we never be baptized!

A sinner has a heart as well as a head; a sinner has emotions as well as thoughts, and we must appeal to both. A sinner will never be converted until his emotions are stirred. Unless he feels sorrow for sin and unless he has some measure of joy in the reception of the Word, you cannot have much hope of him. The Truth must soak into the soul and dye it with its own color. The Word must be like a strong wind sweeping through the whole heart and swaying the whole man, even as a field of ripening corn waves in the summer breeze. Religion without emotion is religion without life.

But, still, we must mind how these emotions are caused. Do not play upon the mind by exciting feelings which are not spiritual. Some preachers are very fond of introducing funerals and dying children into their discourses, and they make the people weep through sheer natural affection. This may lead up to something better, but in itself what is its value? What is the good of opening up a mother's griefs or a widow's sorrows? I do not believe that our merciful Lord has sent us to make men weep over their departed relatives by digging anew their graves and rehearsing past scenes of bereavement and woe.

If our hearers will weep over their sins, and after Jesus, let their tears flow in rivers; but if the object of their sorrow is merely natural and not at all spiritual, what good is done by setting them weeping? There might be some virtue in making people joyful, for there is sorrow enough in the world, and the more we can promote cheerfulness, the better; but what is the use of creating needless misery? What right have you to go through the world pricking everybody with your lancet just to show your skill in surgery? A true physician only makes incisions in order to effect cures, and a wise minister only excites painful emotions in men's minds with the distinct object of blessing their souls.

I have already insisted upon instruction and impression as most needful to soul-winning; but these are not all—they are, indeed, only means to the desired end. A far greater work must be done before a man is saved. A wonder of divine grace must be wrought upon the soul, far transcending anything which can be accomplished by the power of man. Of all whom we would fain win for Jesus it is true, "Except a man be born again, he cannot see the kingdom of God." *The Holy Ghost must work regeneration in the objects of our love,* or they never can become possessors of eternal happiness. They must be quickened into a new life, and they must become new creatures in Christ Jesus. The same energy which accomplishes resurrection and creation must put forth all its power upon them; nothing short of this can meet the case.

Regeneration, or the new birth, works a change in the whole nature of man, and, so far as we can judge, its essence lies in the implantation and creation of a new principle within the man. The Holy Ghost creates in us a new, heavenly, and immortal nature, which is known in Scripture as "the spirit" by way of distinction from the soul. Our theory of regeneration is that man in his fallen nature consists only of body and soul and that when he is regenerated, there is created in him a new and higher nature—"the spirit"—which is a spark from the everlasting fire of God's life and love; this falls into the heart and abides there and makes its receiver "a partaker of the divine nature." Thenceforward, the man consists of three parts, body, soul, and spirit, and the spirit is the reigning power of the three.

As this God-begotten spiritual life in men is a mystery, we shall speak to more practical effect if we dwell upon the signs following and accompanying it, for these are the things we must aim at. First, regeneration will be shown in *conviction of sin*. This we believe to be an indispensable mark of the Spirit's work; the new life as it enters the heart causes intense inward pain as one of its first effects. Though nowadays we hear of persons being healed before they have been wounded and brought into a certainty of justification without ever having lamented their condemnation, we are very dubious as to the value of such healings and justifyings. This style of things is not according to the truth. God never clothes men until He has first stripped them, nor does He quicken them by the gospel till first they are slain by the law. When you meet with persons in whom there is no trace of conviction of sin, you may be quite sure that they have not been wrought upon by the Holy Spirit, for "when he is come, he will reprove the world of sin, and of righteousness, and of judgment."

Equally certain is it that true conversion may be known by the exhibition of *a simple faith in Jesus Christ*. You need not that I speak unto you of that, for you yourselves are fully persuaded of it. The production of faith is the very center of the target at which you aim. The proof to you that you have won the man's soul for Jesus is never before you till he has done with himself and his own merits and has closed in with Christ. Great care must be taken that this faith is exercised upon Christ for a complete salvation and not for a part of it. Numbers of persons think that the Lord Jesus is available for the pardon of past sin, but they cannot trust Him for their preservation in the future. They trust for years past but not for years to come; whereas no such a subdivision of salvation is ever spoken of in Scripture as the work of Christ. Either He bore all our sins or none; and He either saves us once for all or not at all. His death can never be repeated, and it must have made expiation for the future sin of believers, or they are lost, since no further atonement can be supposed and future sin is certain to be committed. Blessed be His name, "by Him all that believe are justified from all things." Salvation by grace is eternal salvation.

Together with undivided faith in Jesus Christ there must also be *unfeigned repentance of sin*. Repentance is an old-fashioned word not much used by modern revivalists. "Oh!" said a minister to me, one day, "It only means a change of mind." This was thought to be a profound observation. "Only a change of mind"; but what a change! A change of mind with regard to everything! Instead of saying, "It is only a change of mind," it seems to me more truthful to say it is a great and deep change—even a change of the mind itself. But whatever the literal Greek word may mean, repentance is no trifle. You will not find a better definition of it than the one given in the children's hymn:

> Repentance is to leave
> The sins we loved before;
> And show that we in earnest grieve,
> By doing so no more.

Another proof of the conquest of a soul for Christ will be found in *a real change of life*. If the man does not live differently from what he did before, both at home and abroad, his repentance needs to be repented of and his conversion is a fiction. Not only action and language but spirit and temper must be changed. "But," says someone, "grace is often grafted on a crab-stock." I know it is; but what is the fruit of the grafting? The fruit will be like the graft, and not after the nature of the original stem. "But," says another, "I have an awful temper, and all of a sudden it overcomes me. My anger is soon over, and I feel very penitent. Though I cannot control myself, I am quite sure I am a Christian." Not so fast, my friend, or I may answer that I am quite as sure the other way. What is the use of your soon cooling if in two or three moments you scald all around you? If a man stabs me in a fury, it will not heal my wound to see him grieving over his madness. Hasty temper must be conquered and the whole man must be renewed or conversion will be questionable. We are not to hold up a modified holiness before our people, and say, "You will be all right if you reach that standard." The Scripture says, "He that committeth sin is of the devil."

There must be a harmony between the life and the profession. A Christian professes to renounce sin; and if he does not do so, his very name is an imposture. A drunken man came up to Rowland Hill, one day, and said, "I am one of your converts, Mr. Hill." "I daresay you are," replied that shrewd and sensible preacher; "but you are none of the Lord's, or you would not be drunk." To this practical test we must bring all our work.

In our converts we must also see *true prayer,* which is the vital breath of godliness. If there is no prayer, you may be quite sure the soul is dead. We are not to urge men to pray as though it were the great gospel duty and the one prescribed way of salvation; for our chief message is, "Believe on the Lord Jesus Christ." It is easy to put prayer into its wrong place and make it out to be a kind of work by which men are to live; but this you will, I trust, most carefully avoid. Faith is the great gospel grace; but still we cannot forget that true faith always prays, and when a man professes faith in the Lord Jesus and yet does not cry to the Lord daily, we dare not believe in his faith or his conversion.

There must also be *a willingness to obey the Lord in all His commandments.* It is a shameful thing for a man to profess discipleship and yet refuse to learn his Lord's will upon certain points, or even dare to decline obedience when that will is known. How can a man be a disciple of Christ when he lives in open disobedience to Him?

If the professed convert distinctly and deliberately declares that he knows his Lord's will but does not mean to attend to it, you are not to pamper his presumption, but it is your duty to assure him that he is not saved. Has not the Lord said, "He that taketh not up his cross, and cometh after me, cannot be my disciple"? Mistakes as to what the Lord's will may be are to be tenderly corrected, but anything like willful disobedience is fatal; to tolerate it would be treason to Him that sent us. Jesus must be received as King as well as Priest; and where there is any hesitancy about this, the foundation of godliness is not yet laid.

> Faith must obey her Maker's will
>   As well as trust His grace;
> A pardoning God is jealous still
>   For His own holiness.

Thus, you see, my brethren, the signs which prove that a soul is won are by no means trifling, and the work to be done ere those signs can exist is not to be lightly spoken of. A soul-winner can do nothing without God. He must cast himself on the Invisible or be a laughing-stock to the devil, who regards with utter disdain all who think to subdue human nature with mere words and arguments. To all who hope to succeed in such a labor by their own strength, we would address the words of the Lord to Job, "Canst thou draw out leviathan with a hook? or his tongue with a cord which thou lettest down? Wilt thou play with him as with a bird? or wilt thou bind him for thy maidens? Lay thine hand upon him, remember the battle, do no more. Behold, the hope of him is in vain: shall not one be cast down even at the sight of him?" Dependence upon God is our strength and our joy: in that dependence let us go forth and seek to win souls for Him.

Spurgeon's Sermon Notes

What man of you, having an hundred sheep, if he lose one of them, does not leave the ninety and nine in the wilderness, and go after that which is lost, until he find it?

And when he hath found it, he layeth it on his shoulders, rejoicing.

And when he cometh home, he calleth together his friends and neighbors, saying unto them, Rejoice with me; for I have found my sheep which was lost.—Luke 15:4-6.

THE LOVE of Jesus is not mere sentiment; it is active and energetic.

It is prevenient love, going after sheep that have no notion of returning to the fold from which they have wandered.

It is engrossing, making him leave all else: making one lost one to be of more present importance than ninety and nine.

It sets him upon resolute, determined, persevering search.

Let us behold our great Shepherd—

I. *In the search.* "Until he find it."

Mark him well, as with his eyes, and heart, and all his faculties, he goes "after that which is lost."

1. No rejoicing is on his countenance. He is anxious for the lost.

2. No hesitation is in his mind. Despite the roughness of the way, or the length of the time, or the darkness of the night, he still pursues his lost one.

3. No anger is in his heart. The many wanderings of the

115

sheep cost him dear, but he counts them as nothing, so that he may but find it.

4. No pausing because of weariness. Love makes him forget himself and causes him to renew his strength.

5. No giving up the search. His varied non-successes do not compel him to return defeated.

Such must our searches after others be.

We must labor after each soul until we find it.

II. *At the capture.* "When he hath found it."

Mark the Shepherd when the sheep is at last within reach.

1. Wanderer held. How firm the grip! How hearty! How entire!

2. Weight borne. No chiding, smiting, driving; but a life, a self-loading, an easing of the wanderer.

3. Distance traveled. Every step is hard for the Shepherd. He must tread painfully all that length of road over which the sheep had wandered so wantonly.

The sheep is carried back with no suffering on its own part.

4. Shepherd rejoicing to bear the burden.

The sheep is so dear that its weight is a load of love. The Shepherd is so good that he finds joy in his own toil.

5. Sheep rejoicing, too. Surely it is glad to be found of the Shepherd and so to have its wanderings ended, its weariness rested, its distance removed, its perfect restoration secured.

III. *In the home-bringing.* "When he cometh home."

Mark well the end of the Shepherd's toil and care: he does not end his care till he has brought the stray one "home."

1. Heaven is home to Christ.

2. Jesus must carry us all the way there.

3. The Shepherd's mission for lost souls is known in glory and watched with holy sympathy: in this all heavenly ones are "his friends and neighbors."

4. Jesus loves others to rejoice with Him over the accomplishment of His design. "He calleth together his friends." See how they crowd around Him! What a meeting!

5. Repentance is also regarded as our being brought home. "I have found" refers to the repenting sinner, and it is a finding which secures salvation, or angels would not rejoice over it.

6. One sinner can make all heaven glad. Let us learn a lesson from each of the three pictures which we have looked upon—

Of perseverance till souls are saved.

Of patience with souls who are newly found.

Of encouragement in expectation of the gathering into glory of those for whom we labor on behalf of Jesus.

SHEEP TRACKS

One evening, in 1861, as General Garibaldi was going home, he met a Sardinian shepherd lamenting the loss of a lamb out of his flock. Garibaldi at once turned to his staff and announced his intention of scouring the mountain in search of the lamb. A grand expedition was organized. Lanterns were brought, and old officers of many a campaign started off, full of zeal, to hunt the fugitive. But no lamb was found, and the soldiers were ordered to their beds. The next morning Garibaldi's attendant found him in bed, fast asleep. He was surprised at this, for the General was always up before anybody else. The attendant went off softly and returned in half-an-hour. Garibaldi still slept. After another delay, the attendant awoke him. The General rubbed his eyes, and so did his attendant when he saw the old warrior take from under the covering the lost lamb and bid him convey it to the shepherd. The General had kept up the search through the night until he had found it. Even so doth the Good Shepherd go in search of His lost sheep until He finds them.—*The Preachers' Monthly.*

Christ a Shepherd.—He is the Good Shepherd that laid down His life for the sheep (John 10:11); the Great Shepherd that was brought again from the dead (Heb. 13:20); the Chief Shepherd who shall appear again (I Peter 5:4); the Shepherd and Bishop of souls (I Peter 2:25); He is the Shepherd of the Sheep who gathers the lambs with His arm and carries them in His bosom (John 10, Isaiah 40:11); the Shepherd of Israel (Ezekiel 34:23); Jehovah's Shepherd (Zechariah 13:7)—*John Bate.*

Why doth he not drive the sheep before him, especially seeing it was lively enough to lose itself? First, because, though it had wildness more than enough to go astray, it had not wisdom enough to go right. Second, because probably the silly sheep had tired itself with wandering. "The people shall weary themselves for very vanity" (Hab. 2:13). Therefore, the kind Shepherd brings it home on His own shoulders.—*Thomas Fuller.*

Yam Sing, on his examination for membership on experience before the Baptist Church, San Francisco, in response to the question, "How did you find Jesus?" answered, "I no find Jesus at all; he find me." He passed.

A little boy in a Chinese Christian family at Amoy wishing to make a profession of religion was told that he was too young to be received into the church. He replied, "Jesus has promised to carry the lambs in His bosom. I am only a little boy; it will be easier for Jesus to carry me."—*The Sunday-School Teacher.*

The Despised Friend

. . . we esteemed him not.—Isa. 53:3.

I T WOULD not be easy for some of us to recall the hour when we first heard the name of Jesus. In very infancy that sweet sound was as familiar to our ear as the hush of lullaby. Our earliest recollections are associated with the house of God, the family altar, the Holy Bible, the sacred song, and the fervent prayer. Like young Samuels, we were lighted to our rest by the lamps of the sanctuary and were awakened by the sound of the morning hymn. Many a time has the man of God, whom a parent's hospitality has entertained, implored a blessing on our head, desiring in all sincerity that we might early call the Redeemer blessed; and to his petition a mother's earnest "Amen" has solemnly responded. Ours were happy portions and goodly heritages; but nevertheless, being "born in sin, and shapen in iniquity," these heavenly privileges did not of themselves avail to give us love to Jesus and pardon by His blood.

We are often compelled to weep over sins aggravated by light as clear as noonday—ordinances undervalued from their very frequence—warnings despised, although accompanied with tears from a parent's eye, and loathings felt in the heart if not expressed by the lips to those very blessings which were the rich benisons of heaven. In our own persons we are witnesses to the fact of innate depravity, the birth-plague of man; and we can testify to the doctrine that grace and grace alone can change the heart. The words of Isaiah are ours with an emphasis, notwith-

119

standing all the hallowed influences which surrounded us: and in uttering the confession, ". . . we esteemed him not," the haunts of our childhood, the companions of our youth, and the sins of our manhood, unanimously confirm our truthfulness.

Starting, then, with our own experience, we are led to infer that those who were denied our advantages will certainly be compelled to adopt the same humble language. If the child of pious parents, who by divine power was in youth brought to know the Lord, feels constrained to acknowledge that once he did not esteem the Saviour, shall the man whose education was irreligion, whose childhood was riot, whose youth was license, and whose maturity was crime, be able to adopt language less humiliating? No; we believe that all men of this class who are now redeemed from the hand of the enemy will readily acknowledge that they were the blind neglecters of the beauties of our glorious Emmanuel. Aye, more, we venture to challenge the "church of the first-born" to produce a single saint who did not once pass by the cross with indifference if not contempt.

Whether we review the "noble army of martyrs," "the goodly fellowship of the prophets," "the glorious company of the apostles," or "the holy church throughout all the world," we shall not discover a single lover of the adorable Redeemer who will not join the general confession, "We esteemed him not."

Pause, attentive reader, and ask thyself whether thou doest esteem Him *now;* for possibly it may happen that thou hast not as yet seen in Him any "beauty that thou shouldest desire him," nor canst thou subscribe to the exclamation of the spouse, "Yea, he is altogether lovely." Should this be thine unhappy condition, a meditation thereon under the Holy Spirit's influence may be of much use to thee; and I beseech thee, while we unfold the secrets of what was once our prison-house, be thou intensely anxious that by any means thou also mayest escape a bondage which deprives thee of joy here and will shut thee out from bliss hereafter.

We propose to endeavor first of all to bring the fact of our light estimation of Jesus vividly before our eye; then, second, we will discuss the causes of this folly; and, third, seek to excite emotions proper to such a mournful contemplation.

I. Let us go to the potter's house and view the unshapen clay which we once were; let us remember "the rock whence we were hewn," and the "hole of the pit from which we were digged," that we may with deeper feeling repeat the text, ". . . we esteemed him not." Let us here seriously peruse the diary of memory, for there the witnesses of our guilt have faithfully recorded their names.

We pause and consider first *our overt acts of sin* for these lie like immense boulders on the sides of the hill of life, sure testifiers to the rock within.

Few men would dare to read their own autobiography if all their deeds were recorded in it; few can look back upon their entire career without a blush. "We have all sinned, and come short of his glory." None of us can lay claim to perfection. True, at times a forgetful self-complacency bids us exult in the virtue of our lives, but when faithful memory awakes, how instantly she dispels the illusion! She waves her magic wand and in the king's palaces frogs arise in multitudes; the pure rivers at her glance become blood; the whole land is creeping with loathsomeness. Where we imagined purity, lo, imperfection ariseth. The snow-wreath of satisfaction melts before the sun of truth; the nectared bowl of gratulation is embittered by sad remembrances; while, under the glass of honesty, the deformities and irregularities of a life apparently correct are rendered, alas! too visible.

Let the Christian whose hair is whitened by the sunlight of heaven tell his life-long story. He may have been one of the most upright and moral, but there will be one dark spot in his history upon which he will shed the tear of penitence, because then he knew not the fear of the Lord. Let yon heroic warrior of Jesus recount his deeds; but he too points to deep scars, the offspring of wounds received in the service of the Evil One. Some amongst our chosen men in their days of unregeneracy were notorious for guilt and could well write with Bunyan (in *Grace Abounding*)— "As for my own natural life, for the time that I was without God in the world, it was, indeed, according to the course of this world and the spirit that now worketh in the children of disobedience (Eph. 2:2, 3). It was my delight to be taken captive by the devil at his will (II Tim. 2:26), being filled with all unrighteousness; the which did also so strongly work, both in my heart and life, that I had but few equals, both for cursing swearing, lying, and blaspheming the holy name of God." Suffice it, however, that by each of us open sins have been committed which manifest that "we esteemed him not."

Could we have rebelled against our Father with so high a hand if His Son had been the object of our love? Should we have so perpetually trampled on the commands of a venerated Jesus? Could we have done such despite to His authority if our hearts had been knit to His adorable person? Could we have sinned so terribly if Calvary had been dear to us? Nay; surely our clouds of transgressions testify our former want of love to Him. Had we esteemed the God-man should we so entirely have neglected His claims? could we have wholly forgotten His loving words of command? Do men insult the persons they admire? Will they commit high treason against a king they love? Will they slight the person they esteem or wantonly make sport of him they venerate? And yet we have done all this and more; whereby the least word of flattery concerning any natural love of Christ is rendered to our now honest hearts as hateful as the serpent's hiss. These iniquities might not so sternly prove us to have despised our Lord had they been accompanied by some little service to Him. Even now, when we do love His name, we are oft unfaithful, but *now* our affection helps us "to creep in service where we cannot go"; but *before* our acts were none of them seasoned with the salt of sincere affection but were all full of the gall of bitterness. O beloved, let us not seek to avoid the weight of this evidence, but let us own that our gracious Lord has much to lay to our charge, since we chose to obey Satan rather than the Captain of salvation and preferred sin to holiness.

Let the self-conceited Pharisee boast that he was born free—we see on our wrists the red marks of the iron; let him glory that he was never blind—our eyes can yet remember the darkness of Egypt in which we discerned not the morning star. Others may desire the honor of a merited salvation—we know that our highest ambition can only hope for pardon and acceptance by grace alone; and well we remember the hour when the only channel of that grace was despised or neglected by us.

The Book of Truth shall next witness against us. The time is not yet erased from memory when this sacred font of living water was unopened by us, our evil hearts placed a stone over the mouth of the well which even conscience could not remove. Bible dust once defiled our fingers; the blessed volume was the least sought after of all the books in the library.

Though now we can truly say that His word is "a matchless temple where we delight to be, to contemplate the beauty, the symmetry, and the magnificence of the structure, to increase our awe, and excite our devotion to the Deity there preached and adored" (Boyle), yet at one sad period of our lives we refused to tread the jeweled floor of the temple, or when from custom's sake we entered it, we paced it with hurried tread, unmindful of its sanctity, heedless of its beauty, ignorant of its glories, and unsubdued by its majesty.

Now we can appreciate Herbert's rapturous affection expressed in his poem:

> Oh book! infinite sweetness! let my heart
>   Suck every letter, and a honey gain,
> Precious for any grief in any part;
>   To clear the breast, to mollify all pain.

But *then* every ephemeral poem or trifling novel could move our hearts a thousand times more easily than this "book of stars," "this god of books." Ah! well doth this neglected Bible prove us to have esteemed Jesus but lightly. Verily, had we been full of affection to Him, we should have sought Him in His Word. Here He does unrobe Himself, showing His inmost Heart. Here each page is stained with drops of His Blood or emblazoned with rays of His Glory. At every turn we see Him, as divine and human, as dying and yet alive, as buried but now risen, as the Victim and the Priest, as the Prince and Saviour, and in all those various offices, relationships and conditions, each of which render Him dear to His people and precious to His saints. Oh let us kneel before the Lord, and own that "we esteemed him not," or else we should have walked with him in the fields of Scripture and held communion with him in the spice-beds of inspiration.

The Throne of Grace, so long unvisited by us, equally proclaims our former guilt. Seldom were our cries heard in heaven; our petitions were formal and lifeless, dying on the lip which carelessly pronounced them. Oh sad state of crime when the holy offices of adoration were unfulfilled, the censer of praise smoked not with a savor acceptable unto the Lord nor were the vials of prayer fragrant with precious odors!

Unwhitened by devotion, the days of the calendar were black with sin; unimpeded by our supplication, the angel of judgment speeded his way to our destruction. At the thought of those days of sinful silence, our minds are humbled in the dust; and never can we visit the mercy seat without adoring the grace which affords despisers a ready welcome.

But why went not "our heart in pilgrimage?" Why sung we not that "tune which all things hear and fear?" Why fed we not at "the church's banquet," on this "exalted manna?" What answer can we give more full and complete than this—"we esteemed him not?" Our little regard of Jesus kept us from His throne: for true affection would have availed itself of the ready access which prayer affords to the secret chamber of Jesus and would thereby have taken her fill of loves. Can we now forsake the throne? No; our happiest moments are spent upon our knees, for there Jesus manifests Himself to us. We prize the society of this best of friends for His divine countenance "giveth such an inward decking to the house where he lodgeth, that proudest palaces have cause to envy the gilding." We delight to frequent the shades of secrecy, for there our Saviour allows us to unbosom our joys and sorrows and roll them alike on Him.

O Lamb of God! our prayerlessness bids us confess that once we considered Thee to have neither form nor comeliness.

Furthermore, our *avoidance of the people of God* confirms the humiliating truth. We who now stand in the "sacramental host of God's elect," glorying in the brotherhood of the righteous, were once "strangers and foreigners." The language of Canaan was to our ear either an unmeaning babble at which we scoffed, a harsh jargon which we sought not to imitate, or an "unknown tongue" above our powers of interpretation. The heirs of life were either despised as "earthen pitchers," the work of the hands of the potter, or we removed from their society, conscious that we were not fit compeers for "the precious sons of Zion, comparable to fine gold." Many have been the weary looks which we cast upon the timepiece when in pious company the theme has been too spiritual for our groveling understanding; full often have we preferred the friendship of the laughing worldling to that of the more serious believer.

Need we ask the source of this dislike? The bitter stream is not like the river of Egypt, silent as to its source: it proclaims its own origin plainly enough; and the ear of self-partiality cannot be deaf to the truthful sound—"Ye loved not the servants, because ye esteemed not their master; ye dwelt not amid the brethren, for ye had no friendship towards the firstborn of the family."

One of the plainest evidences of alienation from God is a want of attachment to His people. In a greater or less degree this once existed in each of us. True, there were some Christians whose presence always afforded us pleasure; but we must be aware that our delight in their company was occasioned more by the affability of their manners or the winning style of their address than by the fact of their intrinsic excellence. We valued the gem for its setting, but a common pebble in the same ring would have equally engrossed our attention. The saints, *as saints,* were not our chosen friends, nor could we say, "I am a companion of *all those* that fear thee."

Such sentiments are the finest products of esteem for the Redeemer, and their former absence is conclusive evidence that we then "esteemed him not." We have no further need of aid in this self-condemnation.

Broken Sabbaths start like warrior clansmen from the wild heath of neglected time; they point to *the deserted sanctuary,* for which they would execute a dread revenge did not the shield of Jesus cover us; for, lo! their bows are stringed with *neglected ordinances,* and their arrows are *despised messages of mercy.*

But wherefore these accusers? *Conscience* the ranger of the soul hath seen enough. He will affirm that he hath beheld the ear closed to the wooing voice of the friend of sinners; that full often the eyes have been averted from the cross when Jesus himself was visibly set forth.

II. We now enter upon an examination of the latent causes of this sin. When the disease is removed, it may be useful to learn its origin, that we may serve others and benefit ourselves.

Our coldness towards the Saviour resulted primarily from *the natural evil of our hearts.* We can plainly discern why the dissolute and reprobate entertain but little affection for purity and excellence: the self-same reason may be given for our disregard of the incarnation of virtue in the person of our Lord Jesus. Sin is a madness, disqualifying the mind for sober judgment; a blindness, rendering the soul incapable of appreciating moral beauty; it is in fact such a perversion of all the faculties, that under its terrible influence men will "call evil good, and good evil; they will put darkness for light, and light for darkness; bitter for sweet, and sweet for bitter" (Isaiah 5:20). To us in our fallen condition fiends often appear more fair than angels, we mistake the gates of hell for the portals of bliss and prefer the garnished lies of Satan to the eternal verities of the Most High. Revenge, lust, ambition, pride, and self-will are too often exalted as the gods of man's idolatry; while holiness, peace, contentment, and humility are viewed as unworthy of a serious thought. O sin, what hast thou done! or rather, what hast thou undone! Thou hast not been content to rob humanity of its crown, to drive it from its happy kingdom, to mar its royal garments, and despoil its treasure; but thou hast done more than this! It sufficed not to degrade and dishonor; thou hast even wounded thy victim; thou hast blinded his eyes, stopped his ears, intoxicated his judgment, and gagged his conscience; yea, the poison of thy venomed shaft hath poured death into the *fountain*. Thy malice hath pierced the *heart* of manhood, and thereby hast thou filled his veins with corruption and his bones with depravity. Yea, O monster, thou hast become a murderer, for thou hast made us dead in trespasses and sins!

This last word opens up the entire mystery, for if we are spiritually dead, it is of course impossible for us to know and reverence the Prince of glory. Can the dead be moved to ecstasies or corpses excited to rapture? Exercise your skill on yonder lifeless body. It has not yet become a carnival for worms. The frame is still complete though lifeless. Bring hither lute and harp; let melodies most sweet and harmonies unequalled attempt to move the man to pleasure: he smileth not at the swelling strain, he weepeth not at the plaintive cadence; yea, could the orchestra of the redeemed pour forth their music he would be deaf to the celestial charm.

Will you assault the city by another gate? Place then before those eyes the choicest flowers that e'er were grown since Eden's plants were blasted. Doth he regard the loveliness of the rose or the whiteness of the lily? Nay, the man knoweth no more of their sweetness than doth the water of Nilus of the lotus which it beareth on its bosom. Come, ye gales of Araby and winds laden with the spicy odors of Ceylon; let the incense of fragrant gums, of frankincense and myrrh, smoke before him; yet, motionless as a statue, the nostril is not distended nor doth pleasure sit upon the lip. Aye, and ye may bring to your aid more powerful means. Ye may combine the crash of the avalanche, the roar of the cataract, the fury of the ocean, the howling of the winds, the rumbling of the earthquake, and the roll of the thunder: but these sounds united into one godlike shout could not arouse the slumberer from his fatal couch. *He is dead,* doth in one word solve the mystery. So also we, though quickened by the Holy Ghost, were once dead in sin and hence "we esteemed him not." Here is the root of all our misdeeds, the source of all our iniquity.

The secondary causes of the folly which we once committed lie very near the surface and may repay a moment's observation. *Self-esteem* had much to do with our ill-treatment of "the sinner's friend." Conceit of our own deserts made us indifferent to the claims of one who had procured for us a perfect righteousness. "The whole need not a physician," and we felt insulted by the language of a gospel which spoke to us as undeserving beings. The cross can have little power where pride conceals the necessity of a pardon; a sacrifice is little valued when we are unconscious of our need thereof. In our own opinion we were once most noble creatures; the Pharisee's oration would have sincerely enough emanated from us. A few little trifles there might be which were not quite correct, but in the main we thought ourselves "rich and increased in goods"; and even when under the powerful voice of law we were made to discern our poverty, we yet hoped by future obedience to reverse the sentence and were utterly unwilling to accept a salvation which required a renunciation of all merit and simple trust on the crucified Redeemer. Never until all the work of our hands had been unraveled and our fingers themselves had become powerless would we cease from our own labor and leaving the spider's-web of man's doings, array ourselves in the garment of free justification. No man will ever think much of Christ till he thinks little of himself. The lower our own views of ourselves become, the higher will our thoughts of Jesus be raised; and only when self-annihilation is complete will the Son of God be our "all in all."

Vainglory and self-esteem are fruitful parents of evil. Chrysostom calls self-love one of the devil's three great nets; and Bernard styles it "an arrow which pierceth the soul through, and slays it; a sly insensible enemy, not perceived." Under the sad influence of this power we commonly love him best who does us the most harm, for the flatterer who feeds our vanity with pleasing cries of "Peace, peace," is far more regarded than that sincere friend, the blessed Jesus, who earnestly warns us of our ill estate. But when self-confidence is removed—when the soul is stripped by conviction—when the light of the spirit reveals the loathsome state of the heart—when the power of the creature fails, how precious is Jesus! As the drowning mariner clutches the floating spar—as the dying man looks to some great physician—as the criminal values his pardon, so do we then esteem the deliverer of our souls as the Prince of the kings of the earth. Self-loathing begets an ardent passion for the gracious "lover of our souls," but self-complacency hides His glories from us.

Love of the world has also its share in using this dear friend so ill. When He knocked at the door, we refused Him admittance because another had already entered. We had each chosen another husband to whom we basely gave away our hearts. "Give me wealth," said one. Jesus replied, "Here am I; I am better than the riches of Egypt, and my reproach is more to be desired than hidden treasures." The answer was, "Thou art not the wealth that I seek for; I pant not for an airy wealth like thine, O Jesus! I do not care for a wealth above in the future—I desire a wealth here in the present; I want a treasure that I can grasp *now;* I want gold that will buy me a house, a farm, and estate; I long for the sparkling jewel that will adorn my fingers; I ask thee not for that which is hereafter; I will seek for that when years have passed away."

Another of us cried, "I ask for health, for I am sick." The best Physician appears and gently promises, "I will heal thy soul, take away thy leprosy, and make thee whole." "Nay, nay," we answered, "I ask not for that, O Jesus! I ask to have a *body* that is strong, that I may run like Asahel or wrestle like an Hercules; I long to be freed from pain of body, but I do not ask for health of soul, that is not what I require." A third implored for happiness. "Listen to me," said Jesus, "my ways are ways of pleasantness, and all my paths are peace." "Not the joy for which I sigh," we hastily replied: "I ask the cup filled to the brim, that I may drink it merrily; I love the jovial evening and the joyous day; I want the dance, the revelry, and other fair delights of this world; give your hereafter to those who are enthusiasts—let them live on hope; I prefer this world and the present."

Thus did we each in a different fashion set our affection on things below and despise the things above. Surely he was no ill painter who thus sketched us to the life with his graphic pencil: "The interpreter took them apart again, and had them into a room where was a man that could look no-ways but downwards, with a muckrake in his hand; there stood also one over his head with a celestial crown in his hand, and proferred him that crown for his muckrake; but the man did neither look up nor regard, but raked to himself the straws and dust of the floor."

While we love the world, "the love of the Father is not in us" (I John 2:15); nor the love of Jesus the son. Two masters we cannot serve. The world and Jesus never will agree. We must be able to sing the first portion of Madame Guion's stanza before we can truly join in its concluding words:

Adieu! ye vain delights of earth,
Insipid sports, and childish mirth,
  I taste no sweets in you;
Unknown delights are in the Cross,
All joy beside to me is dross;
  And Jesus thought so too.

It would be a great omission did we not observe that our *ignorance of Christ* was a main cause of our want of love towards Him. We now see that to know Christ is to love Him. It is impossible to have a vision of His face, to behold His person, or understand His offices, without feeling our souls warmed towards Him. Such is the beauty of our blessed Lord, that all men, save the spiritually blind, pay willing homage to Him. It needs no eloquence to set forth Christ to those who see Him by faith for in truth He is His own orator; His glory speaks, His condescension speaks, His life speaks, and, above all, His death speaks; and what these utter without sound the heart receiveth willingly.

Jesus is "curtained from the sight of the gross world" by the wilful unbelief of mankind or else the sight of Him would have begotten veneration for Him. Men know not the gold which lies in the mine of Christ Jesus, or surely they would dig in it night and day. They have not yet discovered the pearl of great price, or they would have sold their all to buy the field wherein it lies. The person of Christ strikes eloquence dumb when it would describe Him; it palsies the artist's arm when with fair colors he would portray Him; it would o'er-match the sculptor to carve His image even were it possible to chisel it in a massive block of diamond. There is nought in nature comparable to Him. Before His radiance the brilliance of the sun is dimmed; yea, nothing can compete with Him, and heaven itself blushes at its own plainness of countenance when His "altogether lovely" person is beheld. Ah, ye who pass Him by without regard, it is well said by Rutherford, "Oh if we knew Him, and saw His beauty, your love, your heart, your desires, would close with Him and cleave to Him. Love, by nature, when it seeth, cannot but cast out its spirit and strength upon amiable objects, and good things, and things loveworthy; and what fairer thing is there than Christ?" The Jewish world crucified Him because they knew not their king, and we rejected Him because we had not seen His adaptation to our wants and believed not the love He bore to our souls. We can all thus soliloquize with Augustine: "There was a great dark cloud of vanity before mine eyes, so that I could not see the sun of justice and the light of truth; I being the son of darkness, was involved in darkness; I loved my darkness, because I knew not thy light; I was blind, and loved my blindness, and did walk from darkness to darkness; but Lord, thou art my God, who hast led me from darkness and the shadow of death; hast called me into this glorious light, and behold I see."

III. We come now to the practical part of our meditation, and consider the emotions which ought to be excited by it.

First, then, we think *deep penitential sorrow* will well become us. As tears are the fit moisture for the grave, as ashes are a fit crown for the head of mourning, so are penitential feelings the proper mementoes of conduct now forsaken and abhorred. We cannot understand the Christianity of those men who can narrate their past history with a kind of self-congratulation. We have met with some who will recount their former crimes with as much gusto as the old soldier tells his feats in arms. Such men will even blacken themselves to render their case more worthy of regard and glory in their past sins as if they were ornaments to their new life. To such we say, "Not thus thought Paul; when speaking to the Romans, he said, 'whereof ye are now ashamed.'" There are times when it is proper, beneficial, and praiseworthy for a converted man to tell the sad tale of his former life; free grace is thus glorified and divine power extolled, and such a story of experience may serve to bring about faith in others who think themselves too vile; but then let it be done in a right spirit with expressions of unfeigned regret and repentance. We object not to the narration of the deeds of our unregenerate condition but to the mode in which it is too often done. Let sin have its monument, but let it be a heap of stones cast by the hands of execration—not a mausoleum erected by the hands of affection. Give it the burial of Absalom—let it not sleep in the sepulcher of the kings.

Let not a libation of tears be the only offering at the shrine of Jesus; *let us also rejoice with joy unspeakable*. If we have need to lament our sin, how much more to rejoice at our pardon! If our previous state moves us to tears, shall not our new condition cause our hearts to leap for joy? Yes, we must, we will praise the Lord for His sovereign, distinguishing grace. We owe Him an eternal song for this change in our position; He has made us to differ, and this from mere unmerited mercy, since we, like others, "esteemed him not." He certainly did not elect us to the high dignity of union with Himself because of any love we had toward Him, for we confess the very reverse. It is said of the writer's sainted predecessor, Dr. Rippon, that when asked why God chose His people, he replied, "Because He chose them"; and when the question was repeated, he answered yet again. "Because He *did* choose them and if you ask me a hundred times, I can give you no other reason." Verily it is "even so Father, because so it seemed good in thy sight." Let our gratitude for divine grace leap forth in praise; let our whole man be vocal to His honor who has elected us in sovereignty, redeemed us by blood, and called us by grace.

Should we not also be moved to *the deepest prostration of spirit* at the remembrance of our guilt? Ought not the subject of our present contemplation to be a stab in the very heart of pride? Come hither, Christian, and though now arrayed in the garments of salvation, behold here thy former nakedness. Boast not of thy riches, remember how sorry a beggar once thou wast. Glory not in thy virtues, they are exotics in thy heart; remember the deadly plants—the native growth of that evil soil. Stoop thyself to the earth and though thou canst not veil thyself with wings as angels do, let repentance and self-abhorrence serve thee instead thereof. Think not that humility is weakness; it shall supply the marrow of strength to thy bones. Stoop and conquer; bow thyself and become invincible.

If we had right views of *ourselves,* we should judge none too base to be reclaimed and should count it no dishonor to bear upon the shoulders of our sympathy the most wandering of the flock. We have amongst us too much of the spirit of "Stand by, for I am holier than thou." Those whom Jesus would have grasped by the hand, we will scarcely touch with a pair of tongs; such is the pride of many professors that they need but the name to be recognized at once as the true successors of the ancient Pharisees. If we were more like Christ, we should be more ready to hope for the hopeless, to value the worthless, and to love the depraved.

The following anecdote, which the writer received from the lips of an esteemed minister of the Church of England, may perhaps, as a fact, plead more forcibly than words. A clergyman of a parish in Ireland in the course of his visitations had called upon every one of his flock with but one exception. This was a woman of most abandoned character, and he feared that by entering her house he might give occasion of offence to gainsayers and bring dishonor upon his profession. One Sabbath, he observed her among the frequenters of his church, and for weeks after he noticed her attention to the Word of Life. He thought, too, that amid the sound of the responses he could detect one sweet and earnest voice, solemnly confessing sin and imploring mercy. The bowels of his pity yearned over this fallen daughter of Eve; he longed to ask her if her heart were indeed broken on account of sin, and he intensely desired to speak with her concerning the abounding grace which, he hoped, had plucked her from the burning. Still, the same delicacy of feeling forbade him to enter the house; time after time he passed her door with longing look, anxious for her salvation, but jealous of his own honor. This lasted for a length of time, but at last it ended. One day, she called him to her, and with overflowing tears which well betrayed her bursting heart, she said, "*O sir! if your Master had been in this village half as long as you have, He would have called to see me long ago; for surely I am the chief of sinners, and therefore have most need of His mercy.*" We may conceive the melting of the pastor's heart when he saw his conduct thus gently condemned by a comparison with his loving Master. From that time forth he resolved to neglect none but to gather even the "outcasts of Israel." Should we by our meditation be constrained to do likewise, we shall have derived no little benefit, and possibly some soul may have reason to bless God that our thoughts were directed into such a channel. May the gracious Spirit, who has promised to "lead us into all truth" by His holy influences, sanctify to our profit this visit to the house of our nativity, exciting in us all those emotions which are congenial to the subject, and leading us to actions in harmony with the grateful retrospect.

The Empty Sepulcher

An Exposition of Matthew 28

1. *In the end of the sabbath, as it began to dawn toward the first day of the week, came Mary Magdalene and the other Mary to see the sepulchre.*

WHILE THE Jewish Sabbath lasted, they paid to it due respect. They did not even go to *the sepulcher* to perform the kindly offices of embalmment; but when the old Sabbath was dying away and the new and better Sabbath *began to dawn,* these holy women found their way back to their Lord's tomb. Woman must be first at the sepulcher as she was last at the cross. We may well forget that she was first in the transgression; the honor which Christ put upon her took away that shame. Who but *Mary Magdalene* should be the first at the tomb? Out of her Christ had cast seven devils, and now she acts as if into her He had sent seven angels. She had received so much grace that she was full of love for her Lord.

2. *And, behold, there was a great earthquake: for the angel of the Lord descended from heaven, and came and rolled back the stone from the door, and sat upon it.*

Death was being upheaved, and all the bars of the sepulcher were beginning to burst. When the King awoke from the sleep of death, He shook the world; the bedchamber in which He rested for a little while trembled as the heavenly Hero arose from His couch: *Behold, there was a great earthquake.* Nor was the King unattended in His rising: *for the angel of the Lord descended from heaven.* It was not merely one of the angelic host, but some mighty presence-angel, "the angel of the Lord," who came to minister to Him on that resurrection morn. Jesus was put in the prison of the tomb as a hostage for His people; therefore He must not break out by Himself, but the angelic sheriff's officer must bring the warrant for His deliverance and set the captive at liberty. When the angel had *rolled back the stone from the door,* he *sat upon it,* as if to defy earth and hell ever to roll it back again. That great stone seems to represent the sin of all Christ's people which shut them up in prison; it can never be laid again over the mouth of the sepulcher of any child of God. Christ has risen, and all His saints must rise, too.

3, 4. *His countenance was like lightning, and his raiment white as snow: And for fear of him the keepers did shake and became as dead men.*

It took a great deal to alarm Roman soldiers; they were inured to all manner of terrors, but this angel's flashing *countenance and snow-white raiment* paralyzed them with fright until they swooned away *and became as dead men.* He does not appear to have drawn a flaming sword nor even to have spoken to *the keepers;* but the presence of perfect purity overawed these rough legionaries. What terror will strike through the ungodly when all the hosts of angels shall descend and surround the throne of the reigning Christ on the last great day!

5. *And the angel answered and said unto the women, Fear not ye: for I know that ye seek Jesus, which was crucified.*

Let the soldiers tremble, let them lie as if dead through fright but, "*Fear not ye: for I know that ye seek Jesus, which was crucified.*" Those who seek Jesus need not fear. These women were mistaken in seeking the living among the dead, yet their seeking ended in finding. They did fear, although the angel said, "Fear not." Only Jesus can silence the fears of trembling hearts.

6, 7. *He is not here: for he is risen, as he said. Come, see the*

*place where the Lord lay. And go quickly, and tell his disciples
that he is risen from the dead; and, behold, he goeth before you
into Galilee; there shall ye see him: lo, I have told you.*

Jesus always keeps His word: "*He is risen, as he said.*" He
said He would rise from the dead, and He did; He says that His
people also shall rise, and they shall. "*Come, see the place where
the Lord lay. And go quickly*": the angel would not let the
women stay long looking into the sepulcher, for there was work
for them to do. In this world, we cannot afford to spend all our
time in contemplation, however heavenly it may be. Notice the
angel's words: first "See," and then "Go." Make sure about the
fact for yourselves, and then let others know of it. What you
know, tell; and do it "quickly." Swift be your feet; such good
news as you have to carry should not be long on the road. "The
King's business required haste."

"*Tell his disciples that he is risen from the dead; and, behold,
he goeth before you into Galilee; there shall ye see him.*" Matthew
wrote *The Gospel of the Kingdom*, yet in his writings there is
much about that despised region called "Galilee of the Gentiles,"
that border-land which touches us as well as the chosen seed of
Abraham. There, in Galilee, is the place where Jesus will hold the
first general assembly of His church after His resurrection.

The Risen King

8. *And they departed quickly from the sepulchre with fear
and great joy; and did run to bring his disciples word.*

That seems a strange mixture, *fear and great joy,* awe and
delight, doubt and faith; yet the joy was greater than the fear.
It was not joy and great fear, but "fear and great joy." Have we
never had that mixture—drops of grief like April showers, and
peace and joy like sunlight from heaven, making a glorious rainbow reminding us of God's covenant of peace? A holy fear,
mingled with great joy, is one of the sweetest compounds we can

bring to God's altar; such were the spices these holy women took away from Christ's sepulcher. Fear and joy would both make them *run to bring His disciples word*. Either of these emotions gives speed to the feet; but when "fear and great joy" are combined, running is the only pace that accords with the messenger's feelings.

9, 10. And as they went to tell his disciples, behold, Jesus met them, saying, All hail. And they came and held him by the feet, and worshipped him. Then said Jesus unto them, Be not afraid: go tell my brethren that they go into Galilee, and there shall they see me.

Saints running in the way of obedience are likely to be *met by Jesus*. Some Christians travel to heaven so slowly that they are overtaken by follies or by faults, by slumber or by Satan; but he who is Christ's running footman shall meet his Master while he is speeding on his way.

And they came and held him by the feet, and worshipped him. These holy women were not Unitarians; knowing that Jesus was the Son of God, they had no hesitation in worshiping him. There must have been a new attraction about Christ after He had risen from the dead, something more sweet about the tones of His voice, something more charming about the countenance that had been so marred at Gethsemane, and Gabbatha, and Golgotha. Perhaps these timid souls clung to their Lord through fear that He might be again taken from them, so "they held him by the feet, and worshipped him," fear and faith striving within them for the mastery.

Jesus perceived the palpitation of these poor women's hearts, so He repeated the angel's message, *"Be not afraid."* He also confirmed the angel's information about "Galilee," only He spoke of His disciples as *"my brethren."* When Christ's servants, angelic or human, speak what He has bidden them, He will endorse what they say.

FALSEHOOD AND BRIBERY

11. *Now when they were going, behold, some of the watch came into the city, and shewed unto the chief priests all the things that were done.*

While good people were active, bad people were active, too. *Some of the watch* having recovered from their fright, *came into the city* to report the startling scenes they had witnessed. It is noteworthy that they did not go to Pilate; they had been placed at the disposal of *the chief priests,* and therefore, while some of them remained on guard at the sepulcher, others of the soldiers went to their ecclesiastical employers *and showed unto them all the things that were done,* so far as they knew the particulars. A startling story they had to tell, and one that brought fresh terror to the priests and led to further sin on their part.

12-15. *And when they were assembled with the elders, and had taken counsel, they gave large money unto the soldiers, Saying, Say ye, His disciples came by night, and stole him away while we slept. And if this come to the governor's ears, we will persuade him, and secure you. So they took the money, and did as they were taught: and this saying is commonly reported among the Jews until this day.*

For money Christ was betrayed, and for money the truth about His resurrection was kept back as far as it could be: *They gave large money unto the soldiers.* Money has had a hardening effect on some of the highest servants of God, and all who have to touch the filthy lucre have need to pray for grace to keep them from being harmed by being brought into contact with it.

The lie put into the soldiers' mouths was so palpable that no one ought to have been deceived by it: *Say ye, His disciples came by night, and stole him away while we slept.* A Roman soldier would have committed suicide sooner than confess that he had slept at his post of duty. If they were asleep, how did they know what happened? The chief priests and elders were not afraid of

Pilate hearing of their lie; or if he did, they knew that golden arguments would be as convincing with him as with the common soldiers: *If this come to the governor's ears, we will persuade him, and secure you.*

The soldiers acted just as many men have continued to do from their day to ours: *They took the money, and did as they were taught.*

> What makes a doctrine straight and clear?
> About five hundred pounds a year,

is an "old saw" that can be "reset" today. How much even of religious teaching can be accounted for by the fact that "they took the money"! There are many who make high professions of godliness who would soon give them up if they did not pay. May none of us ever be affected by considerations of profit and loss in matters of doctrine, matters of duty, and matters of right and wrong!

And this saying is commonly reported among the Jews unto this day. This lie, which had not a leg to stand upon, lived on till Matthew wrote his Gospel and long afterwards. Nothing lives so long as a lie, except the truth; we cannot kill either the truth or a lie, therefore let us beware of ever starting a falsehood on its terrible career. Let us never teach even the least error to a little child, for it may live on and become a great heresy long after we are dead.

The modern philosophy which is thrust forward to cast a slur upon the great truths of revelation is no more worthy of credence than this lie put into the mouths of the soldiers; yet common report gives it currency, and amongst a certain clique it pays.

THE KING'S LAST COMMAND

16, 17. *Then the eleven disciples went away into Galilee, into a mountain where Jesus had appointed them. And when they saw him, they worshipped him: but some doubted.*

Notice those words, *the eleven disciples.* There were twelve; but Judas, one of the twelve, had gone to his own place; and Peter, who had denied his Lord, had been restored to his place among the apostles. The eleven *went away into Galilee* to the trysting-place their Lord had fixed: *into a mountain where Jesus had appointed them.* Jesus always keeps His appointments, so He met the company that assembled at the selected spot: *and when they saw him they worshipped him.* Seeing their Lord, they began to adore Him and to render divine honors to Him, for to them He was God: *but some doubted.* Where will not Mr. Doubting and other members of his troublesome family be found? We can never expect to be quite free from doubters in the church, since even in the presence of the newly risen Christ "some doubted." Yet the Lord revealed Himself to the assembled company, although He knew that some among them would doubt that it was really their Lord who was risen from the dead.

Probably this was the occasion referred to by Paul when the risen Saviour "was seen of above five hundred brethren at once." It was evidently a meeting for which He had made a special appointment, and His own words to the women, following those of the angel, seem to point this out as the one general assembly of His church on earth before He ascended to His Father. Those who gathered were, therefore, a representative company; and the words addressed to them were spoken to the one church of Jesus Christ throughout all time.

18–20. *And Jesus came and spake unto them, saying, All power is given unto me in heaven and in earth. Go ye therefore, and teach all nations, baptizing them in the name of the Father, and of the Son, and of the Holy Ghost: Teaching them to observe all things whatsoever I have commanded you: and, lo, I am with you alway, even unto the end of the world. Amen.*

What a truly royal speech our King made to His loyal subjects! What a contrast was this scene in Galilee to the groans in Gethsemane and the gloom of Golgotha! Jesus claimed omnipotence and universal sovereignty: *All power is given unto me in heaven and in earth.* This is part of the reward of His humiliation (Phil. 2:6–10). On the cross He was proclaimed King of the Jews, but when John saw Him in his apocalyptic vision "on his head were many crowns," and on his vesture and on his thigh he had a name written, KING OF KINGS, AND LORD OF LORDS.

By virtue of His kingly authority, He issued this last great command to His disciples: *Go ye therefore, and teach,* or *make disciples of all nations, baptizing them in the name of the Father, and of the Son, and of the Holy Ghost: teaching them to observe all things whatsoever I have commanded you.* This is our commission as well as theirs. From it we learn that our first business is to make disciples of all nations, and we can only do that by teaching them the truth as it is revealed in the Scriptures and seeking the power of the Holy Spirit to make our teaching effective in those we try to instruct in divine things. Next, those who by faith in Christ become His disciples are to be baptized into the name of the triune Jehovah, and after baptism they are still to be taught all that Christ commanded. We are not to invent anything new, nor to change anything to suit the current of the age, but to teach the baptized believers to observe "all things whatsoever" our Divine King has commanded.

This is the perpetual commission of the church of Christ; and the great seal of the Kingdom attached to it, giving the power to execute it and guaranteeing its success, is the King's assurance of His continual presence with His faithful followers: *Lo, I am with you alway, even unto the end of the world. Amen.* May all of us realize His presence with us until He calls us to be with Him, "for ever with the Lord"! Amen.

Harvest Time

Is it not wheat harvest to-day?—I Sam. 12:17.

I SHALL not notice the connection, but I shall simply take these words as a motto, and my sermon will be founded upon a harvest field. I shall rather use the harvest for my text than any passage that I find here. "Is it not wheat harvest to-day?" I suppose the dwellers in cities think less of times and seasons than dwellers in the country. Men who were born, trained up, nourished and nurtured among cornfields, harvests, sowings, and reapings, are more likely to notice such things than you who are always engaged in mercantile pursuits and think less of these things than rustics do. But I suppose if it is almost necessary that you should less regard the harvest than others, it ought not to be carried to too great an extent. Let us not be forgetful of times and seasons. There is much to be learned from them, and I would refresh your memories by a harvest field. What a wondrous temple this world is, for in truth it is a temple of God's building wherein men ought to worship Him. What a wondrous temple it is to a mind spiritually enlightened which can bring to bear upon it the resources of intellect and the illuminations of God's Holy Spirit! There is not a single flower in it that does not teach us a lesson, there is not a single wave, or blast of thunder, that has not some lesson to teach to us, the sons of men. This world is a great temple, and as, if you walk in an Egyptian temple, you know that every mark and every figure in the temple has a meaning, so when you walk this world you must believe that everything about you has a meaning. It is no fanciful idea that there are "sermons in stones," and this world is intended to teach us by everything that we see. Happy is the man who only has the mind and the spirit to get these lessons from nature. Flowers, what are they? They are but the thoughts of God solidified, God's beautiful thoughts put into shape. Storms, what are they? They are God's terrible thoughts written out that we may read them. Thunders, what are they? They are God's powerful emotions just opened out that men may hear them. The world is just the materializing of God's thoughts, for the world is a thought in God's eye. He made it first from a thought that came from His own mighty mind, and everything in the majestic temple that He has made has a meaning.

In this temple there are four evangelists. As we have four great evangelists in the Bible, so there are four evangelists in nature; and these are the four evangelists of the seasons—spring, summer, autumn, winter.

First comes spring, and what says it? We look, and we behold that by the magic touch of spring, insects which seemed to be dead begin to awaken, and seeds that were buried in the dust begin to lift up their radiant forms. What says spring? It utters its voice, it says to man, "Though thou sleepest thou shalt rise again; there is a world in which in a more glorious state thou shalt exist; thou art but a seed now, and thou shalt be buried in the dust, and in a little while thou shalt arise." Spring utters that part of its evangel. Then comes summer. Summer says to man, "Behold the goodness of a merciful Creator; 'He makes his sun to shine on the evil and on the good,' He sprinkleth the earth with flowers, He scattereth it with those gems of creation, He maketh it blossom like Eden, and bring forth like the garden of the Lord." Summer utters that; then comes autumn. We shall hear its message. It passes, and forth comes winter, crowned with a coronal of ice, and it tells us that there are times of trouble for man; it points to the fruits that we have stored up in autumn, and it says to us, "Man, take heed that thou store up something for thyself; something against the day of wrath; lay up for thyself the fruits of autumn, that thou mayest be able to feed on them in winter." And when the old year expires, its death-knell tells us that man must die; and when the year has finished its evangelistic mission, there comes another to preach the same lesson again.

We are about to let autumn preach. One of these four evangelists comes forth, and it says, "Is it not wheat harvest to-day?" We are about to take the harvest into consideration in order to learn something from it. May God's most blessed Spirit help His feeble dust and ashes to preach the unsearchable riches of God to your souls' profit!

We shall talk of three joyful harvests and of three sorrowful harvests.

First, we shall speak of three joyful harvests that there will be.

The first joyful harvest that I will mention is the harvest of the field which Samuel alluded to when he said, "Is it not wheat harvest to-day?" We cannot forget the harvest of the field. It is not meet that these things should be forgotten; we ought not to let the fields be covered with corn and to have their treasures stored away in the barns, and all the while to remain forgetful of God's mercy. Ingratitude, that worst of ills, is one of those vipers which makes its nest in the heart of man, and the adder never can be slain until Divine grace comes there and sprinkles the blood of the cross upon man's heart. All vipers die when the blood of Christ is upon them. Let me just lead you for a moment to a harvest field. You shall see there a most luxuriant harvest, the heavy ears bending down almost to touch the ground, as much as to say, "From the ground I came, I owe myself to the ground, to that I bow my head," just as the good Christian does when he is full of years. He holds his head down the more fruit he has upon him. You see the stalks with their heads hanging down, because they are ripe. And it is goodly and precious to see these things.

Now just suppose the contrary. If this year the ears had been blighted and withered; if they had been like the second ears that Pharaoh saw, very lean and very scanty, what would have become of us? In peace we might have speculated on large supplies from Russia to make up the deficiency; now, in times of war,* when nothing can come, what would become of us? We may conjecture, we may imagine, but I do not know that we are able to come to the truth; we can only say, blessed be God, we have not yet to reckon on what would have been; but God seeing one door closed has opened another. Seeing that we might not get supplies from those rich fields in the South of Russia, He has opened another door in our own land. "Thou art My own favored island," says He; "I have loved thee, England, with a special love, thou art My favored one, and the enemy shall not crush thee; and lest thou shouldst starve, because provisions are cut off, I will give thee thy barns full at home, and thy fields shall be covered that thou mayst laugh thine enemy to scorn and say to him, 'Thou thought thou couldst starve us and make us afraid; but He who feeds the ravens has fed his people and has not deserted his favored land.' " There is not one person who is uninterested in this matter. Some say the poor ought to be thankful that there is abundance of bread. So ought the rich. There is nothing which happens to one member of society which does not affect all. The ranks lean upon one another; if there is scarcity in the lower ranks, it falls upon the next, and the next, and even the Queen upon her throne feels in some degree the scarcity when God is pleased to send it. It affects all men.

Now, the second joyful harvest is the harvest of every Christian. In one sense the Christian is the seed, in another he is a sower. In one sense he is a seed sown by God which is to grow, and ripen, and germinate till the great harvest time. In another sense, every Christian is a sower sent into the world to sow good seed and to sow good seed only. I do not say that Christian men never sow any other seed than good seed. Sometimes in unguarded moments they take garlic into their hands instead of wheat; and we may sow tares instead of corn. Christians some-

* Referring to the war in the Crimea.

times make mistakes, and God sometimes suffers His people to fall so that they sow sins; but the Christian never reaps his sins; Christ reaps them for him. He often has to have a decoction made of the bitter leaves of sin, but he never reaps the fruit of it. Christ has borne the punishment. Yet bear in mind, if you and I sin against God, God will take our sin and He will get an essence from it that will be bitter to our taste; though He does not make us eat the fruits, yet still He will make us grieve and sorrow over our crimes. But the Christian, as I have said, should be employed in sowing good seed, and as such he shall have a glorious harvest.

In some sense or other the Christian must be sowing seed. If God calls him to the ministry, he is a seed sower; if God calls him to the Sabbath school, he is a seed sower; whatever his office, he is a sower of seed. I sow seed broadcast all over this immense field; I cannot tell where my seed goes. Some are like barren ground, and they object to the seed that I sow. Let them—I have no objection that any man should do so. I am only responsible to God whose servant I am. There are others, and my seed falls upon them and brings forth a little fruit, but by and by when the sun is up, because of persecution they wither away and they die. But I hope there are many who are like the good ground that God has prepared, and when I scatter the seed abroad, it falls on good ground and brings forth fruit to an abundant harvest. Ah! the minister has a joyful harvest, even in this world, when he sees souls converted.

Every Christian has his harvest. The Sabbath school teacher has his harvest. He goes and he toils and ploughs very stony ground often, but he shall have his harvest. Oh, poor laboring Sabbath school teacher, hast thou seen no fruit yet? Dost thou say, "Who hath believed our report, and to whom is the arm of the Lord revealed?" Cheer up, thou dost labor in a good cause, there must be some to do thy work. Hast thou seen no children converted? Well, fear not, you cannot expect to see the seed spring up very early, but remember—

> Though seed lie buried long in dust,
> It sha'n't deceive your hope,
> The precious grain can ne'er be lost,
> For God insures the crop.

Go on sowing still, and thou shalt have a harvest when thou shalt see children converted. I have known some Sabbath school teachers who could count a dozen, or twenty, or thirty children who one after another have come to join the church and know the Lord Jesus Christ. But if you should not live to see it on earth, remember you are only accountable for your labor and not for your success. Sow still, toil on! "Cast thy bread upon the waters, and thou shalt find it again after many days," for God will not allow His word to be wasted; "It shall not return unto him void, it shall accomplish that which he pleases."

There was a boy once, a very sinful child, who hearkened not to the counsel of his parents; but his mother prayed for him, and now he stands to preach to this congregation every Sabbath. And when his mother thinks of her first-born preaching the gospel, she reaps a glorious harvest that makes her a glad woman. Now, fathers and mothers, such may be your case. However bad your children are at present, still press toward the throne of grace, and you shall have a harvest. What thinkest thou, mother, wouldst thou not rejoice to see thy son a minister of the gospel; thy daughter teaching and assisting in the cause of God? God will not suffer thee to pray and thy prayers be unheeded.

Young man, thy mother has been wrestling for thee a long time, and she has not won thy soul yet. Thou defraudest thy mother of her harvest! If she had a little patch of ground hard by her cottage where she had sown some wheat, wouldst thou go and burn it? If she had a choice flower in her garden, wouldst thou go and trample it under foot? Thou art going on in the ways of the reprobate, thou art defrauding thy father and thy mother of their harvest. Perhaps there are some parents who are weeping over their sons and daughters because they are hardened and unconverted. God, turn their hearts! for bitter is the doom of that man who goes to hell over the road that is washed by his mother's tears, stumbles over his father's reproofs, and tramples on those things which God has put in his way—his mother's prayers and his father's sighs. God help that man who dares to do such a thing as that! And it is wondrous grace if He does help him.

You shall have a harvest whatever you are doing. I trust you are all doing something. If I cannot mention what your peculiar engagement is, I trust you are all serving God in some way, and you shall assuredly have a harvest wherever you are scattering your seed. But suppose the worst—if you should never live to see the harvest in this world, you shall have a harvest when you get to heaven. If you live and die a disappointed man in this world, you shall not be disappointed in the next. I think how surprised some of God's people will be when they get to heaven. They will see their Master, and He will give them a crown. "Lord, what is that crown for?" "That crown is because thou didst give a cup of cold water to one of My disciples." "What! a crown for a cup of cold water?" "Yes," says the Master, "that is how I pay My servants. First I give them grace to give that cup of water, and then, having given them grace, I give them a crown." "Wonders of grace to God belong." He that soweth liberally shall reap liberally, and he that soweth grudgingly shall reap sparingly.

Now, beloved, I must mention very hastily the third joyful harvest. We have had the harvest of the field, and the harvest of the Christian. We are now to have another, and that is the harvest of Christ.

Christ had His sowing times. What bitter sowing times were they! Christ was one who went out bearing precious seed. Oh, I picture Christ sowing the world. He sowed it with tears; He sowed it with drops of blood; He sowed it with sighs; He sowed it with agony of heart; and at last He sowed himself in the ground to be the seed of a glorious crop. What a sowing time His was! He sowed in tears, in poverty, in sympathy, in grief, in agony, in woes, in suffering, and in death. He shall have a harvest, too. Blessings on His name, Jehovah swears it; the everlasting predestination of the Almighty has settled that Christ shall have a harvest. He has sown and He shall reap; He has scattered and He shall win His prize. "He shall see His seed, He shall prolong His days; and the pleasure of the Lord shall prosper in His hands." My friends, Christ has begun to reap His harvest. Yea, every soul that is converted is part of His reward; every one who comes to the Lord is a part of it. Every soul that is brought out of the miry clay and set on the Kings highway, is a part of Christ's crop. But He is going to reap more yet. There is another harvest coming in the latter day when He shall reap armfuls at a time and gather the sheaves into His garner. Now men come to Christ in ones and twos and threes, but then they shall come in flocks, so that the church shall say, "Who are these that come in as doves to their windows?"

There shall be a greater harvest when time shall be no more. "And I heard a voice from heaven saying unto me, Write, Blessed are the dead which die in the Lord from henceforth: Yea, saith the Spirit, that they may rest from their labours; and their works do follow them" (Rev. 14:13). They do not go before them and win them heaven. "And I looked, and behold a white cloud, and upon the cloud one sat like unto the Son of man, having on his head a golden crown, and in his hand a sharp sickle. And another angel came out of the temple, crying with a loud voice to him that sat on the cloud, Thrust in thy sickle, and reap: for the time is come for thee to reap; for the harvest of the earth is ripe. And he that sat on the cloud thrust in his sickle on the earth; and the earth was reaped" (Rev. 14:14–16). That was Christ's harvest.

Notice again, that there was first a harvest and then a vintage. The harvest is the righteous; the vintage is the wicked. When the wicked are gathered, an angel gathers them; but Christ will not trust an angel to reap the righteous. ". . . he that sat on the

throne, thrust in his sickle. . . ." Oh, my soul, when thou comest
to die, Christ will Himself come after thee; when thou art to be
cut down, He that sits upon the throne will cut thee down with a
very sharp sickle, in order that He may do it as easily as possible.
He will be the reaper Himself; no reaper will be allowed to
gather Christ's saints in but Christ the King of saints. Oh, will it
not be a joyful harvest when all the chosen race, every one of
them, shall be gathered in?

But now we are obliged to turn to the three sad harvests.
Alas! alas; the world was once like a Eolian harp; every wind
that blew upon it gave forth melody; now the strings are all un-
strung and they are full of discord so that when we have the
strains of joy, we must have the deep bass of grief to come after it.

The first sad harvest is the harvest of death. We are all living
and for what? For the grave. I have sometimes sat down and had
a reverie like this. I have thought: Man, what is he? He grows,
he grows, till he comes to his prime, and when he is forty-five, if
God spare him, perhaps he has then gained the prime of life.
What does he do then? He continues where he is a little while,
and then he goes down hill: and if he keeps on living, what is it
for? To die. But there are many chances to one, as the world has
it, that he will not live to be seventy. He dies very early. Do not
all of us live to die? But none shall die till they are ripe. Death
never reaps his corn green, he never cuts his corn till it is ripe.
The wicked die, but they are always ripe for hell when they die;
the righteous die, but they are always ripe for heaven when they
die. "That poor thief there who had not believed in Jesus, perhaps an hour before he died—he was as ripe as a seventy years'
saint. The saint is always ready for glory whenever death, the
reaper, comes, and the wicked are always ripe for hell whenever
God pleases to send for them. Oh, that great reaper; he sweeps
through the earth, and mows his hundreds and thousands down!
It is all still; death makes no noise about his movements, and he
treads with velvet footfall over the earth—that ceaseless mower

none can resist. He is irresistible, and he mows, and mows, and cuts them down. Sometimes he stops and whets his scythe; he dips his scythe in blood, and then he mows us down with war; then he takes his whetstone of cholera and mows down more than ever. Still he cries, "More! more! more!" Ceaseless that work keeps on! Wondrous mower! Wondrous reaper! Oh, when thou comest to reap me, I cannot resist thee; for I must fall like others —when thou comest, I shall have nothing to say to thee. Like a blade of corn I must stand motionless, and thou must cut me down! But oh! may I be prepared for thy scythe! May the Lord stand by me, and comfort me, and cheer me; and may I find that death is an angel of life—that death is the portal of heaven; that it is the outward porch of the great temple of eternity; that it is the vestibule of glory!

There is a second sad harvest, and that is the harvest that the wicked man has to reap. Thus saith the voice of inspiration, "Whatsoever a man soweth that shall he also reap." Now, there is a harvest that every wicked man has to reap in this world. No man ever sins against his *body* without reaping a harvest for it. The young man says, "I have sinned with impunity." Stay, thou young man! go there to that hospital, and see the beings writhing in their disease. See that staggering, bloated wretch, and I tell thee, stay thy hand! lest thou become like him. Wisdom bids thee stop; for thy steps lead down to hell. If thou "enterest into the house of the strange women," thou shalt reap a harvest. There is a harvest that every man reaps if he sins against his *fellows*. The man who sins against his fellow creature shall reap a harvest. Some men walk through the world like knights with spurs on their heels and think they may tread on whom they please, but they shall find their mistake. He who sins against others, sins against himself; that is nature. It is a law in nature that a man cannot hurt his fellows without hurting himself. Now you who cause grief to others' minds, do not think the grief will end there; you will have to reap a harvest even here. Again, a man cannot sin against *his estate* without reaping the effects of it. The miserly wretch who hoards up his gold, he sins against his gold. It becomes cankered, and from those golden sovereigns he will have to reap a harvest; yes, that miserly wretch, sitting up at night and straining his weary eyes to count his gold, that man reaps his harvest. And so does the young spendthrift. He will reap his harvest when all his treasure is exhausted. It is said of the prodigal, that "no man gave unto him"—none of those that he used to entertain—and so the prodigal shall find it. No man shall give anything unto him. Ah! but the worst harvest will be that of those who sin against the *church* of Christ. I would not that a man should sin against his body; I would not that a man should sin against his estate; I would not that a man should sin against his fellows; but, most of all, I would not have him touch Christ's church. He that touches one of God's people, touches the apple of His eye.

The third sad harvest is the harvest of Almighty wrath when the wicked at last are gathered in. In the 14th chapter of Revelation, you will see that God commanded the angel to gather the grapes, and they were all put into the winepress together, and after that the angel came and trod them down until the blood ran out so that it was up to the horses' bridles for the space of one hundred and twenty miles. Wonderful figure to express the wrath of God! Suppose, then, some great winepress in which our bodies are put like grapes; and suppose some mighty giant comes and treads us all under foot; that is the idea—that the wicked shall be cast together, and an angel shall crush them under foot until the blood runs out up to horses' bridles. May God grant of His sovereign mercy that you and I may never reap such a harvest as that; that God may never reap us in that fearful harvest; but that rather we may be written amongst the saints of the Lord!

You shall have a harvest in due season if you faint not. Sow on, brother, sow on, sister; and in due time thou shalt reap an abundant harvest.

Faith

Without faith it is impossible to please God.—Hebrews 6:6

THE OLD Assembly's Catechism asks, "What is the chief end of man?" and its answer is, "To glorify God, and to enjoy him forever." The answer is exceedingly correct; but it might have been equally truthful if it had been shorter. The chief end of man is "to please God," for, in so doing, we need not say it because it is an undoubted fact, he will please himself. The chief end of man, we believe, in this life and in the next, is to please God his Maker. If any man pleases God, he does that which conduces most to his own temporal and eternal welfare. Man cannot please God without bringing to himself a great amount of happiness; for, if any man pleases God, it is because God accepts him as a son, gives him the blessings of adoption, pours upon him the bounties of His grace, makes him a blessed man in this life, and insures him a crown of everlasting life which he shall wear and which shall shine with unfading luster, when the wreaths of earth's glory have all been melted away; while, on the other hand, if a man does not please God, he inevitably brings upon himself sorrow and suffering in this life; he puts a worm and a rottenness in the core of all his joys; he fills his death pillow with thorns, and he supplies the eternal fire with fagots of flame which shall forever consume him. He that pleases God is, through divine grace, journeying onward to the ultimate reward of all those that love and fear God; but he who is ill-pleasing to God must, for Scripture has declared it, be banished from the presence of God, and consequently, from

155

the enjoyment of happiness. If, then, we be right in saying that to please God is to be happy, the one important question is, how can I please God? and there is something very solemn in the utterance of our text, "Without faith it is impossible to please God." That it to say, "Do what you may, strive as earnestly as you can, live as excellently as you please, make what sacrifices you choose, be as eminent as you can for everything that is lovely and of good repute," yet none of these things can be pleasing to God unless they be mixed with faith. As the Lord said to the Jews, "With all your sacrifices you must offer salt," so He says to us: "With all your doings you must bring faith, or else 'without faith it is impossible to please God.'"

This is an old law; it is as old as the first man. No sooner were Cain and Abel born into this world and had attained manhood, than God gave a practical proclamation of this law that "without faith it is impossible to please Him." Cain and Abel, one bright day, erected an altar side by side with each other. Cain fetched of the fruits of the trees and of the abundance of the soil and placed them upon his altar; Abel brought of the firstlings of the flock and laid it upon his altar. It was to be decided which God would accept. Cain had brought his best, but he brought it without faith; Abel brought his sacrifice, but he brought it with faith in God. Now, then, which shall best succeed? The offerings are equal in value; so far as they themselves are concerned, they are equally good. Upon which will the heavenly fire descend? Which will the Lord God consume with the fire of his pleasure? O! I see Abel's offering burning, and Cain's countenance has fallen; for, unto Abel and unto his offering the Lord had respect, but unto Cain and his offering the Lord had no respect. It shall be the same till the last man shall be gathered into heaven. There shall never be an acceptable offering which has not been seasoned with faith. Good though it may be, as apparently good in itself as that which has faith, yet, unless faith be with it, God never can and never will accept it; for he here declares, "Without faith it is impossible to please God."

I shall endeavor to pack my thoughts closely this morning and be as brief as I can, consistently with a full *exposition* of what is faith; second, I shall have an *argument,* that without faith it is impossible to be saved; and, third, I shall ask a *question,* "Have you that faith which pleases God?" We shall have, then, an exposition, an argument, and a question.

I. First, for the *exposition*. What is faith?

The old writers, who are by far the most sensible—for you will notice that the books that were written about two hundred years ago by the old Puritans have more sense in one line than there is in a page of our new books and more in a page than there is in a whole volume of our modern divinity—the old writers tell you, that faith is made up of three things: first, knowledge, then assent, and then what they call affiance, or, the laying hold of the knowledge to which we give assent, and making it our own by trusting in it.

1. Let us begin, then, at the beginning. The first thing in faith is *knowledge*. A man cannot believe what he does not know. That is a clear, self-evident axiom. If I have never heard of a thing in all my life and do not know it, I cannot believe it. And yet there are some persons who have a faith like that of the fuller, who, when he was asked what he believed, said, "I believe what the church believes." "What does the church believe?" "The church believes what I believe." "And pray what do you and the church believe?" "Why, we both believe the same thing." Now, this man believed nothing except that the church was right, but in what he could not tell. It is idle for a man to say, "I am a believer," and yet not to know what he believes; but yet I have seen some persons in this position. A violent sermon has been preached which has stirred up their blood; the minister has cried, "Believe! Believe! Believe!" and the people on a sudden have got it into their heads that they were believers and have walked out of their

place of worship and said, "I am a believer." And if they were asked, "Pray, what do you believe?" they could not give a reason for the hope that was in them. They believe they intend to go to chapel next Sunday; they intend to join that class of people; they intend to be very violent in their singing, and very wonderful in their rant; therefore, they believe they shall be saved; but what they believe they cannot tell. Now, I hold no man's faith to be sure faith unless he knows what he believes. If he says, "I believe," and does not know what he believes, how can that be true faith?

The apostle has said: "How can they believe on him of whom they have not heard? and how can they hear without a preacher? and how can they preach except they be sent?" It is necessary, then, to true faith, that a man should know something of the Bible. Believe me, this is an age when the Bible is not so much thought of as it used to be. Some hundred years ago, the world was covered with bigotry, cruelty, and superstition. We always run to extremes, and we have just gone to the other extreme now. It was then said: "One faith is right; down with all others, by the rack and by the sword!" Now it is said, "However contradictory our creeds may be, they are all right." If we did but use our common sense, we should know that it is not so. But some reply, "Such-and-such a doctrine need not be preached and need not be believed." Then, sir, if it need not be preached, it need not be revealed. You impugn the wisdom of God when you say a doctrine is unnecessary, for you do as much as say that God has revealed something which was not necessary, and He would be as unwise to do more than was necessary as if He had done less than was necessary. We believe that every doctrine of God's Word ought to be studied by men, and that their faith should lay hold of the whole matter of the Sacred Scriptures; and more especially upon all that part of the Scripture which concerns the person of our all-blessed Redeemer. There must be some degree of knowledge before there can be faith.

"Search the Scriptures," "for in them ye think ye have eternal life, and they are they which testify of Christ"; and by searching and reading cometh knowledge, and by knowledge cometh faith, and through faith cometh salvation.

2. But a man may know a thing and yet not have faith. I may know a thing and yet not believe it. Therefore, *assent* must go with faith: that is to say, what we know we must also agree unto as being most certainly the verity of God. Now, in order to have faith, it is necessary that I should not only read the Scriptures and understand them, but that I should receive them in my soul as being the very truth of the living God and should devoutly, with my whole heart, receive the complete Scripture as being inspired of the Most High and the whole of the doctrine which he requires me to believe to my salvation. You are not allowed to have the Scriptures and to believe what you please; you are not allowed to believe the Scriptures with a half-heartedness; for if you do this willfully, you have not the faith which looks alone to Christ. True faith gives its full assent to the Scriptures; it takes a page and says, "No matter what is in the page, I believe it"; it turns over the next chapter and says: "Herein are some things hard to be understood which they that are unlearned and unstable do wrest, as they do also the other Scriptures, to their destruction; but, hard though it be, I believe it." It sees the Trinity; it cannot understand the Trinity in Unity, but it believes it. It sees an atoning sacrifice; there is something difficult in the thought, but it believes it; and whatever it be which it sees in revelation, it devoutly puts its lips to the book and says: "I love it all, I give my full, free, and hearty assent to every word of it, whether it be the threatening, or the promise, the proverb, the precept, or the blessing. I believe that since it is all the Word of God, it is all most assuredly true." Whosoever would be saved must know the Scriptures and give full assent unto them.

3. But a man may have all of this and yet not possess true faith; for the chief part of faith lies in the last head, namely, in an *affiance* to the truth; not the believing it merely, but the tak-

ing hold of it as being ours and in the resting on it for salvation. Recumbency on the truth was the word which the old preachers used. You will understand that word. Leaning on it: saying, "This is truth; I trust my salvation on it." Now, true faith in its very essence rests in this—a leaning upon Christ. It will not save me to know that Christ is a Saviour; but it will save me to *trust* Him to be *my* Saviour. I shall not be delivered from the wrath to come by believing that His atonement is sufficient; but I shall be saved by making that atonement my trust, my refuge, and my all. The pith, the essence, of faith lies in this—a casting oneself on the promise. It is not the life buoy on board the ship that saves the man when he is drowning, nor is it his belief that it is an excellent and successful invention. No! he must have it around his loins, or his hand upon it, or else he will sink. To use an old and hackneyed illustration: Suppose there is a fire in the upper room of a house and the people gathered in the street. A child is in the upper story: how is he to escape? He cannot leap down, he would be dashed to pieces. A strong man comes beneath and cries, "Drop into my arms." It is a part of faith to know that the man is there; it is another part of faith to believe that the man is strong; but the essence of faith lies in the dropping down into the man's arms. That is the proof of faith and the real pith and essence of it. So, sinner, thou art to know that Christ died for sin; thou art also to understand that Christ is able to save, and thou art to believe that; but thou art not saved unless in addition to that, thou puttest thy trust in Him to be thy Saviour and to be thine forever.

II. And now we come to the *argument*—why, without faith, we cannot be saved.

There are some gentlemen present who are saying, "Now we shall see whether Mr. Spurgeon has any logic in him." No, you won't, sirs, because I never pretend to exercise it. I hope I have the logic which can appeal to men's hearts, but I am not very prone to use the less powerful logic of the head when I can win the heart in another manner. But, if it were needful, I should not be afraid to prove that I know more of logic and of many other things than the little men who undertake to censure me. It were well if they knew how to hold their tongues, which is at least a fine part of rhetoric. My argument shall be such as, I trust, will appeal to the heart and conscience, although it may not exactly please those who are always so fond of syllogistic demonstration—

> Who could a hair divide
> Between the west and northwest side.

1. "Without faith it is impossible to please God." And I gather it from the fact, that there never has been the case of a man recorded in Scripture who did please God without faith. The eleventh chapter of Hebrews is the chapter of the men who pleased God. Listen to their names: "By faith Abel offered unto God a more excellent sacrifice"; "By faith Enoch was translated"; "By faith Noah built an ark"; "By faith Abraham went out into a place that he should afterwards receive"; "By faith he sojourned in the land of promise"; "By faith Sarah bare Isaac"; "By faith Abraham offered up Isaac"; "By faith Moses gave up the wealth of Egypt"; "By faith Isaac blessed Jacob"; "By faith Jacob blessed the sons of Joseph"; "By faith Joseph, when he died, made mention of the departure of the children of Israel"; "By faith the Red Sea was dried up"; "By faith the walls of Jericho fell down"; "By faith the harlot Rahab was saved"; And what more shall I say? for the time would fail me to tell of Gideon, of Barak, of Samson, of Jephthah, of David and Samuel, and of the prophets. But all these were men of faith. Others mentioned in Scritpure have done something, but God did not accept them. Men have humbled themselves, and yet God has not saved them. Ahab did, and yet his sins were never forgiven. Men have repented, and yet have not been saved because theirs was the wrong repentance. Judas repented and went and hanged himself and was not saved. Men have confessed their sins and have not been saved. Saul did

it. He said to David, "I have sinned against thee, my son David"; and yet he went on as he did before. Multitudes have confessed the name of Christ and have done many marvelous things, and yet, they have never been pleasing to God for this simple reason, that they had not faith. And, if there be not one mentioned in Scripture, which is the history of some thousand years, it is not likely that in the later two thousand years of the world's history there would have been one when there was not one during the first four thousand.

2. But the next argument is: *faith is the stooping grace,* and nothing can make a man stoop without faith. Now, unless man does stoop, his sacrifice cannot be accepted. The angels know this. When they praise God, they do it veiling their faces with their wings. The redeemed know it. When they praise God, they cast their crowns before His feet. Now, a man who has not faith proves that he cannot stoop; for he has not faith for this reason, because he is too proud to believe. He declares, he will not yield his intellect, he will not become a child and believe meekly what God tells him to believe. He is too proud, and he cannot enter heaven because the door of heaven is so low that no one can enter in by it unless he will bow his head. There never was a man who could walk into salvation erect. We must go to Christ on our bended knees; for though He is a door big enough for the greatest sinner to come in, He is a door so low that men must stoop if they would be saved. Therefore, it is that faith is necessary because a want of faith is certain evidence of absence of humility.

3. But now for other reasons. Faith is necessary to salvation, because we are told in Scripture that *works cannot save.* I will tell a very familiar story so that even the poorest may not misunderstand what I say. A minister was one day going to preach. He climbed a hill on his road. Beneath him lay the villages sleeping in their beauty, the cornfields motionless in the sunshine; but he did not look at them for his attention was arrested by a woman standing at her door, and who, upon seeing him, came up to

him with the greatest anxiety and said: "Oh! sir, have you any keys about you? I have broken the key of my drawers, and there are some things that I must get directly." Said he, "I have no keys." She was disappointed expecting that everyone would have some keys. "But suppose," he said, "I had some keys; they might not fit your lock and therefore you could not get the articles you want. But do not distress yourself; wait till someone else comes up. But," said he, wishing to improve the occasion, "have you ever heard of the key of heaven?" "Ah! yes," she said, "I have lived long enough, and I have gone to church long enough to know that if we work hard and get our bread by the sweat of our brow, and act well towards our neighbors, and behave, as the Catechism says, lowly and reverently to all our betters, and if we do our duty in that station of life in which it has pleased God to place us, and say our prayers regularly, we shall be saved." "Ah!" said he, "my good woman, that is a broken key, for you have broken the commandments; you have not fulfilled all your duties. It is a good key, but you have broken it." "Pray, sir," said she, believing that he understood the matter and looking frightened, "What have I left out?" "Why," said he, "the all-important thing, the blood of Jesus Christ. Don't you know it is said that the key of heaven is at His girdle; He openeth, and no man shutteth; He shutteth, and no man openeth?" And, explaining it more fully to her he said, "It is Christ and Christ alone that can open heaven to you and not your good works." "What! minister," said she, "are our good works useless then?" "No," said he, "not after faith. If you believe first, you may have as many good works as you please; but if you believe, you will never trust in them; for if you trust in them, you have spoiled them, and they are not good works any longer. Have as many good works as you please; still, put your trust wholly in the Lord Jesus Christ; for if you do not, your key will never unlock heaven's gate." So, then, my hearers, we must have true faith because the old key of works is so broken by us all that we never shall enter Paradise by it. If any of you pretend that you have no sins, to be very plain with you, you deceive yourselves, and the truth is not in you. If you conceive that by your good works you shall enter heaven, never was there a more fell delusion; and you shall find at the last great day that your hopes were worthless, and that like sere leaves from the autumn trees your noblest doings shall be blown away or kindled into a flame wherein you yourselves must suffer forever. Take heed of your good works; get them after faith, but remember, the way to be saved is simply to believe in Jesus Christ.

4. Again: without faith it is impossible to be saved and to please God; because, without faith, there is *no union with Christ.* Now, union with Christ is indispensable to our salvation. If I come before God's throne with my prayers, I shall never get them answered unless I bring Christ with me. The Molossians of old, when they could not get a favor from their king, adopted a singular expedient: they took the king's only son in their arms and falling on their knees, cried, "O king, for thy son's sake grant our request." He smiled, and said, "I deny nothing to those who plead my son's name."

It is so with God. He will deny nothing to the man who comes having Christ at his elbow; but if he come alone, he must be cast away. Union with Christ is, after all, the great point in salvation. Let me tell you a story to illustrate this: the stupendous falls of Niagara have been spoken of in every part of the world; but while they are marvelous to hear of and wonderful as a spectacle, they have been very destructive to human life when by accident any have been carried down the cataract. Some years ago, two men, a bargeman and a collier, were in a boat and found themselves unable to manage it, the boat being carried so swiftly by the current that they must both inevitably be borne down and dashed to pieces. Persons on the shore saw them but were unable to do much for their rescue. At last, however, one man was saved by floating a rope out to him which he grasped. The same instant that the rope came into his hand, a log floated by the other man. The thoughtless and confused bargeman instead of seizing the rope, laid hold on the log. It was a fatal mistake; they were both in imminent peril, but the one was drawn to shore because he had a connection with the people on the land, while the other, clinging to the log, was borne irresistibly along and never heard of afterwards. Do you not see that here is a practical illustration? Faith is a connection with Christ. Christ is on the shore, so to speak, holding the rope of faith, and if we lay hold of it with the hand of our confidence, he pulls us to shore; but our good works, having no connection with Christ, are drifted along down the gulf of fell despair. Grapple them as tightly as we may, even with hooks of steel, they cannot avail us in the least degree. You will see, I am sure, what I wish to show to you. Some object to anecdotes; I shall use them till they have done objecting to them. The truth is never more powerfully set forth to men than by telling them, as Christ did, a story of a certain man with two sons, or a certain householder who went on a journey, divided his substance, and gave to one ten talents, to another one.

5. Just one more argument and then I have done with it. "Without faith it is impossible to please God," because it is impossible to persevere in holiness without faith. What a multitude of fair weather Christians we have in this age! Many Christians resemble the nautiluses, which in fine, smooth weather swim on the surface of the sea in a splendid little squadron like the mighty ships, but the moment the first breath of the wind ruffles the waves, they take in their sails and sink into the depths. Many Christians are the same. In good company, in evangelical drawing-rooms, in pious parlors, in chapels and vestries, they are tremendously religious; but if they are exposed to a little ridicule, if some should smile at them and call them Methodist, or Presbyterian, or some name of reproach, it is all over with their religion till the next fine day. Then, when it is fine weather and religion will answer their purpose, up go their sails again and they are as

pious as before. Believe me, that kind of religion is worse than ir-religion. I do like a man to be thoroughly what he is, a down-right man; and if a man does not love God, do not let him say he does, but if he be a true Christian, a follower of Jesus, let him say it and stand up for it; there is nothing to be ashamed of in it; the only thing to be ashamed of is to be hypocritical. Let us be honest to our profession, and it will be our glory. Ah! what would you do without faith in times of persecution? You good and pious people that have no faith, what would you do if the stake were again erected in Smithfield and if once more the fires con-sumed the saints to ashes? if the Lollards' tower were again opened, if the rack were again plied, or if even the stocks were used, as they have been used by a Protestant church, as witness the persecution of my predecessor, Benjamin Keach who was once set in the stocks at Aylesbury for writing a book against infant baptism. If even the mildest form of persecution were revived, how would the people be scattered abroad! And some of the shepherds would be leaving their flocks. Another anecdote now and I hope it will lead you to see the necessity of faith, while it may lead me on insensibly to the last part of my discourse. A slaveholding American, on the occasion of buying a slave, said to the person of whom he was purchasing him, "Tell me honestly what are his faults?" Said the seller: "He has no faults that I am aware of but one: that one fault is, he will pray." "Ah!" said the purchaser, "I don't like that, but I know something that will cure him of it pretty soon." So, the next night, Cuffey was surprised by his master in the plantation while in earnest prayer, praying for his new master and his master's wife and family. The man stood and listened but said nothing at the time; but the next morning he called Cuffey and said, "I do not want to quarrel with you, my man, but I'll have no praying on my premises: so you just drop it." "Massa," said he, "me canna leave off praying; me must pray." "I'll teach you to pray if you are going to keep on at it." "Massa, me must keep on." "Well, then, I'll give you five-and-twenty lashes a day till you leave off." "Massa, if you give me fifty, I must pray." "If that's the way you are saucy to your master, you shall have it directly." So, tying him up, he gave him five-and-twenty lashes and asked him if he would pray again. "Yes, massa, me must pray always; me canna leave off." The master looked astonished; he could not understand how a poor saint could keep on praying when it seemed to do no good but only brought persecution upon him. He told his wife of it. His wife said: "Why can't you let the poor man pray? He does his work very well; you and I do not care about praying, but there's no harm in letting him pray if he gets on with his work." "But I don't like it," said the master, "he almost frightened me to death. You should see how he looked at me." "Was he angry?" "No, I should not have minded that, but after I had beaten him, he looked at me with tears in his eyes as if he pitied me more than himself." That night the master could not sleep; he tossed to and fro on his bed; his sins were brought to his remembrance; he remembered he had persecuted a saint of God. Rising in his bed, he said, "Wife, will you pray for me?" "I never prayed in my life," said she; "I cannot pray for you." "I am lost," he said, "if somebody does not pray for me; I cannot pray for myself." "I don't know anyone on the estate who knows how to pray, except Cuffey," said his wife. The bell was rung, and Cuffey was brought in. Taking hold of his black servant's hand, the master said, "Cuffey, can you pray for your master?" "Massa," said he, "me been praying for you eber since you flogged me, and me mean to pray always for you." Down went Cuffey on his knees and poured out his soul in tears, and both husband and wife were converted. That negro could not have done this without faith. Without faith he would have gone away directly, and said, "Massa, me leave off praying; me no like de white man's whip." But because he persevered through his faith, the Lord honored him and gave him his master's soul for his hire.

III. And now in conclusion, *the question,* the vital question.

Dear hearer, have you faith? Dost thou believe on the Lord Jesus
Christ with all thy heart? If so, thou mayest hope to be saved.
Ay, thou mayest conclude with absolute certainty that thou
shalt never see perdition. Have you faith? Shall I help you to
answer that question? I will give you three tests, as briefly as I
can, not to weary you; and then farewell this morning. He that
has faith has renounced his own righteousness. If thou puttest
one atom of trust in thyself, thou hast no faith; if thou dost place
even a particle of reliance upon anything else but what Christ
did, thou hast no faith. If thou dost trust in thy works, then thy
works are antichrist, and Christ and antichrist can never go together. Christ will have all or nothing; He must be a whole
Saviour or no Saviour at all. If, then, you have faith, you can say:

> Nothing in my hand I bring,
> Simply to the cross I cling.

Then true faith may be known by this, that it begets a great
esteem for the person of Christ. Doest thou love Christ? Couldst
thou die for Him? Doest thou seek to serve Him? Doest thou
love His people? Canst thou say:

> Jesus, I love thy charming name
> 'Tis music to my ear.

O! if thou dost not love Christ, thou doest not believe in Him;
for to believe in Christ begets love. And yet more: he that has
true faith will have true obedience. If a man says he has faith
and has no works, he lies; if any man declares that he believes on
Christ and yet does not lead a holy life, he makes a mistake; for
while we do not trust in good works, we know that faith always
begets good works. Faith is the father of holiness, and he has not
the parent who loves not the child. God's blessings are blessings
with both His hands. In the one hand He gives pardon, but in
the other hand He always gives holiness; and no man can have
the one, unless he has the other.

The Sin of Unbelief

And that Lord answered the man of God, and said, Now, behold, if the Lord should make windows in heaven, might such a thing be? And he said, Behold, thou shalt see it with thine eyes, but shalt not eat thereof.—II Kings 7:19.

ONE WISE man may deliver a whole city; one good man may be the means of safety to a thousand others. The holy ones are "the salt of the earth," the means of the preservation of the wicked. Without the godly as a conserve, the race would be utterly destroyed. In the city of Samaria there was one righteous man—Elisha, the servant of the Lord. Piety was altogether extinct in the court. The king was a sinner of the blackest dye; his iniquity was glaring and infamous. Jehoram walked in the ways of his father Ahab and made unto himself false gods. The people of Samaria were fallen like their monarch; they had gone astray from Jehovah; they had forsaken the God of Israel; they remembered not the watchword of Jacob, "The Lord thy God is one God"; and in wicked idolatry they bowed before the idols of the heathens. Therefore the Lord of Hosts suffered their enemies to oppress them until the curse of Ebal was fulfilled in the streets of Samaria, for "the tender and delicate woman who would not adventure to set the sole of her foot upon the ground for delicateness" had an evil eye to her own children and devoured her offspring by reason of fierce hunger. (Deuteronomy, 28:56–58.) In this awful extremity the one holy man was the medium of salvation. The one grain of salt preserved the entire city; the one warrior for God was the means of the deliverance of the whole beleaguered multitude. For Elisha's sake, the Lord sent the promise

169

that the next day food, which could not be obtained at any price, should be had at the cheapest possible rate at the very gates of Samaria. We may picture the joy of the multitude when first the seer uttered this prediction. They knew him to be a prophet of the Lord; he had divine credentials; all his past prophecies had been fulfilled. They knew that he was a man sent of God and uttering Jehovah's message. Surely the monarch's eyes would glisten with delight and the emaciated multitude would leap for joy at the prospect of so speedy a release from famine. "Tomorrow," would they shout, "*tomorrow* our hunger shall be over, and we shall feast to the full!"

However, the lord on whom the king leaned expressed his disbelief. We hear not that any of the common people, the plebeians, ever did so, but an aristocrat did it. Strange it is that God has seldom chosen the great men of this world. High places and faith in Christ do seldom agree. This great man said, "Impossible!" and with an insult to the prophet he added, "If the Lord should make windows in heaven, might such a thing be?" His sin lay in the fact that after repeated seals of Elisha's ministry, he yet disbelieved the assurances uttered by the prophet on God's behalf. He had doubtless seen the marvelous defeat of Moab; he had been startled at tidings of the resurrection of the Shunamite's son; he knew that Elisha had revealed Benhadad's secrets and smitten his marauding hosts with blindness; he had seen the bands of Syria decoyed into the heart of Samaria; and he probably knew the story of the widow whose oil filled all the vessels and redeemed her sons; at all events, the cure of Naaman was common conversation at court; and yet in the face of all this accumulated evidence, in the teeth of all these credentials of the prophet's mission, he yet doubted and insultingly told him that heaven must become an open casement ere the promise could be performed. Whereupon God pronounced his doom by the mouth of the man who had just now proclaimed the promise, "Thou shalt see it with thine eyes, but shalt not eat thereof." And Providence—which always fulfills prophecy just as the paper takes the stamp of the type—destroyed the man. Trodden down in the streets of Samaria, he perished at its gates, beholding the plenty but tasting not of it. Perhaps his carriage was haughty and insulting to the people, or he tried to restrain their eager rush; or, as we would say, it might have been by mere accident that he was crushed to death; so that he saw the prophecy fulfilled but never lived to enjoy it. In his case, seeing was believing, but it was not enjoying.

I shall this morning invite your attention to two things—the man's *sin* and his *punishment*. Perhaps I shall say but little of this man, since I have detailed the circumstances, but I shall discourse upon the sin of unbelief and the punishment thereof.

1. First, the *sin*. His sin was *unbelief*. He doubted the promise of God. In this particular case unbelief took the form of a doubt of the divine veracity or a mistrust of God's power. Either he doubted whether God really meant what He said, or whether it was within the range of possibility that God should fulfill His promise. Unbelief hath more phases than the moon and more colors than the chameleon. Common people say of the devil that he is seen sometimes in one shape and sometimes in another. I am sure this is true of Satan's first-born child, unbelief, for its forms are legion. At one time I see unbelief dressed out as an angel of light. It calls itself humility, and it saith, "I would not be presumptuous; I dare not think that God would pardon me; I am too great a sinner." We call that humility, and thank God that our friend is in so good a condition. I do not thank God for any such delusion. It is the devil dressed as an angel of light; it is unbelief after all. At other times we detect unbelief in the shape of a doubt of God's immutability: "The Lord has loved me, but perhaps He will cast me off tomorrow. He helped me yesterday, and under the shadow of His wings I trust; but perhaps I shall receive no help in the next affliction. He may have cast me off; He may be unmindful of His covenant and forget to

be gracious." Sometimes this infidelity is embodied in a doubt of God's power. We see every day new straits; we are involved in a net of difficulties, and we think, "Surely the Lord can not deliver us." We strive to get rid of our burden, and finding that we can not do it, we think God's arm is as short as ours and His power as little as human might. A fearful form of unbelief is that doubt which keeps men from coming to Christ; which leads the sinner to distrust the ability of Christ to save him; to doubt the willingness of Jesus to accept so great a transgressor. But the most hideous of all is the traitor, in his true colors, blaspheming God and madly denying His existence. Infidelity, deism, and atheism are the ripe fruits of this pernicious tree; they are the most terrific eruptions of the volcano of unbelief.

I am astonished, and I am sure you will be when I tell you that there are some strange people in the world who do not believe that unbelief is sin. Strange people I must call them because they are sound in their faith in every other respect; only to make the articles of their creed consistent, as they imagine, they deny that unbelief is sinful. I remember a young man going into a circle of friends and ministers who were disputing whether it was a sin in men that they did not believe the gospel. While they were discussing it he said, "Gentlemen, am I in the presence of Christians? Are you believers in the Bible, or are you not?" They said, "We are Christians, of course." "Then," said he, "does not the Scripture say, 'of sin, because they believed not on me'? And is it not the damning sin of sinners that they do not believe on Christ?"

I could not have thought that person should be so foolhardy as to venture to assert that "it is no sin for a sinner not to believe on Christ." I thought that however far they might wish to push their sentiments, they would not tell a lie to uphold the truth; and in my opinion that is what such men are really doing. Truth is a strong tower and never requires to be buttressed with error. God's Word will stand against all man's devices. I would never invent a sophism to prove that it is no sin on the part of the ungodly not to believe; for I am sure it is when I am taught in the Scriptures that, "this is the condemnation, that light is come into the world, and men love darkness rather than light"; and when I read, "he that believeth not is condemned already, because he believeth not on the Son of God." I affirm, and the word declares it, *unbelief is* a sin. Surely, with rational and unprejudiced persons it can not require any reasoning to prove it. Is it not a sin for a creature to doubt the word of its Maker? Is it not a crime and an insult to the divinity for me, an atom, a particle of dust, to dare to deny His words? Is it not the very summit of arrogance and extremity of pride for a son of Adam to say, even in his heart, "God, I doubt Thy grace; God, I doubt Thy love; God, I doubt Thy power?" Oh! sirs, believe me, could you roll all sins into one mass; could you take murder, and blasphemy, and lust, and adultery, and fornication, and everything that is vile and unite them all into one vast globe of black corruption, they would not equal even then the sin of unbelief. This is the monarch sin, the quintessence of guilt; the mixture of the venom of all crimes; the dregs of the wine of Gomorrah: it is the A-1 sin; the masterpiece of Satan; the chief work of the devil.

I shall attempt this morning for a little while to show the extremely evil nature of the sin of unbelief.

And, first, the sin of unbelief will appear to be extremely hideous when we remember that *it is the parent of every other iniquity*. There is no crime which unbelief will not beget. I think that the fall of man is very much owing to it. It was in this point that the devil tempted Eve. He said to her, "Yea, *hath* God said, Ye shall not eat of every tree of the garden?" He whispered and insinuated a doubt, "Yea, *hath* God said so?" as much as to say, "Are you *quite* sure He said so?" It was by means of unbelief—that thin part of the wedge—that the other sin entered; curiosity and the rest followed. She touched the fruit, and destruction came into this world. Since that time, unbelief has been the prolific parent of all guilt. An unbeliever is capable of the vilest crime that ever was committed. Unbelief, sirs! why it hardened the heart of Pharaoh; it gave license to the tongue of blaspheming Rabshekah; yea, it became a deicide and murdered Jesus. Unbelief!—it has sharpened the knife of the suicide; it has mixed many a cup of poison; thousands it has brought to the halter, and many to a shameful grave; who have murdered themselves and rushed with bloody hands before their Creator's tribunal because of unbelief. Give me an unbeliever; let me know that he doubts God's Word; let me know that he distrusts His promise and His threatening; and with that for a premise, I will conclude that, by and by, unless there is amazing restraining power exerted upon him, the man will be guilty of the foulest and blackest crimes.

And let me say here, that unbelief in the Christian is of the self-same nature as unbelief in the sinner. It is not the same in its final issue, for it will be pardoned in the Christian; yea it is pardoned. It was laid upon the scape-goat's head of old; it was blotted out and atoned for; but it is of the same sinful nature. In fact, if there can be one sin more heinous than the unbelief of a sinner, it is the unbelief of a saint. For a saint to doubt God's word; for a saint to distrust God after innumerable instances of His love, after ten thousand proofs of His mercy, exceeds everything. In a saint, moreover, unbelief is the root of other sins. When I am perfect in faith, I shall be perfect in everything else.

2. Second; *unbelief not only begets, but fosters sin.* How is it that men can keep their sin under the thunders of the Sinai preacher? How is it that when Boanerges stands in the pulpit, and by the grace of God cries aloud, "Cursed is every man that keepeth not all the commands of the law," how is it that when the sinner hears the tremendous threatenings of God's justice, still he is hardened and walks on in his evil ways? I will tell you: it is because unbelief of that threatening prevents it from having any effect upon him. The devil gives the ungodly man unbelief:

he thus puts up a barrier and finds refuge behind it. Ah, sinners! when once the Holy Ghost knocks down your unbelief; when once he brings home the truth in demonstration and in power, how the law will work upon your soul. If man did not believe that the law is holy, that the commandments are holy, just, and good, how he would be shaken over hell's mouth; there would be no sitting and sleeping in God's house; no careless hearers; no going away and straightway forgetting what manner of men ye are. Again; how is it that men can hear the wooings of the cross of Calvary and yet not come to Christ? How is it that when we preach about the sufferings of Jesus and close by saying, "yet there is room"; how is it that when we dwell upon His cross and passion, men are not broken in their hearts? Methinks the tale of Calvary is enough to break a rock. Rocks did rend when they saw Jesus die. Methinks the tragedy of Golgotha is enough to make a flint gush with tears and to make the most hardened wretch weep out his eyes in drops of penitential love; but yet we tell it you, and after repeat it, but who weeps over it? Who cares about it? Sirs, you sit as unconcerned as if it did not signify to you. Oh! behold and see, all ye that pass by. Is it nothing to you that Jesus should die? You seem to say, "It is nothing." What is the reason? Because there is unbelief between you and the cross.

3. But there is a third point. *Unbelief disables a man for the performance of any good work.* "Whatsoever is not of faith is sin," is a great truth in more senses than one. "Without faith it is impossible to please God." You shall never hear me say a word against morality; you shall never hear me say that honesty is not a good thing, or that sobriety is not a good thing; on the contrary, I would say, they are commendable things; but I will tell you what I will say afterward. I will tell you that they are just like the cowries of Hindoostan: they may pass current among the Indians, but they will not do in England. These virtues may be current here below but not above. If you have not something better than your own goodness, you will never get to heaven.

Some of the Indian tribes use little strips of cloth instead of money; and I would not find fault with them if I lived there; but when I come to England, strips of cloth will not suffice. So honesty, sobriety, and such things may be very good among men, and the more you have of them the better. I exhort you, whatsoever things are lovely, and pure, and of good report, have them; but they will not do up there. All these things put together, without faith, do not please God. Virtues without faith are whitewashed sins; obedience without faith, if it is possible, is a gilded disobedience. Not to believe nullifies everything. It is the fly in the ointment, it is the poison in the pot.

A certain man had an afflicted son possessed with an evil spirit. Jesus was up in Mount Tabor, transfigured; so the father brought his son to the disciples. What did the disciples do? They said, "Oh, we will cast him out." They put their hands upon him, and they tried to do it; but they whispered among themselves and said, "We are afraid we shall not be able." By and by the diseased man began to froth at the mouth; he foamed and scratched the earth, clasping it in his paroxysms. The demoniac spirit within him was alive. The devil was still there. In vain their repeated exorcism; the evil spirit remained like a lion in his den nor could their efforts dislodge him. "Go!" said they; but he went not. "Away to the pit!" they cried; but he remained immovable. The lips of unbelief can not affright the Evil One who might well have said, "Faith I know, Jesus I know, but who are you? you have no faith." If they had had faith as a grain of mustard seed, they might have cast the devil out; but their faith was gone, and therefore they could do nothing. Look at poor Peter's case, too. While he had faith, Peter walked on the waves of the sea. That was a splendid walk; I almost envy him treading upon the billows. Why, if Peter's faith had continued, he might have walked across the Atlantic to America. But presently there came a billow behind him, and he said, "That will sweep me away"; and then another before and he cried out, "That will overwhelm me"; and he thought—how could I be so presumptuous as to be walking on the top of these waves? Down goes Peter. Faith was Peter's life buoy; faith was Peter's charm—it kept him up; but unbelief sent him down. Do you know that you and I, all our lifetime, will have to walk on the water? A Christian's life is always walking on water—mine is—and every wave would swallow and devour him, but faith makes him stand. The moment you cease to believe, that moment distress comes in, and down you go. Oh! wherefore dost thou doubt, then?

4. Our next remark is—*unbelief has been severely punished.* Turn you to the Scriptures! I see a world all fair and beautiful; its mountains laughing in the sun and the fields rejoicing in the golden light. I see maidens dancing and young men singing. How fair the vision! But lo! a grave and reverend sire lifts up his hand and cries, "A flood is coming to deluge the earth: the fountains of the great deep will be broken up, and all things will be covered. See yonder ark! One hundred and twenty years have I toiled with these mine hands to build it; flee there, and you are safe." "Aha! old man; away with your empty predictions! Aha! let us be happy while we may! when the flood comes, then we will build an ark; but there is no flood coming; tell that to fools; we believe no such things." See the unbelievers pursue their merry dance. Hark! unbeliever. Dost thou not hear that rumbling noise? Earth's bowels have begun to move, her rocky ribs are strained by dire convulsions from within; lo! they break with the enormous strain and forth from between them torrents rush unknown since God concealed them in the bosom of our world. Heaven is split in sunder! it rains. Not drops but clouds descend. A cateract like that of old Niagara rolls from heaven with mighty noise. Both firmaments, both deeps—the deep below and the deep above —do clasp their hands. Now, unbelievers, where are you now? There is your last remnant. A man—his wife clasping him round the waist—stands on the last summit that is above the water. See him there! The water is up to his loins even now. Hear his last

shriek! he is floating—he is drowned. And as Noah looks from the ark, he sees nothing. Nothing! It is a void profound. "Sea monsters whelp and stable in the palaces of kings." All is overthrown, covered, drowned. What hath done it? What brought the flood upon the earth? Unbelief. By faith Noah escaped from the flood. By unbelief the rest were drowned.

And, oh! do you not know that unbelief kept Moses and Aaron out of Canaan? They honored not God; they struck the rock when they ought to have spoken to it. They disbelieved; and therefore the punishment came upon them that they should not inherit that good land for which they had toiled and labored.

Let me take you where Moses and Aaron dwelt—to the vast and howling wilderness. We will walk about it for a time; sons of the weary foot, we will become like the wandering Bedouins, we will tread the desert for a while. There lies a carcass whitened in the sun; there another, and there another. What mean these bleached bones? What are these bodies—there a man, and there a woman? What are all these? How came these corpses here? Surely some grand encampment must have been here cut off in a single night by a blast, or by bloodshed. Ah! no, no. Those bones are the bones of Israel; those skeletons are the old tribes of Jacob. They could not enter because of unbelief. They trusted not in God. Spies said that they could not conquer the land. Unbelief was the cause of their death. It was not the Anakim that destroyed Israel; it was not the howling wilderness which devoured them; it was not the Jordan which proved a barrier to Canaan; neither Hivite nor Jebusite slew them; it was unbelief alone which kept them out of Canaan. What a doom to be pronounced on Israel after forty years of journeying: they could not enter because of unbelief!

5. And now to close this point let me remark that you will observe the heinous nature of unbelief in this—*that it is the damning sin*. There is one sin for which Christ never died; it is the sin against the Holy Ghost. There is one other sin for which

Christ never made atonement. Mention every crime in the calendar of evil, and I will show you persons who have found forgiveness for it. But ask me whether the man who died in unbelief can be saved, and I reply, there is no atonement for that man. There is an atonement made for the unbelief of a Christian because it is temporary; but the final unbelief—the unbelief with which men die—never was atoned for.

II. This brings us now to conclude with the punishment. "Thou shalt see it with thine eyes, but shalt not eat thereof." Listen, unbelievers! you have heard this morning your sin; now listen to your doom: "You shall see it with your eyes, but shall not eat thereof." It is so often with God's own saints. When they are unbelieving, they see the mercy with their eyes but do not eat it. Now, here is corn in this land of Egypt; but there are some of God's saints who come here on the Sabbath and say, "I do not know whether the Lord will be with me or not." Some of them say, "Well, the gospel is preached, but I do not know whether it will be successful." They are always doubting and fearing. Listen to them when they get out of the chapel. "Well, did you get a good meal this morning?" "Nothing for me." Of course not. You could see it with your eyes but did not eat it because you had no faith. If you had come up with faith, you would have had a morsel. I have found Christians who have grown up so very critical that if the whole portion of the meat they are to have, in due season, is not cut up exactly into square pieces and put upon some choice dish of porcelain, they can not eat it. Then they ought to go without, and they will have to go without until they are brought to their appetites. They will have some affliction which will act like quinine upon them; they will be made to eat by means of bitters in their mouths; they will be put in prison for a day or two until their appetite returns, and then they will be glad to eat the most ordinary food, off the most common platter, or no platter at all. But the real reason why God's people do not feed under a gospel ministry is because they have not faith.

But, let me apply this chiefly to the unconverted. They often see great works of God done with their eyes, but they do not eat thereof. A crowd of people have come here this morning to see with their eyes, but I doubt whether all of them eat. Men can not eat with their eyes, for if they could, most would be well fed. And, spiritually, persons can not feed simply with their ears, nor simply with looking at the preacher; and so we find the majority of our congregations come just to see: "Ah, let us hear what this babbler would say, this reed shaken in the wind." But they have no faith; they come, and they see, and see, and see, and never eat. There is someone in the front there who gets converted; and someone down below who is called by sovereign grace; some poor sinner is weeping under a sense of his blood-guiltiness; another is crying for mercy to God; and another is saying, "Have mercy upon me, a sinner." A great work is going on in this chapel, but some of you do not know anything about it; you have no work going on in your hearts and why? Because you think it is impossible; you think God is not at work. He has not promised to work for you who do not honor Him. Unbelief makes you sit here in times of revival and of the outpouring of God's grace, unmoved, uncalled, unsaved.

But, sirs, the worst fulfillment of this doom is to come! Good Whitefield used sometimes to lift up both his hands and shout, as I wish I could shout but my voice fails me, "The wrath to come! the wrath to come!" It is not the wrath now you have to fear, but the wrath to come; and there shall be a doom to come when "you shall see it with your eyes, but shall not eat thereof." Methinks I see the last great day. The last hour of time has struck. I heard the bell toll its death-knell—time was, eternity is ushered in; the sea is boiling; the waves are lit up with supernatural splendor. I see a rainbow—a flying cloud, and on it there is a throne, and on that throne sits one like unto the Son of Man. I know Him. In His hand He holds a pair of balances; just before Him the books—the book of life, the book of death, the book of remembrance. I see His splendor, and I rejoice at it; I behold His pompous appearance, and I smile with gladness that He is come to be "admired of all his saints." But there stand a throng of miserable wretches, crouching in horror to conceal themselves and yet looking, for their eyes must look on Him whom they have pierced; but when they look they cry, "Hide me from the face." What face? "Rocks, hide me from the face." What face? "The face of Jesus, the man who died, but now is come to judgment."

But to conclude. Methinks I see thee in some place in hell tied to a rock, the vulture of remorse gnawing thy heart; and up there is Lazarus in Abraham's breast. You lift up your eye and you see who it is: "That is the poor man who lay on my dunghill, and the dogs licked his sores; there he is in heaven, while I am cast down. Lazarus—yes, it is Lazarus; and I who was rich in the world of time am here in hell. Father Abraham, send Lazarus that he may dip the tip of his finger in water to cool my tongue." But no! it can not be, it can not be. And while you lie there, if there be one thing in hell worse than another, it will be seeing the saints in heaven. Oh, to think of seeing my mother in heaven while I am cast out! Oh, sinner, only think, to see thy brother in heaven—he who was rocked in the selfsame cradle and played beneath the same roof-tree—yet thou art cast out. And, husband, there is thy wife in heaven, and thou art among the damned. And seest thou, father! thy child is before the throne; and thou! accursed of God and accursed of man art in hell. Oh, the hell of hells will be to see our friends in heaven and ourselves lost. I beseech you, my hearers, by the death of Christ—by his agony and bloody sweat—by his cross and passion—by all that is holy—by all that is sacred in heaven and earth—by all that is solemn in time or eternity—by all that is horrible in hell or glorious in heaven—by that awful thought, "forever"—I beseech you lay these things to heart and remember that if you are damned, it will be unbelief that damns you. If you are lost, it will be because you believed not on Christ; and if you perish, this shall be the bitterest drop of gall—that you did not trust in the Saviour.

Regeneration

Except a man be born again, he can not see the kingdom of God.—John 3:3.

IN DAILY life our thoughts are most occupied with things that are most necessary for our existence. No one murmured that the subject of the price of bread was frequently on the lips of men at a time of scarcity, because they felt that the subject was one of vital importance to the mass of the population, and therefore they murmured not, though they listened to continual declamatory speeches, and read perpetual articles in the newspapers concerning it. I must offer the same excuse, then, for bringing before you this morning the subject of regeneration. It is one of absolute and vital importance; it is the hinge of the gospel; it is the point upon which most Christians are agreed, yea, all who are Christians in sincerity and truth. It is a subject which lies at the very basis of salvation. It is the very groundwork of our hopes for heaven; and as we ought to be very careful of the basement of our structure, so should we be very diligent to take heed that we are really born again, and that we have made sure work of it for eternity. There are many who fancy they are born again who are not. It well becomes us, then, frequently to examine ourselves; and it is the minister's duty to bring forward those subjects which lead to self-examination and have a tendency to search the heart and try the reins of the children of men.

To proceed at once, I shall first make some remarks upon *the new birth;* second, I shall note *what is meant by not being able to see the kingdom of God if we are not born again;* then I shall go further on to note *why it is that* "*except we are born again we can not see the kingdom of God*"; and then *expostulate with men* as God's ambassador before I close.

I. First, then, *the matter of regeneration.* In endeavoring to explain it, I must have you notice, first of all, *the figure that is employed.* It is said a man must be born again. I can not illustrate this better than by supposing a case. Suppose that in England there should be a law passed that admission to royal courts, preference in office, and any privileges that might belong to the nation, could only be given to persons who were born in England— suppose that birth in this land was made a *sine qua non,* and it was definitely declared that whatever men might do or be, unless they were native born subjects of England they could not enter into her majesty's presence and could enjoy none of the emoluments or offices of the state nor any of the privileges of citizens. I think if you suppose such a case I shall be able to illustrate the difference between any changes and reforms that men make in themselves and the real work of being born again. We will suppose, then, that some man—a red Indian, for instance—should come to this country and should endeavor to obtain the privileges of citizenship, knowing well that the rule is absolute and can not be altered, that a man must be a born subject, or else he can not enjoy them. Suppose he says, "*I will change my name,* I will take up the name of an Englishman; I have been called by my high-sounding title among the Sioux; I have been called the son of the Great Westwind, or some such name; but I will take an English name, I will be called a Christian man, an English subject." Will that admit him? You see him coming to the palace gates and asking for admission. He says, "I have taken an English name." "But are you an Englishman born and bred?" "I am not," says he. "Then the gates must be shut against you, for the law is absolute; and though you may have the name of even the royal family itself upon you, yet because you have not been born here you must be shut out." That illustration will apply to all of us who are here present. At least, nearly the whole of us bear the professing Christion name; living in England, you would think it a disgrace to you if you were not called Christian. You are not heathen, you are not infidel; you are neither Mohammedans nor Jews; you think that the name, Christian, is a creditable one to you, and you have taken it. Be ye quite assured that the name of a Christian is not the nature of a Christian, and that your being born in a Christian land and being recognized as professing the Christian religion is of no avail whatever unless there be something more added to it—the being born again as a subject of Jesus Christ.

"But," says this red Indian, "I am prepared to *renounce my dress* and to become an Englishman in fashion; in fact, I will go to the very top of the fashion; you shall not see me in anything differing from the accepted style of the present day. When I am arrayed in court dress and have decorated myself as etiquette demands, may I not come in before her majesty? See, I'll doff this plume, I will not shake this tomahawk, I renounce these garments. The moccasin I cast away forever; I am an Englishman in dress as well as name." He comes to the gate dressed out like one of our own countrymen; but the gates are still shut in his face because the law required that he must be born in the country; and without that, whatever his dress might be, he could not enter the palace. So how many there are of you who do not barely take the Christian name upon you but have adopted Christian manners; you go to your churches and your chapels, you attend the house of God, you take care that there is some form of religion observed in your family; your children are not left without hearing the name of Jesus! So far so good; God forbid that I should say a word against it! But remember, it is bad because you do not go further. All this is of no avail whatever for admitting you into the kingdom of heaven unless this also is complied with—the being born again. Oh! dress yourselves never so grandly with the habiliments of godliness; put the chaplet of benevolence upon your brow, and gird your loins with integrity; put on your feet the shoes of perseverance, and walk through the earth an honest and upright man; yet, remember, unless you are born again, "that which is of the flesh is flesh," and you, not having the operations of the Spirit in you, still have heaven's gates shut against you because you are not born again.

"Well," says the Indian, "I will not only adopt the dress, but I will *learn the language;* I will put away my brogue and my language that I once spoke on the wild prairie or in the woods far away from my lips. I shall not talk of the Shu-Shuh-gah and of the strange names wherewith I have called my wild fowl and my deer, but I will speak as you speak and act as you act; I will not only have your dress but precisely your manners, I will talk just in the same fashion, I will adopt your brogue, I will take care that it shall be grammatically correct; will you not then admit me? I have become thoroughly Englishized; may I not then be received?" "No," says the keeper of the door, "there is no admittance, for except a man be born in this country, he can not be admitted." So with some of you; you talk just like Christians. Perhaps you have a little too much cant about you; you have begun so strictly to imitate what you think to be a godly man that you go a little beyond the mark, and you gloss it so much that we are able to detect the counterfeit. Still you pass current among most men as being a right down sort of Christian man. You have studied biographies, and sometimes you tell long yarns about divine experience; you have borrowed them from the biographies of good men; you have been with Christians and know how to talk as they do; you have caught a puritanical twang, perhaps; you go through the world just like professors; and if you were to be observed, no one would detect you. You are a member of the church; you have been baptized; you take the Lord's Supper; perhaps you are a deacon or an elder; you pass the sacramental cup around; you are just all that a Christian can be, except that you are without a Christian heart. You are whitewashed sepulchers, still full of rottenness within, though fairly garnished on the outside. Well, take heed, take heed! It is an astonishing thing how near the painter can go to the expression of life and yet the canvas is dead and motionless; and it is equally astonishing how near a man may go to a Christian, and yet, through not being born again, the absolute rule shuts him out of heaven, and with all his profession, with all the trappings of his professed godliness, and with all the gorgeous plumes of experience, yet must he be borne away from heaven's gates.

You are uncharitable, Mr. Spurgeon. I do not care what you say about that. I never wish to be more charitable than Christ. I did not say this; Christ said it. If you have any quarrel with him, settle it there; I am not the maker of this truth but simply the speaker of it. I find it written, "Except a man be born again, he can not see the kingdom of God."

But now note *the manner in which this regeneration is obtained*. I think I have none here so profoundly stupid as to be Puseyites. I can scarcely believe that I have been the means of attracting one person here so utterly devoid of every remnant of brain as to believe the doctrine of baptismal regeneration. Yet, I must just hint at it. There are some who teach that by a few drops of water sprinkled on an infant's brow the infant becomes regenerate. Well, granted. And now I will find out your regenerate ones twenty years afterward. The champion of the prize ring is a regenerated man. Oh! yes, he was regenerated because in infancy he was baptized; and, therefore, if all infants in baptism are regenerated, the prize fighter is a regenerated man. Take hold of him and receive him as your brother in the Lord. Do you hear that man swearing and blaspheming God? He is regenerate; believe me, he is regenerate; the priest put a few drops of water on his brow, and he is a regenerated man. Do you see the drunkard reeling down the street, the pest of the neighborhood, fighting everybody and beating his wife, worse than the brute. Well, he is regenerate, he is one of those Puseyite's regenerates—O! goodly regenerate! Mark you the crowd assembled in the streets! The gallows is erected, Palmer is about to be executed; the man whose name should be execrated through all eternity for his villainy! Here is one of the Puseyite's regenerates. Yes, he is regenerate because he was baptized in infancy; regenerate while he mixes his strychnine; regenerate while he administers his poison slowly, that he may cause death and infinite pain all the while he is causing it. Regenerate, forsooth! If that be regeneration, such regeneration is not worth having; if that be the thing that makes us free of the kingdom of heaven, verily, the gospel is indeed a licentious gospel; we can say nothing about it. If that be the gospel, that all such men are regenerate and will be saved, we can only say, that it would be the duty of every man in the world to move that gospel right away, because it is so inconsistent with the commonest principles of morality that it could not possibly be of God but of the devil.

Neither is a man regenerated, we say, in the next place, *by his own exertions.* A man may reform himself very much, and that is well and good; let all do that. A man may cast away many vices, forsake many lusts in which he indulged, and conquer evil habits; but no man in the world can make himself to be born in God; though he should struggle never so much, he could never accomplish what is beyond his power. And, mark you, if he could make himself to be born again, still he would not enter heaven because there is another point in the condition which he would have violated—"unless a man be born of the *Spirit,* he can not see the kingdom of God." So that the best exertions of the flesh do not reach this high point, the being born again of the Spirit of God.

And now we must say that regeneration consists in this God, the Holy Spirit, in a supernatural manner—mark, by the word supernatural I mean just what it strictly means, supernatural, more than natural—works upon the hearts of men, and they by the operations of the divine Spirit become regenerate men; but without the Spirit they never can be regenerated. And unless God, the Holy Spirit, who "worketh in us to will and to do," should operate upon the will and the conscience, regeneration is an absolute impossibility, and therefore so is salvation. "What!" says one, "do you mean to say that God absolutely interposes in the salvation of every man to make him regenerate?" I do indeed; in the salvation of every person there is an actual putting forth of the divine power whereby the dead sinner is quickened, the unwilling sinner is made willing, the desperately hard sinner has his conscience made tender; and he who rejected God and despised Christ is brought to cast himself down at the feet of Jesus. This is called fanatical doctrine, perhaps; that we can not help; it is scriptural doctrine, that is enough for us. "Except a man be born of the Spirit he can not see the kingdom of God; that which is born of the flesh is flesh, and that which is born of the Spirit is spirit."

III. I think I may just pass over the second point without remark and to the third place, *why it is that "Unless a man be born again he can not see the kingdom of God"*? And I will confine my remarks to the kingdom of God in the world to come.

Why, he can not see the kingdom of God because *he would be out of place in heaven*. A man that is not born again could not enjoy heaven. There is an actual impossibility in his nature which prevents him from enjoying any of the bliss of Paradise. You think, perhaps, that heaven consists in those walls of jewels, in those pearly gates, in those gates of gold; not so, that is the habitation of heaven. Heaven dwells there, but that is not heaven. Heaven is a state that is made here, that is made in the heart; made by God's Spirit within us, and unless God the Spirit has renewed us and caused us to be born again, we can not enjoy the things of heaven. Why, it is a physical impossibility that ever a swine should deliver a lecture on astronomy; every man will clearly perceive that it must be impossible that a snail should build a city; and there is just as much impossibility that an unmended sinner should enjoy heaven. Why, there would be nothing there for him to enjoy; if he could be put into the place where heaven is, he would be miserable; he would cry, "Let me away, let me away; let me away from this miserable place!" I appeal to yourselves; a sermon is too long for you very often; the singing of God's praises is dull, dry work; you think that going up to God's house is very tedious. What will you do where they praise God day without end? If just a short discourse here is very wearying, what will you think of the eternal talkings of the redeemed through all ages of the wonders of redeeming love? If the company of the righteous is very irksome to you, what will be their company throughout eternity? I think many of you are free to confess that psalm-singing is not a bit to your taste, that you care naught about any spiritual things; give you your bottle of wine, and set you down at your ease, that is heaven for you! Well, there is no such a heaven yet made; and therefore there is no heaven for you. The only heaven there is, is the heaven of spiritual men, the heaven of praise, the heaven of delight in God, the heaven of acceptance in the beloved, the heaven of communion with Christ. Now, you do not understand anything about this; you could not enjoy it if you were to have it; you have not the capabilities for doing so.

But there are some other reasons; there are reasons why

> Those holy gates for ever bar
> Pollution, sin, and shame.

There are reasons, besides those in yourselves, why you can not see the kingdom of God unless you are born again. *Ask yon spirits* before the throne: "Angels, principalities, and powers, would ye be willing that men who love not God, who believe not in Christ, who have not been born again, should dwell here?" I see them as they look down upon us and hear them answering, "No! Once we fought the dragon and expelled him because he tempted us to sin; we must not and we will not have the wicked here. These alabaster walls must not be soiled with black and lustful fingers;

the white pavement of heaven must not be stained and rendered filthy by the unholy feet of ungodly men. No!" I see a thousand spears bristling, and the fiery faces of a myriad seraphs thrust over the walls of Paradise. "No, while these arms have strength and these wings have power, no sin shall ever enter here." I address myself moreover to the saints in heaven redeemed by sovereign grace: "Children of God, are ye willing that the wicked should enter heaven as they are without being born again? Ye love men, say, say, say, are ye willing that they should be admitted as they are?" I see Lot rise up, and he cries, "Admit them into heaven! No! What! must I be vexed with the conversation of Sodomites again as once I was?" I see Abraham coming forward, and he says, "No; I can not have them here. I had enough of them while I was with them on earth—their jests and jeers, their silly talkings, their vain conversation, vexed and grieved us. We want them not here." And, heavenly though they be and loving as their spirits are, yet there is not a saint in heaven who would not resent with the utmost indignation the approach of any one of you to the gates of paradise if you are still unholy and have not been born again.

But all that were nothing. We might perhaps scale the ramparts of heaven, if they were only protected by angels, and burst the gates of paradise open if only the saints defended them. But there is another reason than that—*God has said it Himself*—"Except a man be born again, he can not see the kingdom of God." What sinner, wilt thou scale the battlements of Paradise when God is ready to thrust thee down to hell? Wilt thou with impudent face brazen Him out? God has said it, God hath said it, with a voice of thunder, "Ye shall not see the kingdom of heaven." Can ye wrestle with the Almighty? Can ye overthrow Omnipotence? Can ye grapple with the Most High? Worm of the dust! canst thou overcome thy Maker? Trembling insect of an hour, shaken by the lightnings when far overhead they flash far athwart the sky, wilt thou dare the hand of God? Wilt thou venture to defy Him to His face? Ah! He would laugh at thee. As the snow melteth before the sun, as wax runneth at the fierceness of the fire, so wouldst thou if His fury should once lay hold of thee. Think not that thou canst overcome Him. He has sealed the gate of Paradise against thee, and there is no entrance. The God of justice says, "I will not reward the wicked with the righteous; I will not suffer my goodly, godly Paradise to be stained by wicked ungodly men. If they turn, I will have mercy upon them; but if they turn not, as I live, I will rend them in pieces, and there shall be none to deliver."

IV. Now, my friends, a little *expostulation* with you, and then farewell. I hear one man say, "Well, well, well, I see it. *I will hope that I shall be born again after I am dead.*" O, sir, believe me, you will be a miserable fool for your pains. When men die their state is fixed.

> Fixed as their everlasting state,
> Could they repent, 'tis now too late.

Our life is like that wax melting in the flame; death puts its stamp on it, and then it cools, and the impress never can be changed. You today are like the burning metal running forth from the cauldron into the mold; death cools you in your mold, and you are cast in that shape throughout eternity. The voice of doom crieth over the dead, "He that is holy let him be holy still; he that is unjust let him be unjust still; he that is filthy, let him be filthy still." The damned are lost forever; they can not be born again; they go on cursing, even being cursed; ever fighting against God and ever being trampled beneath His feet; they go on ever mocking, ever being laughed at for their mockery; ever rebelling and ever being tortured with the whips of conscience because they are ever sinning. They can not be regenerated because they are dead.

"Well," says another, "*I will take care that I am regenerated first before I die.*" Sir, I repeat, thou art a fool in talking thus; how knowest thou that thou shalt live? Hast thou taken a lease of thy life as thou hast of thy house? Canst thou insure the breath within thy nostrils? Canst thou say in certainty that another ray of light shall ever reach thine eye? Canst thou be sure that as thine heart is beating a funeral march to the grave thou wilt not soon beat the last note; and so thou shalt die where thou standest or sittest now? O man! if thy bones were iron and thy sinews brass and thy lungs steel, then mightest thou say, "I shall live." But thou art made of dust; thou art like the flower of the field; thou mayest die now. Lo! I see death standing yonder, moving to and fro the stone of time upon his scythe, to sharpen it; today, to-day, for some of you he grasps the scythe—and away, away, he mows the fields, and you fall one by one. You must not and you can not live. God carries us away as a flood, like a ship in a whirl-pool; like the log in a current, dashed onward to the cataract. There is no stopping any one of us; we are all dying now! and yet you say you will be regenerated ere you die! Ay sirs, but are you regenerated now? For if not, it may be too late to hope for to-morrow. Tomorrow you may be in hell, sealed up forever by adamantine destiny which never can be moved.

"Well," cries another, "*I do not care much about it;* for I see very little in being shut out of Paradise." Ah, sir, it is because thou dost not understand it. Thou smilest at it now, but there will be a day when thy conscience will be tender, when thy mem-ory will be strong, when thy judgment will be enlightened, and when thou wilt think very differently from what thou dost now. Sinners in hell are not the fools they are on earth; in hell they do not laugh at everlasting burnings; in the pit they do not despise the words "eternal fire." The worm that never dieth when it is gnawing, gnaws out all joke and laughter; you may despise God now and despise me now for what I say, but death will change your note. O my hearers, if that were all, I would be willing. You may despise me, yes you may; but O! I beseech you, do not despise yourselves; O! be not so foolhardy as to go whistling to hell and laughing to the pit; for when you are there, sirs, you will find it a different thing from what you dream it to be now. When you see the gates of Paradise shut against you, you will find it to be a more important matter than you judge of now. You came to hear me preach today as you would have gone to the opera or playhouse; you thought I should amuse you. Ah! that is not my aim, God is my witness, I came here solemnly and in earnest to wash my hands of your blood. If any one of you is damned, it shall not be because I did not warn you.

But ah! my friends, I can not speak as I wish. This morning I think I feel something like Dante when he wrote his *Il Inferno*. Men said of him that he had been in hell; he looked like it. He had thought of it so long that they said, "He has been in hell," he spoke with such an awful earnestness. Ah! if I could, I would speak like that too. It is only a few days more, and I shall meet you face to face; I can look over the lapse of a few years when you and I shall stand face to face before God's bar. "Watchman, watchman," saith a voice, "didst thou warn them? didst thou warn them?" Will any of you then say I did not? No, even the most abandoned of you at that day will say, "We laughed, we scoffed at it, we cared not for it; but O Lord, we are obliged to speak the truth; the man was in earnest about it; he told us of our doom, and he is clear." Will you say so? I know you will.

Looking Unto Jesus

They looked unto him, and were lightened: and their faces were not ashamed.—Psalm 34:5.

From the connection we are to understand the pronoun "him" as referring to the word "Lord" in the preceding verse. "They looked unto the Lord Jehovah, and were lightened." But no man ever yet looked to Jehovah God, as He is in Himself, and found any comfort in Him, for "our God is a consuming fire." An absolute God, apart from the Lord Jesus Christ, can afford no comfort whatever to a troubled heart. We may look to him, and we shall be blinded for the light of Godhead is insufferable; and as mortal eye can not fix its gaze upon the sun, no human intellect could ever look unto God and find light, for the brightness of God would strike the eye of the mind with eternal blindness. The only way in which we can see God is through the Mediator Jesus Christ.

> Till God in human flesh I see,
> My thoughts no comfort find.

God shrouded and veiled in the manhood—there we can with steady gaze behold Him for so He cometh down to us, and our poor finite intelligence can understand and lay hold upon Him. I shall therefore use my text this morning, and I think very legitimately, in reference to our Lord and Saviour Jesus Christ— "They looked unto him, and were lightened"; for when we look at God, as revealed in Jesus Christ our Lord, and behold the Godhead as it is apparent in the incarnate Man who was born of the

Virgin Mary and was crucified by Pontius Pilate, we do see that which enlightens the mind and casts rays of comfort into our awakened heart.

To illustrate my text, I shall first invite you to look to Jesus Christ in His life on earth, and I hope there are some of you who will be lightened by that. We shall then look to Him on His cross. Afterward, we shall look to Him in His resurrection. We shall look to Him in His intercession; and last, we shall look to Him in His second coming; and it may be as we look upon Him with faithful eye, the verse will be fulfilled in our experience, which is the best proof of a truth when we prove it to be true in our own hearts. We shall "look unto him" and we shall "be lightened."

I. First, then, we shall look to the Lord Jesus Christ in His life. And here the troubled saint will find the most to enlighten him. In the example, in the patience, in the sufferings of Jesus Christ, there are stars of glory to cheer the midnight darkness of the sky of your tribulation. Come hither, ye children of God, and whatever now are your distresses, whether they be temporal or spiritual, you shall find in the life of Jesus Christ and His sufferings, sufficient to cheer and comfort you if the Holy Spirit will now open your eyes to look unto Him. Perhaps I have among my congregation, indeed I am sure I have, some who are plunged in the depths of poverty. You are the children of toil; with much sweat of your brow you eat your bread; the heavy yoke of oppression galls your neck; perhaps at this time you are suffering the very extremity of hunger; you are pinched with famine, and though in the house of God, your body complains, for you feel that you are brought very low. Look unto Him thou poor distressed brother in Jesus; look unto Him and be lightened.

> Why doest thou complain of want or distress,
> Temptation or pain?—he told thee no less;
> The heirs of salvation, we know from his word,
> Through much tribulation must follow their Lord.

See Him there! Forty days He fasts and He hungers. See Him again; He treads the weary way and at last, all athirst, He sits upon the curb of the well of Sychar; and He the Lord of glory, He who holds the clouds in the hollow of His hand, said to a woman, "Give me to drink." And shall the servant be above his master and the disciple above his Lord? If He suffered hunger, and thirst, and nakedness, O heir of poverty, be of good cheer; in all these thou hast fellowship with Jesus; therefore be comforted, and look unto Him and be lightened.

Perhaps your trouble is of another cast. You have come here today smarting from the forked tongue of that adder-slander. Your character, though pure and spotless before God, seems to be lost before man; for that foul slanderous thing hath sought to take away that which is dearer to you than life itself, your character, your good fame, and you are this day filled with bitterness and made drunken with wormwood because you have been accused of crimes which your soul loathes. Come, thou child of mourning, this indeed is a heavy blow; poverty is like Solomon's whip, but slander is like the scorpion of Rehoboam; to fall into the depths of poverty is to have it on thy little finger, but to be slandered is to have it on thy loins. But in all this thou mayest have comfort from Christ. Come and look unto Him and be lightened. The King of kings was called a Samaritan; they said of Him that He had a devil and was mad; and yet infinite wisdom dwelt in Him though He was charged with madness. And was He not ever pure and holy? And did they not call Him a drunken man and a winebibber? He was His Father's glorious Son, and yet they said He did cast out devils through Beelzebub the prince of the devils. Come, poor slandered one; wipe that tear away! "If they have called the Master of the house Beelzebub, how much more shall they call them of his household?" If they had honored Him, then might you have expected that they would honor you; but inasmuch as they mocked Him and took away His glory and His character, blush not to bear the reproach and the shame for He is with you, carrying His cross before you, and that cross was heavier than yours. Look, then, unto Him and be lightened.

But I hear another say, "Ah! but my trouble is worse than either of those. I am not today smarting from slander, nor am I burdened with penury; but, sir, the hand of God lies heavy upon me; He hath brought my sins to my remembrance; He hath taken away the bright shining of His countenance. Once I did believe in Him, and could 'read my title clear to mansions in the skies,' but today I am brought very low: He hath lifted me up and cast me down; like a wrestler, He has elevated me that He might dash me to the ground with the greater force; my bones are sore vexed, and my spirit within me is melted with anguish." Come, my tried brother, "Look unto Him and be lightened." No longer groan over thine own miseries, but come thou with me and look unto Him if thou canst. Seest thou the Garden of Olives? It is a cold night, and the ground is crisp beneath thy feet for the frost is hard; and there in the gloom of the olive garden kneels thy Lord. Listen to Him. Canst thou understand the music of His groans, the meaning of His sighs? Surely, thy griefs are not so heavy as His were when drops of blood were forced through His skin and a bloody sweat did stain the ground! Say, are thy wrestlings greater than His? If, then, He had to combat with the powers of darkness, expect to do so also; and look thou to Him in the last solemn hour of His extremity, and hear Him say, "My God, my God, why hast thou forsaken me?" And when thou hast heard that, murmur not as though some strange thing had happened to thee, as if thou had to join in His "lama sabbacthani," and had to sweat some few drops of His bloody sweat. "They looked unto him, and were lightened."

II. And now I have to invite you to a more dreary sight; but, strange it is, just as the sight becomes more black, so to us does it grow more bright. The more deeply the Saviour dived into the depths of misery, the brighter were the pearls which He brought up—the greater His griefs, the greater our joys, and the deeper His dishonor, the brighter our glories. Come, then—and this time I shall ask poor, doubting, trembling sinners and saints to come with me—come ye now to Calvary's cross. There on the summit of that little hill outside the gates of Jerusalem where common criminals were ordinarily put to death—the Tyburn of Jerusalem, the Old Bailey of that city, where criminals were executed—there stand three crosses, the center one is reserved for one who is reputed to be the greatest of criminals. See there! They have nailed Him to the cross. It is the Lord of life and glory before whose feet angels delight to pour full vials of glory. They have nailed Him to the cross: He hangs there in mid-heaven, dying, bleeding; He is thirsty and He cries. They bring him vinegar and thrust it into His mouth. He is in suffering, and He needs sympathy, but they mock at Him, and they say, "He saved others; himself he can not save." They misquote His words; they challenge Him now to destroy the temple and build it in three days; while the very thing is being fulfilled, they taunt Him with His powerlessness to accomplish it. Now see Him, ere the veil is drawn over agonies too black for eye to behold. See Him now! Was ever face marred like that face? Was ever heart so big with agony? And did ever eyes seem so pregnant with the fire of suffering as those great wells of fiery agony? Come and behold Him, come and look to Him now. The sun is eclipsed, refusing to behold Him! earth quakes; the dead rise; the horrors of His sufferings have startled earth itself;

He dies! the friend of sinners dies;

and we invite you to look to this scene that you may be lightened. What are your doubts this morning? Whatever they are, they can find a kind and fond solution here by looking at Christ on the cross. You have come here, perhaps, doubting God's mercy; look to Christ upon the cross, and can you doubt it then? If God were not full of mercy and plenteous in His compassion, would

He have given His Son to bleed and die? Think you that a father would rend His darling from His heart and nail Him to a tree, that He might suffer ignominious death for our sakes and yet be hard, merciless, and without pity? God forbid the impious thought! There must be mercy in the heart of God or else there had never been a cross on Calvary.

But do you doubt God's power to save? Are you saying within yourself this morning, "How can he forgive so great a sinner as I am?" Oh! look there, sinner, look there to the great atonement made, to the utmost ransom paid. Dost thou think that that blood has not an efficacy to pardon and to justify? True, without that cross it had been an unanswerable question—"How can God be just, and yet the justifier of the ungodly?" But see there the bleeding substitute! and know that God has accepted His sufferings as an equivalent for the woes of all believers; and then if thy spirit can, let it dare to think that there is not sufficient in the blood of Christ to enable God to vindicate His justice and yet have mercy upon sinners.

But I know you say, "My doubt is not of His general mercy, nor of His power to forgive, but of His willingness to forgive me." Now I beseech you by Him that liveth and was dead, do not this morning look into your own heart in order to find an answer to that difficulty; do not now sit down and look at your sins; they have brought you into the danger—they can not bring you out of it. The best answer you will ever get is at the foot of the cross. Sit down in quiet contemplation for half an hour when you get home this morning; sit at the foot of the cross and contemplate the dying Saviour, and I will defy you then to say, "I doubt His love for me." Looking at Christ begets faith. You can not believe on Christ except as you see Him, and if you look to Him, you will learn that He is able to save; you will learn His loving-kindness, and you can not doubt Him after having once beheld Him. Dr. Watts says,

> His worth, if all the nations knew,
> Sure the whole world would love him too;

and I am sure it is quite true if I read it another way—

> His worth, if all the nations knew,
> Sure the whole world would trust him too.

Oh, that you would look to Him now, and your doubts would soon be removed; there is nothing that so speedily kills all doubt and fear as a look into the loving eye of the bleeding, dying Lord. "Ah," says one, "but my doubts are concerning my own salvation in this respect; I can not be so holy as I want to be." "I have tried very much," says one, "to get rid of all my sins, and I can not; I have labored to live without wicked thoughts and without unholy acts, and I still find that my heart is 'deceitful above all things,' and I wander from God. Surely I can not be saved while I am like this." Stay! Look to Him and be lightened. What business have you to be looking to yourself? The first business of a sinner is not with himself but with Christ. Your business is to come to Christ, sick, weary, and soul-diseased, and ask Christ to cure you. You are not to be your own physician and then go to Christ, but go just as you are; the only salvation for you is to trust implicitly, simply, nakedly, on Christ. As I sometimes put it—make Christ the only pillar of your hope and never seek to buttress or prop Him up. "He is able, he is willing." All He asks of you is just to trust Him. As for your good works, they shall come afterwards. They are after-fruits of the Spirit: but your first business is not to do but to believe. Look to Jesus, and put your only trust in Him.

"Oh," another cries, "sir, I am afraid I do not feel my need of a Saviour as I ought." Looking to yourselves again! all looking to yourselves you see! This is all wrong. Our doubts and fears all arise from this cause—we will turn our eyes the wrong way. Just look to the cross again as the poor thief did when he was dying; he said, "Lord, remember me when thou comest into thy kingdom." Do the same. You may tell Him, if you please, that you do not feel your need of Him as you ought; you may put this among your other sins, that you fear you have not a right sense of your great and enormous guilt. You may add to all your confessions this cry, "Lord help me to confess my sins better; help me to feel them more penitently." But recollect, it is not your repentance that saves you; it is just the blood of Christ streaming from His hands, and feet, and side. Oh! I beseech you by Him whose servant I am, to turn your eyes this very morning to the cross of Christ. There He hangs this day; He is lifted up in your midst. As Moses lifted up the serpent in the wilderness, even so is the Son of man lifted up today in your eyes, that whosoever believeth in Him may not perish, but have everlasting life.

And you children of God, I turn to you, for you have your doubts too. Would you get rid of them? Would you rejoice in the Lord with faith unmoved and confidence unshaken? Then look to Jesus; look again to Him and you shall be lightened. I know not how it is with you, my beloved friends, but I very often find myself in a doubting frame of mind; and it seems to be a question whether I have any love for Christ or not. And despite the fact that some laugh at the hymn, it is a hymn that I am forced to sing:

> 'Tis a point I long to know,
>   Oft it causes anxious thought,
> Do I love the Lord or no?
>   Am I his, or am I not?

And really I am convinced that every Christian has his doubts at times and that the people who do not doubt are just the people that ought to doubt; for he who never doubts about his state perhaps may do so when it is too late. I knew a man who said he never had a doubt for thirty years. I told him that I knew a person who never had a doubt about him for thirty years. "How is that?" said he, "that is strange." He thought it a compliment. I said, "I knew a man who never had a doubt about you for thirty years. He knew you were always the greatest hypocrite he ever met;

he had no doubt about you." But this man had no doubt about himself: he was a chosen child of God, a great favorite of the Most High; he loved the doctrine of election, wrote it on his very brow; and yet he was the hardest driver and most cruel oppressor of the poor I ever met, and when brought to poverty himself, he might very frequently be seen rolling through the streets. And this man had not a doubt for thirty years, and yet the best people are always doubting. Some of those who are living just outside the gates of heaven are afraid of being cast into hell after all; while those people who are on the high road to the pit are not the least afraid. However, if you would get rid of your doubts once more, turn to Christ. You know what Dr. Carey had put on his tomb-stone—just these words for they were his comfort:

> A guilty, weak, and helpless worm,
>   Into Christ's arms I fall;
> He is my strength and righteousness,
>   My Jesus and my all.

Remember what that eminent Scotch divine said when he was dying. Some one said to him, "What are you doing now?" Said he, "I am just gathering all my good works up together, and I am throwing them all overboard; and I am lashing myself to the plank of free grace, and I hope to swim to glory on it." So do you; every day keep your eye only on Christ; and so long as your eye is single, your whole body must and shall be full of light. But if you once look cross-eyed, first to yourself and then to Christ, your whole body shall be full of darkness. Remember, then, Christian, to hie away to the cross. When that great black dog of hell is after you, away to the cross! Go where the sheep goes when he is molested by the dog; go to the Shepherd. The dog is afraid of the shepherd's crook; you need not be afraid of it, it is one of the things that will comfort you. "Thy rod and thy staff they comfort me."

III. And now I invite you to a glorious scene—Christ's Resurrection. Come you here, and look at Him as the old serpent bruises his heel!

> He dies! the friend of sinners dies,
> And Salem's daughters weep around.

He was wrapped in His graveclothes and put into His grave, and there He slept three days and nights. And on the first day of the week, He, who could not be holden by the bands of death and whose flesh did not see corruption, neither did his soul abide in Hades—He arose from the dead. In vain the bands that swaddled Him; He unfolded them by Himself, and by His own living power wrapped them in perfect order and laid them in their place. In vain the stone and the seal; the angel appeared and rolled away the stone and forth the Saviour came. In vain the guards and watchmen; for in terror they fled far away, and He rose the conqueror over death—the first-fruits of them that slept. By His own power and might, He came again to life. I see among my congregation not a few wearing the black weeds of sorrow. Some of you have lost the dearest of your earthly relatives. There are others here who I doubt not are under the constant fear of death. You are all your lifetime subject to bondage because you are thinking upon the groans and dying strife which fall upon men when they near the river Jordan. Come, come, I beseech you, ye weeping and timid spirits, behold Jesus Christ risen! For remember this is a great truth—"Now is Christ risen from the dead, and become the first-fruits of them that slept." And the verse of our song just embodies it:

> What though our inbred sins require
> Our flesh to see the dust,
> Yet as the Lord our Saviour rose,
> So all his followers must.

There, widow, weep no longer for your husband if he died in Jesus. See the Master; He is risen from the dead; no specter is He. In the presence of His disciples He eats a piece of broiled fish and part of a honeycomb. No spirit is He; for He saith, "Handle me and see; a spirit hath not flesh and blood as ye see me have." That was a real resurrection. And when you weep, learn then, beloved, to restrain your sorrows for thy loved ones shall live again. Not only shall their spirits live but their bodies too.

> Corruption, earth, and worms,
>   Do but refine this flesh;
> At the archangel's sounding trump,
>   We put it on afresh.

Oh! think not that the worm has eaten up your children, your friends, your husband, your father, your aged parents—true the worms seem to have devoured them. Oh! what is the worm after all but the filter through which our poor filthy flesh must go? For in the twinkling of an eye at the last trump we shall be raised incorruptible, and the living shall be changed; you shall see the eye that just now has been closed, and you shall look on it again; you shall again grasp the hand that just now fell motionless at the side; you shall kiss the lips that just now were clay-cold and white, and you shall hear again the voice that is silent in the tomb. They shall live again. And you that fear death—why fear to die? Jesus died before you, and He passed through the iron gates, and as He passed them before you, He will come and meet you. Jesus who lives can

> Make the dying bed
> Feel soft as downy pillows are.

Why should you weep? for Jesus rose from the dead; so shall you. Be of good cheer and confidence. You are not lost when you are put into the tomb; you are but seed sown to ripen against the eternal harvest. Your spirit mounts to God; your body slumbers for a while to be quickened into eternal life; it can not be quickened except it die; but when it dies, it shall receive a new life; it shall not be destroyed. "They looked to him, and were lightened."

IV. And with the greatest possible brevity, I invite you to look at Jesus Christ ascending into Heaven. After forty days, He takes His disciples to the hill, and while He discourses with them, suddenly He mounts upward, and is separated from them, and a cloud receives Him into glory. Perhaps I may be allowed a little poetical license if I try to picture that which occurred after He ascended into the clouds. The angels came from heaven—

> They brought his chariot from on high
> To bear him to his throne;
> Clapped their triumphant wings and cried,
> The glorious work is done.

I doubt not that with matchless triumph He ascended the hill of light and went to the celestial city, and when He neared the portals of that great metropolis of the universe, the angels shouted, "Lift up your heads, O ye gates; and be ye lift up ye everlasting doors," and the bright spirits from burning battlements cried out, "Who is this King of Glory—who?" And the answer came, "The Lord mighty in battle, and the Lord of Hosts; he is the King of Glory." And then both they upon the walls and they who walk with the chariot join the song once more, and with one mighty sea of music beating its melodious waves against the gates of heaven and forcing them open, the strain is heard, "Lift up your heads, O ye gates, and be ye lift up ye everlasting doors, that the King of Glory may come in"—and in He went. And at His feet the angelic hosts all cast their crowns and forth came the blood-washed and met Him, not casting roses at His feet as we do at the feet of conquerors in our streets, but casting immortal flowers, imperishable wreaths of honor that never can decay; while again, again, again, the heavens did ring with this melody, "Unto him that hath loved us, and washed us from our sins in his blood, and hath made us kings and priests unto God and his Father—unto him be glory for ever and ever." And all the saints and all the angels said, "Amen." Now look ye here, Christian, here is your comfort; Jesus Christ won the victory, and He ascended to His throne of glory. You are fighting today and wrestling with spiritual enemies, not with flesh and blood but with principalities and powers; you are at war today, and perhaps the enemy has thrust sore at you and you have been ready to fall; it is a marvel to you that you have not turned your back in the day of battle, for you have often feared lest you should be made to fly like a coward from the field. But tremble not, your Master was more than conqueror and so shall you be. The day is coming when with splendor less than His but yet the same in its measure, you too shall pass the gates of bliss; when you are dying, angels shall meet you in the mid-stream, and when your blood is cooling with the cold current, then shall your heart be warming with another stream, a stream of light and heat from the great fountain of all joy, and you shall stand on the other side of Jordan, and angels shall meet you clothed in their immaculate garments; they shall attend you up the hill of light, and they shall chant the praise of Jesus and hail you as another trophy of His power. And when you enter the gates of heaven, you shall be met by Christ your Master who will say to you—"Well done, good and faithful servant, enter thou into the joy of thy Lord." Then will you feel that you are sharing in His victory as once you shared in His struggles and His war. Fight on, Christian, your glorious Captain has won a great victory and has secured for you in one and the same victory, a standard that never yet was stained with defeat though often dipped in the blood of the slain.

V. And now once more, "Look unto him, and be lightened." See there, He sits in heaven; He has led captivity captive, and now sits at the right hand of God forever making intercession for us. Can your faith picture Him today? Like a great high priest of old He stands with outstretched arms; there is majesty in His mien for He is no mean, cringing suppliant. He does not beat His breast, nor cast His eyes on the ground, but with authority He pleads, enthroned in glory now. There on His head is the bright, shining miter of His priesthood, and look you, on His breast are glittering the precious stones whereon the names of his elect are everlastingly engraven; hear Him as He pleads, hear you not what it is?—is that your prayer that He is mentioning before the throne? The prayer that this morning you offered ere you came to the house of God, Christ is now offering before His Father's throne. The vow which just now you uttered when you said, "Have pity and have mercy"—He is now uttering there. He is the Altar and the Priest and with His own sacrifice He perfumes our prayers. And yet, perhaps you have been at prayer many a day and had no answer; poor, weeping suppliant, thou hast sought the Lord and He hath not heard thee, or at least not answered thee to thy soul's delight; thou hast cried unto Him, but the heavens have been as brass, and He hath shut out thy prayer; thou art full of darkness and heaviness on account of this: "Look to him, and be lightened." If thou dost not succeed, He will; if thy intercession be unnoticed, His can not be passed over; if thy prayers can be like water spilled on a rock which cannot be gathered up, yet His prayers are not like that; He is God's Son, He pleads and must prevail; God can not refuse His own Son what He now asks, He who once bought mercies with His blood. Oh! be of good cheer, continue still thy supplication. "Look unto him, and be lightened."

VI. In the last place, there are some of you here weary with this world's din and clamor and with this world's iniquity and vice. You have been striving all your life long to put an end to the reign of sin, and it seems as if your efforts have been fruitless; the pillars of hell stand as fast as ever, and the black palace of evil is not laid in ruins; you have brought against it all the battering rams of prayer and all the might of God, you have thought—and yet the world still sins, its rivers still roll with blood, its plains are still defiled with the lascivious dance, and its ear is still polluted with the filthy song and profane oath. God is not honored; man is still vile; and perhaps you are saying, "It is vain for us to fight on; we have undertaken a task which can not be accomplished; the kingdoms of this world never can become the kingdoms of our Lord and of his Christ." But, Christian, "Look unto him, and be lightened." Lo! He cometh, He cometh, He cometh quickly; and what we can not do in six thousand years, He can do in an instant. Lo! He comes, He comes to reign; we may try to build His throne, but we shall not accomplish it. But when He comes, He shall build His throne Himself on solid pillars of light and sit and judge in Jerusalem amidst His saints, gloriously. Perhaps today, the hour we are assembled, Christ may come—"For of that day and hour knoweth no man; no, not the angels in heaven." Christ Jesus may, while I yet speak, appear in the clouds of glory. We have no reason to be guessing at the time of His appearing; He will come as the thief in the night; and whether it shall be at cock-crowing, or broad day, or at midnight, we are not allowed to guess; it is left entirely in the dark, and vain are the prophecies of men, vain your "Apocalyptic Sketches," or aught of that. No man knoweth anything of it except that it is certain He will come; but when He comes, no spirit in heaven or on earth should pretend to know. Oh! it is my joyous hope that He may come whilst yet I live. Perhaps there may be some of us here who shall be alive and remain at the coming of the Son of man. Oh, glorious hope! we shall have to sleep, but we shall all be changed. He may come now, and we that are alive and remain shall be forever with Him. But if you die, Christian, this is your hope. "I will come again, and receive you to myself, that where I am, there ye may be also." And this is to be your duty, "Watch, therefore, for in such an hour as ye think not, the Son of man cometh." Oh, will I not work on for Christ is at the door! Oh! I will not give up toiling never so hard for my Master cometh, and His reward is with Him, and His work before Him, giving unto every man according as his work shall be. Oh, I will not lie down in despair, for the trump is sounding now. Methinks I hear the trampling of the conquering legion; the last of God's mighty heroes are even now, perhaps, born into the world. The hour of this revival is the hour of turning to the battle; thick has been the fight and hot and furious the struggle, but the trump of the conqueror is beginning to sound, the angel is lifting it now to his lips. The first blast has been heard across the sea, and we shall hear it yet again; or if we hear it not in these our days, yet still it is our hope. He comes, He comes, and every eye shall see Him, and they that have crucified Him shall weep and wail before Him, but the righteous shall rejoice and shall magnify Him exceedingly. "They looked unto him, and were lightened."

Spiritual Religion

It is the spirit that quickeneth: the flesh profiteth nothing.
—John 6:63.

To a casual reader it looks as if the meaning of this passage lay upon the very surface, but he that has studied the chapter will find that it is a sentence replete with many difficulties as to the exact interpretation of it. I shall not, however, waste your time by entering into any critical discussion of it, but shall try only to give you what I believe to be the mind of the Spirit as uttered by the lips of Jesus in this passage, and after I have done that, I shall then revert to what I shall call the meaning which any person would give to it who is not a usual student of Scripture. That being true, although not the truth taught in the passage, I shall enlarge upon it briefly. "It is the spirit that quickeneth; the flesh profiteth nothing." I suppose there is not a man in the world who could form any intelligent idea of what a spirit is. It is very easy for persons to define a spirit by saying what it is not, but I query whether there is, or ever could be, any man who could form any idea of what it is. We sometimes talk about seeing a spirit; ignorant persons in ages gone by, and some now in benighted villages, talk about seeing spirits by night. They must know that they talk contradictions. Matter can be seen, but a spirit if it clothed itself in any light substance, could not even then be seen; it would only be the substance that would be seen. The spirit itself is a thing which can neither be tasted, handled, seen, nor discerned in any way whatever by our senses, for if it could be it

210

would then be proof positive that it was not a spirit at all but belonged to the realm of matter. We divide all things into matter and spirit, and whatsoever can be recognized by the senses in any way is matter, depend on it. Spirit is itself a thing too subtle either to be seen or in any other way recognized by the senses. I say, then, I suppose there is no man living and never will be any man in this mortal state who will be able to define a spirit as to what it is, though he may say what it is not.

Now, there is a region where there are spirits dwelling without body. It is certain that in the world to come in that state which now intervenes between the death of the saints and the day of the resurrection, they are dwelling before the throne of God in a disembodied state—pure spirits without any embodiment whatever. It may be that angels have some form of bodies; we could not imagine what angels were if they had some kind of semblance of appearance; but it is quite certain that the saints before the throne have no semblance of shapes whatever. They are pure spirits; beings whose substance we cannot imagine; purely immaterial as they are also immaculate. But on earth you will find no such a thing as a pure spirit. We are all spirits in bodies, and, somehow, from the fact that wherever we find souls and spirits, they are always found in bodies, we are very apt to confound bodies and spirits together. But let us always understand that bodies and spirits are distinct things; and though it hath pleased God in this world never to make a spirit without making a house called the body for it to dwell in, yet the body is not the spirit. "It is the spirit that quickeneth; the flesh profiteth nothing."

Now, you will easily learn this, for in man's body no one can tell where the life is. In vain the surgeon lays the body on the table and dissects it; he will find life neither in the brain nor in the heart; he may cut the body in pieces as he pleases—he will not find anything that he can lay hold upon tangibly and really say, "That is life." He can see all the effects—he can see the parts moving, he can see all the appearances of life caused by a super-natural something, but life he cannot see. It is altogether beyond his ken, and after all his searching he would lay down his scalpel and say at once, "There now, the task is all over, there is a spirit that quickeneth this body, but in my search after life this flesh profiteth me nothing. I might as well search for a soul within a stone or within one of the pillars that support this house as search for a soul within mere flesh and blood if I look for something which I can see, which I can lay hold of, or which by either taste, sight smelling, or anything else I can distinguish and designate as being a spirit."

Now, then, brethren, this illustration just brings me to a truth. We are here assembled at this moment spirits, souls. Here we are, bodies; but these bodies are not ourselves; they are the houses in which we live. I question whether there is any man who can define himself; the most any man can say is, "I am; I know I have an existence; but what kind of thing my spirit is I do not know; I cannot tell; I have no knowledge of what it is. I feel it; I know it moves my body; I feel its outward manifestations; I am certain of my existence; but what I am I know not; God alone can say." "I am that I am," is comprehensible to Himself; but man is a being himself incomprehensible; and though God may allow him to say, "By God's grace I am what I am," he cannot tell what he is; he understandeth not his own existence. Understand, then, that as in our being there is a mystery in our flesh, so religion, the true religion of the blessed God, in order to be made like unto us and to be a something which would suit us must be a religion of spirit; but because we have a body it must have a body in which to clothe itself. Allow me, if I can, to try to make this plain; for if you do not understand it now, I am certain you will before I have done. We are spirits in bodies. Well, then, in order to meet our cases, the great work of God in us must be a spiritual thing; but in order that I may be able to talk about it to you and that you may be able to hear it with your ears, that spiritual thing must be encased in a body; or else if it were a pure spiritual thing, I could not talk to you about it, any more than I could talk to you about a spirit if there were no body in which a spirit could be found and no body in which I should be able to live to talk about it. I want to show you this because there are some persons that are so busy about the body of religion that they forget that religion has a spirit at all.

Now, what Jesus meant in this passage was, "The mere embodiment of religion profiteth nothing; it is the spirit that quickeneth. Just as, to use my figure over again, in order to perform an act, the mere flesh and blood and arms and legs profit nothing; it is the spirit that quickens all the bones and makes the nerves ply as they ought to do and the sinews work as they should. And religion has its outward form, it has its ceremonies, it has its outward developments, its body, but the mere outward body of religion is of no use whatever except the spirit quickeneth it.

I. To begin, then, I will first show you this order as I think our Saviour meant it when He first of all stated it. There were some people in our Saviour's day who admired Christ. They admired Him as a man, and they thought there was some marvelous efficacy in His flesh and blood. Now, Jesus Christ said to them in the words of our text, "Even my flesh will profit you nothing: it is the spirit that quickens." We would state this truth very cautiously but very plainly. When our Saviour was upon earth there were some, we say, who admired His person. You remember those who said, "Blessed is the womb that bare thee and the paps that gave thee suck"; and you remember our Saviour rebuked them. He would not have people admire His flesh and think so much of His mere humanity. "No," said he, "blessed are they that hear the word of God and do it." There were some again who wanted to take the Lord Jesus and make Him a king. Said He to them, "My flesh, if you exalt it to a throne, will profit you nothing. I did not come here that you might bow down and venerate my mere flesh, that you might think the mere admiration of myself is religion. It is the spirit, the gospel that I came to preach, that will benefit you. It is not these outward acts; it is the thoughts and words of which they are the exponents." Hear what the Saviour says in the next sentence. "It is not your admiration of my flesh that is of any use to you, for my flesh profits nothing; it is the spirit that quickens, and if you want to know what is the spirit of my incarnation, I tell you that the words that I speak unto you are spirit and life. It is not your venerating my flesh and blood; it is your venerating my doctrines that will be the soul and heart of the religion that I desire you to feel."

Our Saviour, however, was led to make these remarks from the fact that when He talked about eating His flesh and blood, the poor Jews thought that He meant they were to turn cannibals and eat Jesus Christ up. Now, any man may smile at so ridiculous an idea, but we know that the idea is still rife in the church of Rome. The Romanist priest solemnly assures us that the people who eat the bread and wine, or stuff he calls bread and wine which he hands round, do actually act the part of cannibals and eat the body of Christ and drink His blood. You ask him seriously; you say to him, "You mean they do it in a figure, my dear sir, spiritually?" "No," says he, "I don't; I mean to say that after I have pronounced certain words over that bread, it becomes Christ's flesh, and after I have said a certain hocus pocus over that wine, it becomes actual blood." "Well," we reply to him, "it is very singular, certainly, and I should say that you do not expect us to believe you whilst God allows our heads to be occupied by brains; but even if we do believe you, my dear sir, we refer you to this passage here that says, 'The flesh profiteth nothing, it is the spirit that quickeneth,' and you tell the people that they do actually and really receive body and blood. Suppose they do, the mere body and blood of Christ is of no earthly use to them, and even if they could carnally press it with their teeth and drink it with their throats, it would be of no more use to them than the eating of the flesh and blood of any other man; it could be of no service whatever to them, for He himself denounces the error of transubstantiation, and He declares that even His flesh profiteth nothing. It is only the spirit, the spiritual receiving of that flesh and blood that can be of any avail whatever."

While I am here just allow me to say one word; for Popery prevails in this day and that happens to be the bulwark of Popery, the doctrine that the bread and wine are turned into the body and blood of Christ. Dr. Carson, of Coleraine, has settled off Dr. Cahill in a remarkable way. He has challenged Dr. Cahill to prove that he can turn the bread and wine used in the sacrament into Christ's body and blood. He offers to give Dr. Cahill a hundred pounds if he will let him make a wafer for him and if Dr. Cahill will then put it on his own tongue and swallow it in Mr. Carson's own presence. "If the Doctor is not dead in an hour," says Dr. Carson, "I'll give him a hundred pounds." "No," says one, "that is not fair." "Oh! but if he can turn it into the body and blood of Christ, it cannot hurt him, whatever I make it of." "What! would you make it of poison, then?" "Yes, the deadliest I could find." "Would you give him poison?" "I should not give it to him; he would swallow it himself; he would do it of his own voluntary choice." And Dr. Cahill backs out of that; he cannot turn it into the body and blood of Christ; if he could, Dr. Carson says it could not hurt him, for the body and blood of Christ would poison no one. But some wise Romanist says, "That is not fair; the Doctor does not pretend to turn poison into the body and blood of Christ; it is only clean bread." "Very well," says Dr. Carson, "I'll try him another way. I will let him choose a youth from seven or eight Catholic boys; he shall take a quart of wine, and turn this wine in his own peculiar way into the blood of Christ. The boy shall drink the quart, and if he is not drunk in six hours, I'll pay the hundred pounds." "Now," says Dr. Carson, "if that is the blood of Christ, it will not make him drunk; he might drink a hogshead of it, and it would not make him intoxicated." But Dr. Cahill dare not come to such a trial as that, for I think it would very soon be found that the wine would make the boy intoxicated as much as any other wine; therefore, it could not have been turned into anything like the blood of Christ, even by the great Doctor himself. The fact is that the lie is so palpable, the delusion so absurd, that any child of any age would as soon think of believing the cock and bull story we used to read in our childish days about what the bull said and what the cock said to be actual truth, as to imagine it to be a literal fact that any priest or any man in the world could ever turn bread and wine into flesh and blood. But even if they could, hear the words of the text: "The flesh profiteth nothing; it is the spirit that quickeneth." So, then, after all, if the Roman Catholic sacrament, be actually a cannibal's feast upon the body and blood of Christ, it is of no earthly use; but that sacrament wherein we do spiritually receive the flesh and blood of Jesus and in a spirtiual way hold communion with Him is that which quickeneth and that only.

Now, this brings me to the truth that I want specially to be arrived at. As Christ Jesus in His flesh was the embodiment of His own doctrine, and yet not His flesh but the spirit of His doctrine quickeneth souls, so the outward forms and ceremonies which Christ has made to be the body to contain the spirit are of no earthly use at all unless the Spirit of God be in them. We come to baptism; there are the pool and the water; that pool and that water are, so to speak, the flesh and blood of dedication; that holy ordinance signifies that we do devote ourselves to the Lord Jesus. Suppose, however, our hearts are in a wrong condition or that we are not converted persons—suppose there is no influence of the Spirit resting upon us during the act of baptism, then the act of baptism is like the flesh to the body, it is a dead thing, it profiteth nothing because it is without the soul. We come the next Sabbath to the Lord's table: there is the bread broken by God's servant, there is the wine decently handed round by the deacons of the church, and it is sipped; but, mark you, however reverently it is performed, except the Spirit of the living God breathes through the whole divine ordinance, "the flesh," that is, the mere embodiment of communion, will profit you nothing. You might sit at a thousand Sacraments, and you might be baptized in a myriad of pools, but all this would not avail one jot or tittle for your salvation unless you had the spirit that quickened you. Nay, to go farther, it is not just these two outward ordinances only that need in them the Spirit; it is so in everything else. You have sometimes read, dear friends, of some great Christians that grew to have much fellowship with Christ by prayer. Perhaps you imbibed the idea that if you were to go home and spend as many hours in your closet as they did, you would get as much profit by it; and not thinking about the Holy Spirit, you simply devote yourself to your closet as you would do any manual exercise with a hope of profiting by the closet alone. I tell you, you might be on your knees till your knees were bare, and you might be in your closet till the steam of your devotion ran down the walls; but unless the Spirit of the Lord was in that closet with you, the mere fleshly exercise of praying would no more avail you and profit you than if you had been chanting songs to the moon or standing in the street to sell your goods. Another hears that a certain person had been very much blessed by reading a text of Scripture. "Oh!" says he, "has that text been blessed to such a one? I'll go and read the same passage too." You think that if you do the same act as he does you will be equally blessed; and you are marvelously surprised that when you read the passage, it does no good to you. It made his spirit leap for joy, it filled his soul with the wine of the kingdom, but to you it is like a dry well or an empty bottle. Why is this? The mere letter in which the promise is put profiteth you nothing; it is the spirit of the promise; it is the life of the Spirit running through the veins of the promise that alone can profit you. You hear that another man meditates on God's Law day and night and becomes like a tree planted by the rivers of water. You say, "I will take care that every morning I will read a chapter, and that every night I will read two chapters." There are certain people who think if they read a good long bit of Bible, they've done a great deal. In that spirit they might just as well read a bit of Hudibras, for they just read it straight through without thinking of understanding it. Many of our ministers think they must read a certain quantity of the Scriptures, and they take perhaps three long chapters out of Ezekiel, and not a soul knows what they are at. If they were to read a Dutch sermon in an English church, it would do about as much good. There is a lot about ephahs and wheels within wheels, but no one understands much about them. Instead of reading as Ezra did and expounding to the people, they must go on reading—hedge, hedge, ditch, ditch—one continual steeplechase! Instead of stopping to break the shells and give the kernels of truth to the people, they must read right on. To such persons we would simply say, "Your Bible reading is but the flesh; it is no use to you; it is the spirit that quickeneth; the mere flesh, the mere outward fashion and form of Bible reading will not profit anybody. One bit of Bible prayed over, and bedewed with the Spirit, and made alive, though it be only a short sentence of six words, will profit you more than a hundred chapters without the Spirit because the hundred chapters without the Spirit are flesh—dead; but the one verse with the Spirit is the thing that quickeneth."

I do not know whether I have as yet brought my full meaning out; but I want to let everyone understand that it is not the mere outward embodiment of our religion that saves the soul and that profits us; it is the inner spirit of the thing that does it. Mark, I would not find fault with any of these forms, any more than I would find fault with our bodies, because they are not spirits; our bodies are good things for the spirits to live in, and the forms are good things for the spirit to live in, but the form without the spirit though it be the most decorous and apparently the most devout that can be performed can be of no use for our soul's eternal profit and ultimate salvation. "It is the Spirit that quickeneth; the flesh profiteth nothing."

Now, my dear friend, Mr. So-and-so, if you will just take your pencil out and cast up your accounts for all the years of your life, they will come to very little if what I say be true. "I think," say you, "I am a tolerably good sort of man; I have a few faults, but look now what I have done. I have been to chapel twice every Sunday almost since I was a boy—I don't know that I missed once except when I was ill; that has been very good of me and no mistake. I always read the Bible every morning; I always have family prayer; that is very good of me; another down to my account. I say my prayers when I go to bed at night, and when I get up in the morning; I very frequently go to prayer-meetings; I don't think anyone can find fault with me; really I think I do everything to make me a truly religious man." Ah! and did you put at the end of it, "Lord, I thank thee that I am not as other men are, unjust, extortioners," and so on, or even like that poor fellow, a Sabbath-breaker, that you saw going the opposite way and not going to your place of worship. Pity you didn't finish it up; but, however, if you did not in words, you finished it up in your heart. But I pray God to show you that all these beautiful things of yours are good for nothing. There you are—there are your chapel-goings—all flesh; there are your Bible readings—flesh; there are your family prayers—all flesh; there are your good works and excellences—all flesh. You have never received the Spirit of the living God: you dare not say you have. Well, then, all these things will profit you nothing whatever. It is the spirit alone can quicken; for you know, my dear sir, and let me speak very pointedly—you know you never enter into the spirit of the thing; though you go to your church or chapel regularly, yet you know you might very often as well be at home; for when they sing, you do not sing with all your heart; and when the minister preaches, it is seldom there is much that touches you unless it is a good intellectual discourse and happens to fit you, and you believe it, and it meets your views, and so on. You know that into the inward soul, and marrow, and bowels of devotion you have never yet learned to plunge. You know your devotion is like that ox which was slain once in the time of siege in Rome and was said to portend ill because when the augur slew it, he declared he could not find a heart anywhere. He looked through all the entrails, and no heart could he discover; and hence, the Romans said their city must be destroyed. It was a solemn augury they said when the sacrifice had no heart in it. It is just the same with you. You have done all these things; oh! yes, and there has been as much reality in what you have done as there was devotion in the poor Kalmuck's windmill when he tied the prayer to it and put it up in the garden, and every time it blew round that was just one more prayer. There was as much heart in your prayer as there was in his windmill; that is to say, none at all. There it is! How far have you got? Go on no longer with this useless round of performances. I would not have you give the performances up. Stop awhile, and ask God to give you that inward spirit that quickeneth, for that is what is needed; "The flesh profiteth nothing."

But I must speak to you that are the children of God, and I must say to you, "How often do you forget this?" I know it is not often of a morning that I would leave my chamber without prayer: but oh, brethren, I have often left my chamber without having the spirit of prayer; I should not like to pass a day without reading the Scriptures, but I am afraid it is very often the mere "flesh" of Scripture reading and not the spirit breathing in the Word that I get. And how often is our conscience satisfied with the mere form without the spirit! Now, if we were what we ought to be, we should never be content with the form unless we could see the spirit in it. Mother, would you be content to have a child at home that was dead? Suppose someone should say to you, "Why, this child is just as good a child as ever it was! Look at it! It has not lost a leg, or arm, or anything!" "Ah, but," you say, "it is dead." "Oh!" says one, "there is no difference. It looks as beautiful now as ever it did." "Ah!" she says, "but there is a vast deal of difference between what it was when it was alive and what it is now it is dead." And now just transfer that to your poor dead prayers, and your poor dead Bible reading, and your poor dead sacraments, and your poor dead goings to chapel, and all that! Ah! how many of our sacrifices are just poor dead things. When we bring them, they have died in the night, and then we come and offer them before God! How frequently do we satisfy ourselves with having the "flesh," the embodiment of the sacrifice and forget the spirit! But let us remember, God only looks for the life: He does not look for the body; so in all we do for Him, we ought to take care, first of all, for the spirit, and then we may rest quite sure the flesh and blood of the devotion will take care of themselves.

II. This, I believe, is the meaning of the passage. But the common rendering of it if anyone read it without noticing the context would be, "Why, that means, it is the Spirit that quickeneth; that is to say, it is the Holy Spirit that quickeneth; the flesh profiteth nothing." Our friends will excuse me when I say it cannot mean that; you notice the "s" in the text has got no capital to it. If it meant the Holy Spirit, it would always be noted so to separate it from the spirit to which I have just referred— the inward spirit, the life of a thing. This word "spirit" here does not mean the Holy Spirit; still, almost every ordinary reader would make that mistake and say, "It is the Spirit that quickeneth; the flesh profiteth nothing." Well, it is a mistake that will not do him any hurt because if it does not say so there, it does say so somewhere else; and if it is not true in this one particular text, it is true all over the Bible, and it is true in a Christian's experience, so that a man may make a great many worse mistakes than that. Well, then, let us make that mistake, and then let us get at the truth of it: "It is the spirit that quickeneth; the flesh profiteth nothing."

How often have I thought, "There is a young woman in the gallery, or a young man: how interested they look during the sermon!" I have met with them, I have admired their characters; they have had an amiable carriage and deportment; there has been much in them that everybody would tell others to imitate and emulate. I have said, "Ah! I shall soon have them added to the church; there is so much good about them it will be such an easy transition for them; they are so moral and excellent it will be very easy for them surely to take a step into the kingdom of heaven." I don't say I have said so in words to my heart, but that has been about what I have thought. Well, there has been a fellow who came into chapel one evening, a queer looking object certainly; he came running in one Thursday evening towards the end of the service, not washed or anything; he only just came to hear something that would make him laugh as he thought. I did not expect to see him converted. The next time I sat to hear inquiries, in he came, cleaned and washed a bit; but I recognized him for all that and I said to him, "Didn't you come in one Thursday night after you had been hammering and tinkering somewhere? I thought you looked a strange one, certainly." "Yes," said he, "and the Lord met with me." Now, I sat many and many a night, and I did not see the young man or the young woman come. Why was this? The Lord meant to teach his servant that "the flesh profiteth nothing." "No," said He, "that man seemed far from God, that young man and that young woman seemed very near to me: I will just let you see that all their morality and all their goodness did not put them near the kingdom of heaven or help me a bit, I could save one as well as the other, and if I chose to show my sovereignty, I might even let publicans and harlots enter the kingdom of heaven before those who becoming proud of their morality would not stoop before me." Have you not sometimes met with a person of such a peculiar character that you have said, "Is it not a pity someone cannot talk with that man?" I often have notes; a father writes, "I wish you could get hold of my son; he is a very interesting young man; if you were to put the truth before him to suit his turn of mind, he would be sure to lay hold of it, for if you knew how his mind was constituted, you would say at once there was a peculiar adaptation in his mind for the reception of the gospel." Well, I have been told that a dozen times, but I never found it true once—never. "The flesh profiteth nothing." No peculiar adaptation of mind is any more susceptible of gospel influences than another. Dead sinners are all dead and all dead alike. Some may be black, and some may be white; some may be well washed and dressed, and some may have all the mire and filth of sensuality about them. They are all dead alike, and when converting grace comes to deal with them, it finds as much for its exercise in the one case as in the other; it finds as much to help it in the one heart as in the other—that is to say, it finds nothing to help it at all. It brings it all within itself: it kindles its own fire with its own torch, it blows the fire with its own breath and asks for nothing in the sinner be he who he may.

Then, again, we have sometimes said, "If such a one were converted, dear me, what a shining Christian he would make! He is a man of brilliant talent, of great intellectual power, and of extensive fortune. Oh if he were converted, what a jubilee it would be to the church of God! How much he would do!" Well, do you know, I have always found that these fine people, who when they were converted were to be somebody, if they have been converted and we have got them, have not turned out to be quite so great after all! I knew a minister once who with great joy and gladness baptized a man. It was on a New Year's Day, and I remember with what self-congratulation he said, "The Lord has sent me one of the best New Year's gifts I ever had"; and he looked upon that man and said, "Ah! this is a brother; he is a great gain to the church; he is a man of such active spirit, of such excellent turn of mind—he is everything that could be desired." Well, I have just happened to live long enough to see that man rend the church in sunder and drive the minister out of his pulpit, and he is alive still, a thorn in the side of that church and a huge prickly bramble that they would be glad enough to eradicate, but that they scarcely have power enough to do. No; the Lord will show us that "the flesh profiteth nothing." "You may have him," says the Lord, "if he is such a fine fellow; take him, take him; you will find he will not be so much after all. I will let you know that 'the flesh profiteth nothing'; it is the spirit alone 'that quickeneth.'" On the other hand, we have seen some come whose flesh could not help them. They were the poor, the mean, the illiterate, the despised; and we have seen the grace of God blaze up in their hearts to an eminence of fervor, and we have seen them stand confident and strong, notwithstanding the nothingness of the flesh; and then we have said, "Verily, O God, it is marvelous how when the flesh is weak, thy grace is strong"; and we have heard an answer from "the excellent Glory," which said, "Ah! the flesh profiteth nothing; it is the spirit that quickeneth."

Now, I do not believe that there is any form of our flesh, nor any act of our flesh, nor anything that our flesh can do, or attempt to do, or think of, or suggest, that can in any way assist in the great spiritual work of our salvation. It is the spirit alone that quickeneth; and you will find till you die that "the flesh profiteth nothing" except the devil, and it often profits him; but in God's ways and in God's holy Gospel you will always find the flesh lusting against the spirit and the spirit against the flesh.

Now, my brethren, in conclusion, I will ask thee the question—hast thou received the influence of the Holy Spirit? and have those influences led thee to worship God, who is a spirit, "in spirit and in truth?" For if not, though some may put thee in the cradle of ceremonies and rock thee to sleep, I will not be one of them. Although men may tell thee thou art right enough because thou art so outwardly religious, because thou art no sabbath-breaker, no swearer, no drunkard, I warn thee that unless thou art born again from above thou canst not see the kingdom of

God; and when drunkards, and harlots, and all manner of ungodly persons, shall be driven from the presence of God, you also shall share their fate, for you are dead in sin and must be quickened by the spirit. No more shall I say, but solemnly entreat the Spirit of the blessed God to touch your hearts with this solemn thought, and lead you to renounce the works of the flesh, and put your trust in Him who is "the Saviour of all men, especially of them that believe."

How a Man's Conduct Comes Home to Him

The backslider in heart shall be filled with his own ways; and a good man shall be satisfied.—Proverbs 14:14.

A COMMON PRINCIPLE is here laid down and declared to be equally true in reference to two characters who in other respects are a contrast. Men are affected by the course which they pursue; for good or bad their own conduct comes home to them. The backslider and the good man are very different, but in each of them the same rule is exemplified—they are both filled by the result of their lives. The backslider becomes filled by that which is within him as seen in his life, and the good man also is filled by that which grace implants within his soul. The evil leaven in the backslider leavens his entire being and sours his existence, while the gracious fountain in the sanctified believer saturates his whole manhood and baptizes his entire life. In each case the fulness arises from that which is within the man and is in its nature like the man's character; the fulness of the backslider's misery will come out of his own ways, and the fulness of the good man's content will spring out of the love of God which is shed abroad in his heart.

The meaning of this passage will better come out if we begin with an illustration. Here are two pieces of sponge, and we wish to fill them: you shall place one of them in a pool of foul water, it will be filled and filled with that which it lies in; you shall put the other sponge into a pure crystal stream, and it will also become full, full of the element in which it is placed. The backslider lies asoak in the dead sea of his own ways, and the brine fills him; the good man is plunged like a pitcher into "Siloa's brook which flows hard by the oracle of God," and the river of the water of life fills him to the brim. A wandering heart will be filled with sorrow, and a heart confiding in the Lord will be satisfied with joy and peace. Or take two farmsteads; one farmer sows tares in his field and in due time his barns are filled therewith; another sows wheat, and his garners are stored with precious grain. Or follow out our Lord's parable: one builder places his frail dwelling on the sand, and when the tempest rages, naturally enough he is swept away in it; another lays deep the foundations of his house and sets it fast on a rock, and as an equally natural consequence, he smiles upon the storm protected by his well-founded dwelling place. What a man is by sin or by grace will be the cause of his sorrow or his satisfaction.

I. I shall take the two characters without further preface, and first, let us speak awhile about the backslider. This is a very solemn subject, but one which it is needful to bring before the present audience since we all have some share in it. I trust there may not be many present who are backsliders in the worst sense of the term, but very, very few among us are quite free from the charge of having backslidden in some measure at some time or other since conversion. Even those who sincerely love the Master sometimes wander, and we all need to take heed lest there be in any one of us an evil heart of unbelief in departing from the living God.

There are several kinds of persons who may with more or less propriety be comprehended under the term "backsliders," and these will each in his own measure be filled with his own ways.

There are, first, apostates, those who unite themselves with the church of Christ and act for a time as if they were subjects of a real change of heart. These persons are frequently very zealous for a season and may become prominent, if not eminent, in the church of God. They did run well, like those mentioned by the apostle, but by some means they are, first of all, hindered and slacken their pace; after that they linger and loiter and leave the crown of the causeway for the side of the road. By and by in their hearts they go back into Egypt and at last, finding an opportunity to return, they break loose from all the restraints of their profession and openly forsake the Lord. Truly the last end of such men is worse than the first. Judas is the great type of these pre-eminent backsliders. Judas was a professed believer in Jesus, a follower of the Lord, a minister of the gospel, an apostle of Christ, the trusted treasurer of the college of the apostles, and after all turned out to be the "son of perdition" who sold his Master for thirty pieces of silver. He ere long was filled with his own ways, for tormented with remorse he threw down the blood-money he had so dearly earned, hanged himself, and went to his own place. The story of Judas has been written over and over again in the lives of other traitors. We have heard of Judas as a deacon and as an elder; we have heard Judas preach, we have read the works of Judas the bishop and seen Judas the missionary. Judas sometimes continues in his profession for many years, but sooner or later the true character of the man is discovered; his sin returns upon his own head and if he does not make an end of himself, I do not doubt but what, even in this life, he often lives in such horrible remorse that his soul would choose strangling rather than life. He has gathered the grapes of Gomorrah, and he has to drink the wine; he has planted a bitter tree, and he must eat the fruit thereof. Oh sirs, may none of you betray your Lord and Master. God grant I never may.

This title of backslider applies also to another class, not so desperate but still most sad of which not Judas but David may serve as the type: we refer to backsliders who go into open sin. There are men who descend from purity to careless living, and from careless living to indulgence of the flesh, and from indulgence of the flesh in little matters into known sin, and from one sin to another till they plunge into uncleanness. They have been born again, and therefore the trembling and almost extinct life within must and shall revive and bring them to repentance; they will come back weary, weeping, humbled, and brokenhearted, and they will be restored, but they will never be what they were before; their voices will be hoarse like that of David after his crime, for he never again sung so jubilantly as in his former days. Life will be more full of trembling and trial and manifest less of buoyancy and joy of spirit. Broken bones make hard traveling, and even when they are set, they are very subject to shooting pains when ill weathers are abroad. I may be addressing some of this sort this morning, and if so I would speak with much faithful love. Dear brother, if you are now following Jesus afar off, you will ere long like Peter deny Him. Even though you will obtain mercy of the Lord, yet the text will certainly be fulfilled in you, and you will be "filled with your own ways." As certainly as Moses took the golden calf and ground it into powder, and then mixed it with the water which the sinful Israelites had to drink till they all tasted the grit in their mouths, so will the Lord do with you if you are indeed His child: He will take your idol of sin and grind it to powder, and your life shall be made bitter with it for years to come. When the gall and wormwood are most manifest in the cup of life, it will be a mournful thing to feel "I procured this unto myself by my shameful folly." O Lord, hold thou us up and keep us from falling by little and little, lest we plunge into overt sin and continue in it for a season; for surely the anguish which comes of such an evil is as terrible as death itself. If David could rise from his grave and appear before you with his face seamed with sorrow and his brow wrinkled with his many griefs, he would say to you "Keep your hearts with all diligence, lest ye bring woe upon yourselves. Watch unto prayer, and guard against the beginnings of sin lest your bones wax old through your roarings and your moisture be turned into the drought of summer." O beware of a wandering heart, for it will be an awful thing to be filled with your own backslidings.

But there is a third sort of backsliding, and I am afraid a very large number of us have at times come under the title—I mean those who in any measure or degree, even for a very little time, decline from the point which they have reached. Perhaps such a man hardly ought to be called a backslider because it is not his predominant character, yet he backslides. If he does not believe as firmly, and love as intensely, and serve as zealously as he formerly did, he has in a measure backslidden, and any measure of backsliding, be it less or be it more, is sinful and will in proportion as it is real backsliding fill us with our own ways. If you only sow two or three seeds of the thistle, there will not be so many of the ill weeds on your farm as if you had emptied out a whole sack, but still there will be enough and more than enough. Every little backsliding, as men call it, is a great mischief; every little going back even in heart from God if it never comes to words or deeds yet will involve us in some measure of sorrow. If sin were clean removed from us, sorrow would be removed also, in fact we should be in heaven since a state of perfect holiness must involve perfect blessedness. Sin in any degree will bear its own fruit, and that fruit will be sure to set our teeth on edge; it is ill therefore to be a backslider even in the least degree.

Having said so much, let me now continue to think of the last two kinds of backsliders and leave out the apostate. Let us first read his name, and then let us read his history, we have both in our text.

The first part of his name is "backslider." He is not a back runner, nor a back leaper, but a backslider, that is to say he slides back with an easy, effortless motion, softly, quietly, perhaps unsuspected by himself or anybody else. The Christian life is very much like climbing a hill of ice. You cannot slide up, nay, you have to cut every step with an ice axe; only with incessant labor in cutting and chipping can you make any progress; you need a guide to help you, and you are not safe unless you are fastened to the guide for you may slip into a crevasse. Nobody ever slides up, but if great care be not taken, he will slide down, slide back, or in other words backslide. This is very easily done. If you want to know how to backslide, the answer is leave off going forward and you will slide backward, cease going upward and you will go downward of necessity for stand still you never can. To lead us to backslide, Satan acts with us as engineers do with a road down the mountain's side. If they desire to carry the road from yonder alp right down into the valley far below, they never think of making the road plunge over a precipice or straight down the face of the rock, for nobody would ever use such a road; but the road makers wind and twist. See, the track descends very gently to the right, you can hardly see that it does run downwards; anon it turns to the left with a small incline, and so, by turning this way and then that, the traveler finds himself in the vale below. Thus the crafty enemy of souls fetches saints down from their high places; whenever he gets a good man down it is usually by slow degrees. Now and then, by sudden opportunity and strong temptation, the Christian man has been plunged right from the pinnacle of the temple into the dungeon of despair in a moment, but it is not often the case; the gentle decline is the devil's favorite piece of engineering, and he manages it with amazing skill. The soul scarcely knows it is going down, and it seems to be maintaining the even tenor of its way, but ere long it is far below the line of peace and consecration.

Think again of this man's name. He is a "backslider," but what from? He is a man who knows the sweetness of the things of God and yet leaves off feeding upon them. He is one who has been favored to wait at the Lord's own table, and yet he deserts his honorable post, backslides from the things which he has known, and felt, and tasted, and handled, and rejoiced in—things that are the priceless gifts of God. He is a backslider from the condition in which he has enjoyed a heaven below; he is a backslider from the love of Him who bought him with His blood; he slides back from the wounds of Christ, from the works of the Eternal Spirit, from the crown of life which hangs over his head, and from a familiar intercourse with God which angels might envy him. Had he not been so highly favored he could not have been so basely wicked. O fool and slow of heart to slide from wealth to poverty, from health to disease, from liberty to bondage, from light to darkness; from the love of God, from abiding in Christ, and from the fellowship of the Holy Ghost into lukewarmness, worldliness, and sin.

The text, however gives the man's name at greater length, "The backslider in heart." Now the heart is the fountain of evil. A man need not be a backslider in action to get the text fulfilled in him, he need only be a backslider in heart. All backsliding begins within, begins with the heart's growing lukewarm, begins with the love of Christ being less powerful in the soul. Perhaps you think that so long as backsliding is confined to the heart it does not matter much; but consider for a minute, and you will confess your error. If you went to your physician and said, "Sir, I feel a severe pain in my body," would you feel comforted if he replied, "There is no local cause for your suffering, it arises entirely from disease of the heart"? Would you not be far more alarmed than before? A case is serious indeed when it involves the heart. The heart is hard to reach and difficult to understand, and moreover it is so powerful over the rest of the system and has such power to injure all the members of the body that a disease in the heart is an injury to a vital organ, a pollution of the springs of life. A wound there is a thousand wounds, a complicated wounding of all the members at a stroke. Look ye well then to your hearts and pray, "O Lord cleanse Thou the secret parts of our spirit and preserve us to Thy eternal kingdom and glory!"

Now let us read this man's history—"he shall be filled with his own ways." From which it is clear that he falls into ways of his own. When he was in his right state he followed the Lord's ways, he delighted himself in the law of the Lord, and he gave him the desire of his heart; but now he has ways of his own which he prefers to the ways of God. And what comes of this perverseness? Does he prosper? No; he is before long filled with his own ways; we will see what that means.

The first kind of fulness with his own ways is absorption in his carnal pursuits. He has not much time to spend upon religion; he has other things to attend to. If you speak to him of the deep things of God, he is weary of you and even of the daily necessaries of godliness he has no care to hear much, except at service time. He has his business to see to, or he has to go out to a dinner party, or a few friends are coming to spend the evening: in any case, his answer to you is "I pray thee have me excused." Now, this pre-occupation with trifles is always mischievous, for when the soul is filled with chaff, there is no room left for wheat; when all your mind is taken up with frivolities, the weighty matters of eternity cannot enter. Many professed Christians spend far too much time in amusements which they call recreation, but which, I fear, is far rather a redestruction than a recreation. The pleasures, cares, pursuits, and ambitions of the world swell in the heart when once they enter, and by-and-by they fill it completely. Like the young cuckoo in the sparrow's nest, worldliness grows and grows and tries its best to cast out the true owner of the heart. Whatever your soul is full of if it be not full of Christ, it is an evil case.

Then backsliders generally proceed a stage further and become full of their own ways by beginning to pride themselves upon their condition and to glory in their shame. Not that they really are satisfied at heart, on the contrary, they have a suspicion that things are not quite as they ought to be, and therefore they put on a bold front and try to deceive themselves and others. It is rather dangerous to tell them of their faults, for they will not accept your rebuke but will defend themselves and even carry the war into your camp. They will say, "Ah, you are puritanical, strict, and straight-laced, and your manners and ways do mischief rather than good." They would not bring up their children as you do yours so they say. Their mouths are very full because their hearts are empty, and they talk very loudly in defence of themselves because their conscience has been making a great stir within them. They call sinful pleasure a little unbending of the bow, greed is prudence, covetousness is economy, and dishonesty is cleverness. It is dreadful to think that men who know better should attempt to excuse themselves. Generally the warmest defender of a sinful practice is the man who has the most qualms of conscience about it. He himself knows that he is not living as he should, but he does not intend to cave in just yet, nor at all if he can help it. He is filled with his ways in a boasted self-content as to them.

Ere long this fulness reaches another stage for if the backslider is a gracious man at all, he encounters chastisement and that from a rod of his own making. A considerable time elapses before you can eat bread of your own growing; the ground must be ploughed and sown, and the wheat has to come up, to ripen and to be reaped, and threshed and ground in the mill, and the flour must be kneaded and baked in the oven; but the bread comes to the table and is eaten at last. Even so the backslider must eat of the fruit of his own ways. "Be not deceived; God is not mocked, whatsoever a man soweth, that shall he also reap." Now look at the backslider reaping the fruit of his ways. He neglected prayer and when he tries to pray, he cannot; his powers of desire, emotion, faith, and entreaty have failed: he kneels awhile, but he cannot pray; the Spirit of supplications is grieved and no longer helps his infirmities. He takes down his Bible; he commences to read a chapter, but he has disregarded the word of God so long that he finds it to be more like a dead letter than a living voice though it used to be a sweet book before he became a backslider. The minister, too, is altered; he used to hear him with delight; but now the poor preacher has lost all his early power so the backslider thinks. Other people do not think so, the place is just as crowded, there are as many saints edified and sinners saved as before; but the wanderer in heart began criticizing and now he is entangled in the habit, and he criticizes everything but never feeds upon the truth at all. Like a madman at table he puts his fork into the morsel and holds it up, looks at it, finds fault with it, and throws it on the floor. Nor does he act better towards the saints in whose company he once delighted; they are dull society and he shuns them. Of all the things which bear upon his spiritual life he is weary, he has trifled with them, and now he cannot enjoy them. Hear him sing or rather sigh—

> Thy saints are comforted, I know
> And love thy house of prayer;
> I sometimes go where others go
> But find no comfort there.

How can it be otherwise? He is drinking water out of his own cistern and eating the bread of which he sowed the corn some years ago. His ways have come home to him.

Chastisement also comes out of his conduct in other ways. He was very worldly and gave gay parties, and his girls have grown up and grieved him by their conduct. He himself went into sin, and now that his sons outdo his example, what can he say? Can he wonder at anything? Look at David's case. David fell into a gross sin, and soon Amnon his son rivaled him in iniquity. He murdered Uriah the Hittite, and Absalom murdered his brother Amnon. He rebelled against God, and lo, Absalom lifted up the standard of revolt against him. He disturbed the relationships of another man's family in a disgraceful manner, and behold his own family rent in pieces and never restored to peace; so that even when he lay a-dying he had to say, "My house is not so with God." He was filled with his own ways; and it always will be so even if the sin be forgotten. If you have sent forth a dove or a raven from the ark of your soul, it will come back to you just as you sent it out. May God save us from being back-sliders lest the smooth current of our life should turn into a raging torrent of woe.

The fourth stage, blessed be God, is at length reached by gracious men and women, and what a mercy it is they ever do reach it! At last they become filled with their own ways in another sense; namely, satiated and dissatisfied, misearable and discontented. They sought the world and they gained it, but now it has lost all charm for them. They went after other lovers, but these deceivers have been false to them, and they wring their hands and say, "Oh that I could return to my first husband for it was far better with me then than now." Many have lived at a distance from Jesus Christ, but now they can bear it no longer; they cannot be happy till they return. Hear them cry in the language of the fifty-first psalm, "Restore unto me the joy of thy salvation; and uphold me with thy free spirit." But I tell you they cannot get back very easily. It is hard to retrace your steps from backsliding, even if it be but a small measure of it; but to get back from wanderings is hard indeed, much harder than going over the road the first time.

Beloved friends, let all go straight away to the cross at once for fear we should be backsliders—

> Come, let us to the Lord our God
> With contrite hearts return;
> Our God is gracious, nor will leave
> The penitent to mourn.

Let us confess every degree and form of backsliding, every wandering of heart, every decline of love, every wavering of faith, every flagging of zeal, every dullness of desire, every failure of confidence. Behold the Lord says unto us, "Return"; therefore let us return. Even if we be not backsliders, it will do us no hurt to come to the cross as penitents, indeed, it is well to abide there evermore. O Spirit of the living God, preserve us in believing penitence all our days.

II. I have but little time for the second part of my subject. Excuse me, therefore, if I do not attempt to go into it very deeply. As it is true of the backslider that he grows at last full of that which is within him and his wickedness, it is true also of the Christian that in pursuing the paths of righteousness and the way of faith, he becomes filled and contented too. That which grace has placed within him fills him in due time.

Here then we have the good man's name and history.

Notice first, his name. It is a very remarkable thing that as a backslider if you call out his name will not as a rule answer to it, even so a good man will not acknowledge the title here assigned him. Where is the good man? I know that every man here who is right before God will pass the question on saying, "There is none good save One, that is God." The good man will also question my text and say, "I cannot feel satisfied with myself." No, dear friend, but mind you read the words aright. It does not say, "satisfied with himself," no truly good man ever was self-satisfied, and when any talk as if they are self-satisfied, it is time to doubt whether they know much about the matter. All the good men I have ever met have always wanted to be better; they have longed for something higher than as yet they have reached. They would not own to it that they were satisfied, and they certainly were by no means satisfied with themselves. The text does not say that they are, but it says something that reads so much like it that care is needed. Now, if I should seem to say this morning that a good man looks within and is quite satisfied with what he finds there, please let me say at once, I mean nothing of the sort. I should like to say exactly what the text means, but I do not know quite whether I shall manage to do it, except you will help me by not misunderstanding me even if there should be a strong temptation to do so. Here is the good man's history, he is "satisfied from himself," but first I must read his name again, though he does not own to it, what is he good for? He says, "good for nothing," but in truth he is good for much when the Lord uses him. Remember that he is good because the Lord has made him over again by the Holy Spirit. Is not that good which God makes? When He created nature, at the first He said of all things that they were very good; how could they be otherwise, since He made them? So in the new creation a new heart and a right spirit are from God and must be good. Where there is grace in the heart the grace is good and makes the heart good. A man who has the righteousness of Jesus and the indwelling of the Holy Spirit is good in the sight of God.

A good man is on the side of good. If I were to ask, who is on the side of good? we would not pass on that question. No, we would step out and say "I am. I am not all I ought to be, or wish to be, but I am on the side of justice, truth, and holiness; I would live to promote goodness and even die rather than become the advocate for evil." And what is the man who loves that which is good? Is he evil? I trow not. He who truly loves that which is good must be in a measure good himself. Who is he that strives to be good and groans and sighs over his failures, yea and rules his daily life by the laws of God? Is he not one of the world's best men? I trust without self-righteousness the grace of God has made some of us good in this sense, for what the Spirit of God has made is good, and if in Christ Jesus we are new creatures, we cannot contradict Solomon nor criticize the Bible if it calls such persons good, though we dare not call ourselves good.

Now, a good man's history is this, "He is satisfied from himself."

That means first, that he is independent of outward circumstances. He does not derive satisfaction from his birth, or honors, or properties; but that which fills him with content is within himself. Our hymn puts it so truly—

I need not go abroad for joys,
  I have a feast at home,
My sighs are turned into songs,
  My heart has ceased to roam.

Down from above the blessed Dove
  Is come into my breast,
To witness thine eternal love
  And give my spirit rest.

Other men must bring music from abroad if they have any, but in the gracious man's bosom there lives a little bird that sings sweetly to him. He has a flower in his own garden more sweet than any he could buy in the market or find in the king's palace. He may be poor, but still he would not change his estate in the kingdom of heaven for all the grandeur of the rich. His joy and peace are not even dependent upon the health of his body, he is often well in soul when sick as to his flesh; he is frequently full of pain and yet perfectly satisfied. He may carry about with him an incurable disease which he knows will shorten and eventually end his life, but he does not look to this poor life for satisfaction, he carries that within him which creates immortal joy: the love of God shed abroad in his soul by the Holy Ghost yields a perfume sweeter than the flowers of Paradise. The fulfilment of the text is partly found in the fact that the good man is independent of his surroundings.

And he is also independent of the praise of others. The backslider keeps easy because the minister thinks well of him and Christian friends think well of him, but the genuine Christian who is living near to God thinks little of the verdict of men. What other people think of him is not his chief concern; he is sure that he is a child of God, he knows he can say, "Abba, Father," he glories that for him to live is Christ and to die is gain, and therefore he does not need the approbation of others to buoy up his confidence. He runs alone and does not need to be carried in arms like a weakly child. He knows whom he has believed, and his heart rests in Jesus; thus he is satisfied, not from other people and from their judgment, but "from himself."

Then, again, the Christian man is content with the well of upspringing water of life which the Lord has placed within him. There, my brethren, up on the everlasting hills is the divine reservoir of all-sufficient grace, and down here in our bosom is a spring which bubbles up unto everlasting life. It has been welling up in some of us these five-and-twenty years, but why is it so? The grand secret is that there is an unbroken connection between the little spring within the renewed breast and that vast unfathomed font of God, and because of this the well-spring never fails; in summer and in winter it continues to flow. And now if you ask me if I am dissatisfied with the spring within my soul which is fed by the all-sufficiency of God, I reply, no, I am not. If you could by any possibility cut the connection between my soul and my Lord I should despair altogether, but as long as none can separate me from the love of God, which is in Christ Jesus our Lord, I am satisfied and at rest. Like Naphtali we are "satisfied with favor and full of the blessing of the Lord."

Faith is in the good man's heart and he is satisfied with what faith brings him, for it conveys to him the perfect pardon of his sin. Faith brings him nearer to Christ. Faith brings him adoption into the family of God. Faith secures him conquest over temptation. Faith procures for him everything he requires. He finds that by believing he has all the blessings of the covenant daily to enjoy. Well may he be satisfied with such an enriching grace. The just shall live by faith.

In addition to faith, he has another filling grace called hope which reveals to him the world to come and gives him assurance that when he falls asleep he will sleep in Jesus, and that when he awakes he will arise in the likeness of Jesus. Hope delights him with the promise that his body shall rise, and that in his flesh he shall see God. This hope of his sets the pearly gates wide open before him, reveals the streets of gold, and makes him hear the music of the celestial harpers. Surely a man may well be satisfied with this.

The godly heart is also satisfied with what love brings him; for love though it seems but a gentle maid is strong as a giant and becomes in some respects the most potent of all the graces. Love first opens wide herself like the flowers in the sunshine and drinks in the love of God, and then she joys in God and begins to sing:

I am so glad that Jesus loves me.

She loves Jesus, and there is such an interchange of delight between the love of her soul for Christ and the love of Christ for her that heaven itself can scarce be sweeter. He who knows this deep mysterious love will be more than filled with it, he will need to be enlarged to hold the bliss which it creates. The love of Jesus is known, but yet it passeth knowledge. It fills the entire man so that he has no room for the idolatrous love of the creature; he is satisfied with himself and asks no other joy.

Beloved, when the good man is enabled by divine grace to live in obedience to God, he must, as a necessary consequence, enjoy peace of mind. His hope is alone fixed on Jesus, but a life which evidences his possession of salvation casts many a sweet ingredient into his cup. He who takes the yoke of Christ upon him and learns of Him finds rest unto his soul. When we keep His commandments, we consciously enjoy His love which we could not do if we walked in opposition to His will. To know that you have acted from a pure motive, to know that you have done the right is a grand means of full content. What matters the frown of foes or the prejudice of friends if the testimony of a good conscience is heard within? We dare not rely upon our own works, neither have we had any desire or need to do so for our Lord Jesus has saved us everlastingly; still, "Our rejoicing is this, the testimony of our conscience, that in simplicity and godly sincerity, not with fleshly wisdom, but by the grace of God, we have had our conversion in the world."

The Only Door

I am the door: by me if any man enter in, he shall be saved, and shall go in and out, and find pasture.—John 10:9.

THE WORD of God tells us that in the midst of the great mass of men there are to be found a special people—a people who were chosen of God out of the common race before the stars began to shine; a people who were dear to God's heart before the foundation of the world; a people who were redeemed by the precious blood of Jesus beyond and above the rest of mankind; a people who are the especial property of Christ, the flock of his pasture, the sheep of his hand; a people over whom Providence watches, shaping their course amid the tangled maze of life; a people who are to be produced at the last, every one of them faultless before the eternal throne and fitted for the exalted destiny which, in the ages to come He shall reveal. All through Scripture you read about this particular and special people. Sometimes they are called a "seed," at other times "a garden," at other times "a treasure," and sometimes, as in the chapter we have read, "a flock." The common name in the New Testament for them is "the church," "the church of God which he hath purchased with his own blood." "Christ loved the church, and gave himself for it; that he might sanctify and cleanse it with the washing of water by the word."

Now, the grand question, is, how to obtain admission into this church? Where is this community to be found? Who are the members of it? What is the way to become a partaker of the privileges which belong to it? Jesus Christ here tells us two things: First, how to enter the church. The way is through Himself as the door. Second, what are the benefits we shall receive through being members of Christ's church—we shall be saved and shall go in and out and find pasture.

I. How a man can become a member of that church which is elected, redeemed, and will be saved is simply, briefly solved by our Lord's assertion.

Christ tells us that the only way to enter the church is through Himself. He is the door, the only door. There is no other mode of admission into His church but through Himself. Let it be understood, then, once for all, that we cannot get into the church of Christ through baptism. There are tens of thousands; ay, there have been millions who have been baptized after a fashion; that is to say, they have been sprinkled and thousands have been immersed who never were admitted into the church of Christ. In consideration of the ordinance as it was administered to them, with or more commonly without their consent, they were recognized by some persons as being Christians; but let me tell you that unless they came to Christ by true faith, they are nothing better than baptized Pagans; they are sprinkled heathens still. Why, you might hold a man in an everlasting shower, but you could not make him "a member of Christ" thereby; or you might drag him through the Atlantic Ocean, and if he survived the immersion, yet still he would not be one jot the better. The door is not baptism but Christ. If thou believest in Christ, thou art a member of His church. If thy trust is stayed upon Christ who is God's great way of salvation, thou hast evidence that thou wast chosen of Him from before the foundation of the world; and that faith of thine entitles thee to all the privileges which Christ has promised in His Word to believers.

If Christ be the door, then it follows that men do not get into the church by birthright. The Society of Friends has been one of the most useful communities in the world, and it has maintained a good testimony upon most important points for many years; but it seems to me that the great evil in it, that which has done them the most mischief, is the admission of birthright membership. Do they not receive into their fellowship the children of their members as though they were necessarily proper persons to be received into the visible church? My brethren, it is a great privilege to have Christian parents; it may prove a very great advantage if you use it rightly; but it involves a great responsibility, and if you use it wrongly, instead of being a blessing to you, it may be a fearful curse. Though you may be one of a long line of saints, "Except a man be born again, he cannot see the kingdom of God." The most pious example, the most godly training cannot insure conversion, and without conversion, depend upon it, you cannot be Christ's. "Except ye be converted and become as little children, ye shall in no wise enter into the kingdom of heaven." Through our not practicing infant baptism, we do not so readily fall into this error as some denominations; still it is necessary to say even here that you have no right to gospel privileges because of your mothers and fathers. You must be born again yourselves. You have no right to the covenant of grace, nor to the blessings and promises thereof, except as by your own personal and individual faith you come to Christ. It is not your father nor your mother that can be the door into Christ's church for you, but Christ Himself. "I," saith He, "I am the door." If you get Christ, you are in His church. If you have laid hold on Him, you are a member of that secret and invisible community of His elect and His redeemed; but it is not by baptism nor by birthright that you can ever be so.

Moreover, as Christ is the door, it is evident that a man does not come to be a member of the church of Christ by making a profession of being so. He may prove himself to be a detestable hypocrite, but he cannot prove himself to be a genuine Christian by mere profession. Men do not get rich in this world by a lavish expenditure or by a profession of being wealthy. They must hold the title-deeds of their estate and have the cash in the strong box, or else they are poor in spite of all their pretensions. And you cannot become a Christian by coming forward and asking to be admitted into the church, declaring that you believe, and avowing that you repent. No, verily, but you must repent truly or you shall perish; you must believe truly or you shall have no part nor lot in this matter. The mere saying "Yes, yes, I am willing to profess this, I am willing to say that" no more makes you a Christian than it would make cotton to be silk to call it so, or make mud to be gold by labeling it with that title. Beware of a false profession for it is doubly hazardous. The man who has no grace is in danger, but the man who makes a profession of having it when he has not is in double danger, for he is the least likely to be awakened, and he is certain, unless sovereign grace prevent, to make his profession a pillow for his wicked and his slumbering head till he sleeps himself into hell.

Further, and perhaps this may touch the point more closely still, a man does not get to be one of the Lord's people or to be one of Christ's sheep by being admitted into any visible church. He ought not to try to get into any visible church until he is in the true church. He has no right to join the external organization until he has first got into the secret conclave by a living faith in Christ. If he leaves the door alone and gets over the wall and comes into the outward church without being a believer in Christ, so far from being saved, Christ will say to him, "Thou art a thief and a robber, for thou has climbed up some other way, and thou camest not in by the door." I believe we do rightly to subject the admission of members to the voice of all the church; I believe we do rightly to examine candidates to see whether they make a creditable profession and whether they know what they are at. But our examination—oh, 'tis nothing better than skin deep. We cannot search the heart, and the best judgment of never so many Christian men, though honest and deserving to be treated with great respect, would be a very poor thing to rest upon. If you have not Christ, your church certificates are waste paper and your membership with any people, however pure and apostolic they may be, is but a name to live while you are dead, for the only way, the sole way, of getting into the real, vital, living church of Christ, is by coming to Christ who is Himself the door.

The plain English of this metaphor, then, is just this—To be one of God's people, the essential thing is a simple dependence upon Jesus Christ. If you have not this—no matter who baptizes you, or who gives you the consecrated bread and wine, or who maudles to you about a hope of salvation for which there is no warrant—you will die in your sins, notwithstanding all your sacraments, except you come to Christ. No other admittance to heaven can there be but by a simple dependence upon Him who has bled and died on Calvary's cross; the preaching of any other system is a mere delusion against which the warning voice went forth or ever the snare was laid to trap the unwary.

Mark you, simple faith, where it is genuine, makes it plain that you do enter by Christ the door because such faith leads to obedience. How canst thou suppose that thou art a member of His church if thou art not obedient to Christ? It is necessary that the man who trusts Christ should become the servant of Christ. Real faith never kicks at this but rather delights in it. "If ye love me," saith Christ, "keep my commandments." Except we do keep Christ's commandments out of a principle of love for Him, our religion is vain. "Without holiness no man shall see the Lord." We may talk as we will about inward experiences and believings, but "by their fruits ye shall know them." The Spirit of God is the spirit of holiness. When Christ comes into the soul, all iniquity must be purged out of the soul. You know how Malachi describes His advent. He proclaims to us the promise that the Lord whom we seek shall suddenly come to His temple: that is, seekers shall be finders; do you know what he adds? "But who may abide the day of his coming? for he shall be like a refiner's fire, and like fullers' soap." Now, the refiner's fire burns up the dross and fullers' soap takes out the stains; and so, if Christ be in you, you will pass through a refining that will burn up your outward sin, and you will be subjected to a washing like that of the fullers' soap which will cleanse you from all your iniquities. "Be not deceived, God is not mocked, whatsoever a man soweth that shall he also reap." If ye live after the flesh ye shall die, but if through the grace of Christ ye are living in Him, trusting in Him, and serving Him —service being the evidence of trust, and trust being the evidence of your election—ye have then come into the church through the door, and it is well with you.

Now, if it be so that Christ is the door into the church, and if we have entered the church through that door, it does not signify much to us what the old gentleman at Rome thinks of us. He may excommunicate us. This he is very fond of doing. He is a rare hand at cursing. What does it matter? If I be a new creature in Christ Jesus, it signifies not one jot how much the Pope may rail at me. Besides, there are plenty of revilers now-a-days who are saying, "You Nonconformists are only a pack of heretics; we have the apostolical succession; we have the sacraments and the priests." Ah! they vaunt themselves as being "Catholic," though their claim is disallowed alike by the Babylon which is here below and by the Jerusalem which is above. Let them vaunt if they will. As long as we have Christ, they may keep their apostolical succession, and all their other rubbish; He is the door, and if we have come through Him, it is well enough. I like that story of the Sandwich Islanders who had been converted through some of our missionaries, and the gospel had been preached to them for years. At last, two or three gentlemen in long black gowns landed there, and the people asked them what they had come for. They said they were come to instruct them in the true faith and to teach them. Well, they said, they should be glad to hear it. If their teaching was true and like the Scriptures, they would listen to them. By and by, a little diagram was exhibited to the natives after the similitude of a tree. This tree had many branches. The twigs which were farthest off were the different saints, the believers, those who do good works; then the limbs, which were a little larger, were the priests; the bigger boughs were bishops; the biggest boughs were the cardinals; and at last, these all joined on to the trunk which was the Pope, and that went all the way down to the bottom till it came to Peter who was the root, deriving his authority immediately from Christ. So the natives asked about all these twigs, and branches, and specially about certain rotten branches that were tumbling off into a fire. What were they? They were Luther, and Calvin, and other heretics who had been cut off from the true tree of the church. "Well," said one of the islanders, "and pray what is the root of the tree?" Of course, that was allowed to be Jesus Christ. So they clapped their hands at once for joy and said, "Never mind about the branches, and stems, and twigs; we have never heard of them, but we have got the root, and that will do to grow on." In like manner, brethren, we can say tonight, if we have got Christ, we have got "the root out of the dry ground." We have got the root of the matter, the basis, the sum, the substance of it.

> Let others trust what forms they please,
> Their hopes we'll not contest.

Let them go about their business and rejoice in their fancies; but Christ is the door. We have Christ, we have entered by the door, we have believed in Him, we have entered through Him into faith, and into joy, and into peace. We will be content with this; let others clamber up some other way if they please.

Before I leave this point, a question suggests itself, Have we all entered by the door? We are agreed that Christ is the door. Have we entered by the door? You who are growing old—I always feel much pleasure in seeing grey heads, the type of mellowed years, in the concourse of worshipers—but have you all believed in Jesus? You know the truth, you would not like to hear anything but the simple gospel preached; but, have you laid hold on the gospel? A man may starve with bread upon the table if he does not eat, and he may perish with thirst though he be up to his neck in water if he does not drink. Have you trusted Christ? If not, how can you remain in a state of unbelief, for "he that believeth not is condemned already, because he believeth not on the Son of God." Men and women in middle life, struggling with the cares of business, have you entered into Christ? I know your thoughts are much taken up, and necessarily so, with the world; but, have you not time to think upon this question, or dare you neglect it; "Dost thou believe on the Son of God?" If not, O man, thy life hangs on a thread, and that snapped, thy ruin is certain. And, oh, you young people, what a mercy it is to see you willing to come and hear the Word! But, have you all heard it with your inward ears? Have you looked to my Master? Oh, it is sweet to come to Christ in the early morning of life, to have a long day of happiness before you! May it be the blessedness of each one of us! It is vain to look at the door unless you enter. God give you grace to come in if you never have entered before.

II. Our Lord and Master tells us what are the privileges of entering through Him, the door.

The man who enters by Christ shall be saved, he shall go in and out and he shall find pasture.

He shall be saved. The man who believes in Jesus Christ shall be saved; he is saved, and he shall be saved. A man has by accident killed his fellow man. The next of kin to the murdered man will be sure to kill the man-slayer out of revenge if he can get at him. Therefore, the poor homicide takes flight as quickly as he can towards the city of refuge. How his heart beats, how his footsteps bound, how he flies with all his might. There is a handpost with the word "Refuge" upon it, and on he continues his way. But presently, while he is running, he turns his head and finds that the avenger of blood is after him. He sees that he is gaining upon him, he feels that he will probably overtake him. Oh! how he picks his steps lest he should trip against a stone, how he skims the ground, swift as a doe. He runs until he can see the city gates.

"That is the fair city of refuge," saith he. But, he does not rest then, for a sight of the city will not secure him, so he quickens his speed as if he would outstrip the wind, till he shoots through the archway, and he is in the broad street of the city. Now he stops. Now he breathes. Now he wipes the hot sweat from his brow. "Now I am safe," saith he, "for no avenger of blood dares cross that threshold; he that once escapes here is delivered." So with the sinner when sin pursues him, when he discovers that he has offended God. He hears the furious coursers of divine vengeance coming on swiftly behind him, and his conscience flies, and his soul speeds towards the cross. He gets a little hope. He hears of a Saviour; but that is not enough. He will never rest, he will never say he is at peace until he has passed the gate of faith and can say, "Now I do believe that Jesus died for me."

He that enters in by the door shall be saved. Noah's ark was built in the olden times to preserve Noah and his family from the great flood. It could not be said that Noah would be saved till he had passed through the door; but when he had done that, a divine hand, quite unseen, put the door to, and as Noah heard it fastened and understood that the Lord had shut him in, he felt quite safe. If God shuts us in, the floods from beneath cannot drown us, and the rains from above cannot penetrate to injure us. He must be safe whom God shuts in. The moment that a poor sinner trusts in Christ, God shuts the door. There he is and there he shall be till time shall be no more. He is secure. The infernal powers shall not destroy him, and the vengeance of God cannot touch him. He has passed the door, and he shall be saved.

I read a story the other day of some Russians crossing wide plains studded over here and there with forests. The villages were ten or a dozen miles from each other, the wolves were out, the horses were rushing forward madly, the travelers could hear the baying of the wolves behind them; and, though the horses tore along with all speed, yet the wolves were fast behind and they only escaped, as we say, "by the skin of their teeth," managing just to get inside some hut that stood in the road and to shut the door. Then they could hear the wolves leap on the roof; they could hear them dash against the sides of the hut; they could hear them gnawing at the door, and howling, and making all sorts of dismal noises; but the travelers were safe because they had entered in by the door, and the door was shut. Now, when a man is in Christ, he can hear, as it were, the devils howling like wolves all fierce and hungry for him; and his own sins, like wolves, are seeking to drag him down to destruction. But he has got in to Christ, and that is such a shelter that if all the devils in the world were to come at once, they could not start a single beam of that eternal refuge: it must stand fast, though the earth and heaven should pass away. Now, to every man and woman Christ says that if they have entered in by the door, they shall be saved. Do not have any doubt about it. Do not let anybody raise the question whether you may be, or you may not be; you shall be. Oh, clutch at that blessed "shall." Sir, if you have been a drunkard, yet, if you trust in Christ, you shall be saved. You shall not go back to your old drunkenness, but you shall be saved from it if you believe in him. O woman, if thou has stained thy character to the worst, yet, if thou believest in Christ, none of thy old sins shall ruin thee, but thou shalt be saved. Ah! though you be tempted every day of your lives, tempted as none ever were before, yet God is true, and cannot lie—if you come through Christ the door you shall be saved. Do you understand what it is to come through the door? it is to depend upon Jesus, to give ourselves to Him, to rest on Him. When you hang up your jugs and mugs on the nail in the cupboard, what keeps them from falling? Nothing but the nail, and if that holds well, nothing can fall that hangs on it. Now, you must trust in Christ as the vessel hangs on the nail, and if you do so, He is fastened as a nail in a sure place, and you cannot and shall not perish. That is the first privilege—he shall be saved.

He that entereth in by the door shall go in. The man who believes in Christ shall go into rest and peace for there is no condemnation to them that are in Christ Jesus. He shall go in to secret knowledge. He shall become a scholar and shall be taught by Christ as his rabbi. He shall go in unto God with holy boldness in prayer. He shall go in unto that which is within the veil and speak to God from before the mercy seat. He shall go in unto the child's place and shall stand as an adopted heir of heaven. He shall go in unto close communion with God. He shall speak with his Maker. The Lord shall lift up the light of His countenance upon him. He shall go in unto the highest attainment in spiritual things. He shall go in to the treasure house of the covenant and say, "All this is mine." He shall go into the storehouse of the promises and take whatsoever his soul needeth. He shall go in, passing from circle to circle, till he comes in to the innermost place where the love of God is most graciously spread abroad.

He that enters in by the door shall be saved, and he shall go in. If you know what this means—go in; go in farther; go in more constantly. Do not stop where you are, but go in till you have got a little more. If you love Christ, come nearer to Him, and nearer, and nearer still. Let your prayer be—

> Nearer, my God, to thee,
>   Nearer to thee;
> E'en though it be a cross that raiseth me,
>   Still this my cry shall be,
> Nearer to thee; nearer to thee.

But if you want to get into anything that is divine, you must get in through Christ. O you who open your Bibles and want to understand a text, the way to get into the meaning of a text is through the door, Christ. O you who want to get more holiness, come through the door; the way to holiness is not through Moses but through Christ. O you who would have closer communion with your heavenly Father, the way to come in is not through your own efforts but through Christ. You came to Christ at first to get salvation; you must come to Christ still to get sanctification.

Never look for another door for there is but one and that one door will let you into life, love, peace, knowledge, and sanctification. It will let you into heaven. Christ is the master key of all the rooms in the palace of mercy and if you get Christ, you shall go in. Nothing shall keep you out of any of the secret chambers. You shall go in, in God's name, through Christ, the door.

The next privilege is that he shall go out. Putting the two together—he shall go in and out—they signify liberty. The Christion does not come into the church as into a prison, but he comes in as a free man walking in and out of his own house. But, what does it mean to go out? I think it means this, brethren. The men that trust in Christ go out to their daily business through Christ, the door. I wonder how many of you ever thought of this? You know sometimes you get up, put on your things, and go blundering out to work, and then you find yourselves very weak all day. Well, I do not wonder at it for you do not go out through Christ, the door. Oh, suppose you had given yourselves to Christ for the day, and thought you had time but for a few minutes' prayer, yet you had put it thus—"Lord, I am thine; take care of me today; I am going out where there will be many to tempt me and try me. I do not know what may happen, but, Lord, I am going out in Thy name and resting in Thy strength; if there is anything that I can do for Thee, I desire to do it. If there is anything to suffer, I wish to suffer it for Thy sake, but take care of me, Lord. I will not go out and face my fellow men until I have seen Thy face, and I do not want to speak to them until I have spoken to Thee, nor to hear what they have to say till I have heard what God the Lord will speak." Depend upon it, it is blessed going out when you go through the door. You will be sure to come home happy when you go out after this sort.

May not this going out also mean to go out to suffering? You and I are called sometimes to bear great bodily pain, or losses, or bereavements. Well, now, what a sweet thing it is to go out to suffer these things through the door, and to be able to say, "Now, my Master, this is a cross, but I will carry it, not in my own strength, but in Thine. Do what thou wilt with me; I shall drink the cup because Thou appointest it. Whenever you can see Christ's hand in it, it makes the bitter sweet, and heavy things soon grow light. Go to your sick bed as you hope to go to your dying bed, through the door, that is, through Christ.

And when, as sometimes happens, we have to go out, as it were, away from fellowship with Christ to fight with our inward sins, the right way is to go out to resist them through the door. If you ever try to fight with sin in your own strength, or on a legal footing, or because you feel that you will be condemned if you do not overcome those sins, you will be as weak as water. The manner of victory is through the blood of the Lamb. There is no killing sin except by throwing the blood of Christ upon it. When once the blood of Christ comes into contact with the besetting sin, that sin withers straight away. Go to your spiritual conflicts through the door.

And so, beloved, we ought in all that we do for the Lord to go out through the door. It is always sweet preaching for me when I feel that I come forth in the name of my Master, when I do not come to tell you what ideas I have woven out of my own brains, nor to put attractive figures before you as I would like to do sometimes; but, rather, when I come to tell you just what my Lord would have you know, telling it as a message to you from your God and cherishing in my own heart His great love towards perishing sinners. Then, indeed, to minister is joy.

Well, now, the last privilege named in the text is, "And shall find pasture." I suppose this is what you come here for, you who love the Lord, you come here for pasture. It is a great blessing if when we come to hear the gospel, it becomes real pasture to us. We do know some who say that the troubles of the week become unbearable because they have such barren Sabbaths. Ah, if you are members of a church that is rent with discord, where the ministry abounds in anything but Christ, you will soon begin to cry out, and you will value the privilege of hearing Jesus Christ lifted up among you. But who are the people who get the pasture where Jesus Christ is preached? Not all who hear Him, nor yet all believers; there are times when you may hear a sermon that is of no use to you, and yet your brother or sister by your side may be greatly instructed and comforted thereby. In such a case, I should not wonder if it was because your friend came in to the service through the door, and you did not.

Do you remember the story of Mr. Erskine and the good lady who went to hear him preach at the communion? It was such sweet preaching, she thought she had never heard the like. So, after service, she asked, Who the gentleman was that preached today; and, on being told that it was Mr. Ebenezer Erskine she said, "I will come and hear him again next Sunday morning." She went, she listened, and she thought to herself, "Well, this is very dry, very heavy preaching." She was not at all comforted by it; then, like a foolish woman, as I should think she must have been, she went into the vestry and said, "Oh, Mr. Erskine, I heard you last Sabbath with much pleasure, sir; I never was so edified; and, I came again this morning, but I have been dreadfully disappointed." So the good man said very calmly, "Pray madam, when you came to the kirk last Sunday, what did you come for?" She said, "I came to communion, sir." "To have fellowship with Christ, I suppose?" he asked. "Yes, sir." "Well, you came for it, and you had it. And pray, what did you come here this morning for?" Said she, "I came to hear you, sir." "And, you had it, woman," said he, "you had it, and you had not anything else because you did not come for anything more than that." Well, now when people come merely to hear a minister, or for custom's sake, or for form's sake, do they not always get what they come for? If people come to find fault, we always give them plenty of our imperfections to be entertained with so they need not be disappointed. If others come merely out of custom, they say, "Well this is my work, I have performed my duty." Of course it is, but if you had come in through the door—that is, looking to Christ, looking for Christ, desiring not to see the preacher but the Lord, not to get the word of man but the Word of God to your soul— I believe you would have found pasture.

I think the text may mean that he who rests in Christ shall have all his wants supplied. If this text does not mean so, another does: "The Lord is my shepherd, I shall not want; he maketh me to lie down in green pastures, he leadeth me beside the still waters." Some of you are very poor, but if you have trusted in Christ, you may plead this promise—"Thou has said I shall find pasture." Come to Christ and tell Him that He Himself has said it—"No good thing will he withhold from them that walk uprightly."

I would to God that some who have never yet entered into the fold might now be drawn to Jesus. Oh, that ye would come through the door into these four choice privileges. You may never have such another opportunity. You may never feel any of the motions of the Spirit of God again. Oh! that without delay, ye would just cast your helpless souls upon the Saviour's gracious arms who is able and willing to save that ye might be saved now.